Authenticity and the Cultural Politics of Work

Authenticity and the Cultural Politics of Work: New Forms of Informal Control

by
Peter Fleming

OXFORD
UNIVERSITY PRESS

OXFORD

UNIVERSITY PRESS

Great Clarendon Street, Oxford OX2 6DP

Oxford University Press is a department of the University of Oxford.
It furthers the University's objective of excellence in research, scholarship,
and education by publishing worldwide in

Oxford New York

Auckland Cape Town Dar es Salaam Hong Kong Karachi
Kuala Lumpur Madrid Melbourne Mexico City Nairobi
New Delhi Shanghai Taipei Toronto

With offices in

Argentina Austria Brazil Chile Czech Republic France Greece
Guatemala Hungary Italy Japan Poland Portugal Singapore
South Korea Switzerland Thailand Turkey Ukraine Vietnam

Oxford is a registered trade mark of Oxford University Press
in the UK and in certain other countries

Published in the United States
by Oxford University Press Inc., New York

British Library Cataloguing in Publication Data
Data available

Library of Congress Cataloging in Publication Data
Data available

Typeset by SPI Publisher Services, Pondicherry, India
Printed in Great Britain
on acid-free paper by
the MPG Books Group, Bodmin and King's Lynn

ISBN 978–0–19–954715–9 (hbk.)

1 3 5 7 9 10 8 6 4 2

Contents

Contents

Preface

> What the philosophers once knew as life has become the sphere of private existence and now of mere consumption, dragged along as an appendage of the process of material production, without autonomy or substance of its own.
>
> (Adorno, 1974: 15)

Is Adorno off the mark here? The corporation cannot exist on its own without some kind of autonomous sub-labour that provides it life, ideas, and sustenance. We now know that the machine of industrial production is not self-sustaining. Along with so many other crucial raw materials, life, cooperation, and association are but resources to be prospected, objectified, and put to work. A veritable economy of non-corporatized effort is required from us before the corporate system can even become what it is. Realized in the thousand moments of common association, this pre-profit stratum of social interaction persists despite the antisocial code of the corporation. Adorno thought that capitalism was against life. He was right, of course, but he did not foresee how it now requires a *life of sorts*, parasitically feeding upon a creative bio-sociality to sustain its unsustainable nature.

And then we arrive at the office, the shop floor, the retail store, etc. It is time to start work. How can anyone *be him- or herself* in organizations when so many there conceal their 'true' feelings and expressions, grudgingly accepting the artificial roles of subordination and faking their way through yet another half-baked team-building exercise? Why do we feel less ourselves at work compared to within those non-work domains associated with pleasure, relaxation, and 'being at home'? The nagging and sometimes painful sense of being at odds with oneself in organizations has always been a keen concern in management theory and practice. A deep seam of thought runs through industrial ideology in which the post-somatic adjustment to the liturgy of work is a paramount objective for reasons we shall soon discuss. Nothing in the deployment of these mechanisms to achieve the 'happy' and 'harmonious' worker at the coalface of accumulation indicates the basic causes of such malaise. Because the composition of capitalist employment now seems like an eternal and edgeless universe with no end, such adaptation is an unsurprising response to the shock of work. This book focuses on the latest manifestation of this managerial concern in which *personal authenticity* is the primary refrain in a growing number of corporations. The guiding motto for workers here is to 'Just be yourself!' and to freely express those aspects of identity that were once relegated to non-work. My objective in writing this book is to develop a kind of ideology critique whereby the appearance of this discursive practice is unpacked to reveal half-hidden structures, contradictions, and even unintended opportunities for real progressive change.

As it enters the phraseology of corporate discourse the idea that we might now express our authentic selves in an environment renowned for its hierarchical and anti-democratic tendencies appears to be a liberating gesture. And ironically many of the attempts to 'humanize' such structures (commitment, empowerment, job enrichment programmes, etc.) often themselves create feelings of alienation, as employees easily see through them. This unsurprising response among the workforce might result from a pre-emptive expectation regarding the brutal 'right-sizing' that frequently follows such initiatives. But workers also chide these maladroit attempts to soften the crunch of capitalist employment because they seem unreal. Like so much other dross proffered by consultants and pop-management pundits, the discursive facade of work is manipulated without going to the heart of problem: a fundamental *lack of life* at work, which is perhaps an inescapable part of the capitalist labour process since life and work hardly ever go together. The celebration of personal authenticity involving expressions of difference and diverse identities is both a continuation of past attempts to inject a modicum of life into work and an official response to earlier failures.

The recent call for personal authenticity in corporate environments notorious for their alienating modes of life entails an intersection of liberalist political thought and a peculiar radical chic. Especially salient are the notions of difference, diversity, dissent, and the evocation of non-work themes within the conventional boundaries of the firm. This book does not aim to critique the laudable efforts to render the demographic make-up of work more diverse in terms of ethnicity, race, sexual orientation, and so forth. Decisive advances remain to be made here and the importance of a particular pluralism is obvious if a more progressive and just employment environment is to prevail. The chapters that follow are more interested in what happens to the so-called unique individual and the expression of difference once it is objectified and put to work in the corporation. I will argue that difference, diversity, and the *sui generis* of individual actualization become expressive instruments that reinforce the conservative politics of accumulation. Difference is especially transmuted into a forced visibility that effaces its radical potential in significant ways that we shall soon explore.

The analysis that follows is particularly interested in the corporate characterization of authenticity that calls upon the apparent freedoms of *non-work* to enter the office, the factory, the call centre, etc. Managerial ideology has been notoriously suspicious about the disruptive effects that non-work might have on the smooth order inside the firm. This is not surprising given that non-work might be associated with forms of life ostensibly ungoverned by industrial efficiency such as sex, leisure, time wasting, and so forth. The corporate turn to personal authenticity changes this relationship, since non-work associatives are considered important for pinpointing what is unique and different about us. The assumption is that the 'truth of being' is expressed when we are free to be ourselves, and this is usually somewhere far away from the oppressive rituals of work. It is almost as if the corporation today is trying to pretend that the sphere of production is not what it is but something outside itself. This is an important development that can best be explained with reference to the Italian autonomist movement. These theorists argue that capitalism maintains itself by parasitically drawing on a sub-commons of cooperative association that persists despite the antisocial rhythms of the market and the corporate form (what Marx once ironically called the communism of capital). The non-work sphere of the sub-commons inspires the corporate appreciation of personal authenticity and thus contains deep points of transformative antagonism.

This book has been helped along by a number of people who have read and critically engaged with the ideas it explores. First and foremost, the book is indebted to a collaborative project with Andy Sturdy around the notion of neo-normative control. Chapter 1 draws significantly upon themes discussed in our unpublished paper, 'Towards Neo-normative Control'. I thank him for allowing me to build on these arguments in that chapter and for the rich discussion we have shared over the last few years. Other chapters were presented in seminars that helped tremendously to fine-tune the arguments. I thank Todd Bridgman and Deborah Jones at the Victoria University Management School, Wellington, New Zealand, for hosting my presentation on designer resistance. Christina Garsten and her group at Stockholm Centre for Organizational Research gave very useful feedback on my presentation of authenticity at work. Helpful comments were also received from participants at the Latin American European Meeting on Organization Studies in Rio de Janerio, Brazil. My good friend André Spicer, as always, has been so generous in discussing with me ideas regarding authenticity in the workplace. Andy Sturdy and I presented the neo-normative control paper at Cardiff University Business School, and the intense discussion that followed with the participants was valuable for allowing us to conceptually connect authenticity and control. They included Rick Delbridge, Hugh Willmott, Tom Keenoy, Mike Reed, and Andrea Whittle. Marc Jones also assisted in developing these concepts in the many discussions we have had on this topic and beyond. And finally, I would like to express great gratitude to my colleagues at Queen Mary College, University of London, who read and discussed the chapters of this book, especially Stefano Harney, Gerry Hanlon, Palo Do, Matteo Mandarini, and Arianna Bove.

List of Abbreviations

3Fs	Focus, fun, and fulfilment
BAT	British and American Tobacco
BP	British Petroleum
CEO	Chief Executive Officer
CMS	Critical Management Studies
CSR	Corporate Social Responsibility
HRM	human resource management
IT	information technology
PR	public relations
WOBS	Warwick Organization Behaviour Staff

Introduction: Authenticity at Work

Corporate life is the antechamber of depression

(Ehrenberg, 1998: 199)

From its far-flung scope to its trivial daily rituals, there is no doubt that corporatized work represents one of the more asinine things we have invented. The overbearing figure of capitalist employment casts a formidable shadow over social life and signifies a number of contradictory things to the millions who labour therein. Work remains something that many of us would rather avoid if we had the chance. Its social compact still implies profound unfreedoms: when at work, we generally 'do as we are told' in order to make a living. It is also a domain bracketed from the rest of our lives, where petty mortifications are condoned and the artificial is silently tolerated. But work also has more positive connotations. It provides its own temporary means of escape since pay affords access to the leisure and entertainment industries. Work is also a place to evade the unfair demands and humiliations of domestic life. Some find partners there, while others make friends and gather stories and anecdotes with which to regale loved ones. This contradictory nature of organized work, especially in the context of the modern corporation, is no more evident than in the prominence of authenticity in recent managerial discourse, which is the topic this book seeks to investigate further.

Authenticity – the truth of oneself or what philosophers like to call 'self-identity' – has usually been realized anywhere but in the workplace. Employment has typically been a space (and time) where we temporarily forego our true feelings and values, momentarily sacrificing them to the concertive pursuit of organized capitalism. It is only when the workday is done (or in those covert and underground 'informal' facets of the organization) that we can truly be ourselves. This is why a major tradition of social criticism focuses on the dehumanizing effects of the corporation. Not only does organized work suck away our time like a sponge, and unfairly exploit our most alert hours and years only to later discard us 'like an orange peel', it also distorts the very fundamentals of our humanity. From Marx and Weber to more contemporary criticisms found in the Critical Management Studies (CMS) movement, the 'corrosion of character' and the alienating constituents of organizational life have featured as key reasons to question the corporate form.

It is with respect to this image of work – as a site of coercion, control, and subjugation – that the recent invitation for employees to 'just be themselves' must be studied. A growing number of managerial commentators, consultants, and practitioners, especially in the United States and the United Kingdom, argue that authenticity is today a pivotal reference point for understanding worker motivation and productive performance. Internet coaching firms are dedicated to facilitating authentic business strategies, crafting authentic marketing and branding policies, and illustrating the benefits accrued when employees are permitted to express their unique individuality. When workers bring their whole selves to the workplace ('warts and all'), firms are able to exploit a hitherto untapped reservoir of creativity, innovation, and entrepreneurial ingenuity. Popular management writers who defined the contours of the first wave of 'liberation management' in the early 1990s, such as Tom Peters and Deal and Key (as well as a new crop of corporate observers like Sutton and Bains), now espouse a paradoxical *anti-managerial* view since workers ought to be free to voice aspects of personhood once abnegated by corporate managerialism. Rather than deny the rich multiplicity of real individuals in favour of a contrived, staid, and uniform identity, employees are now 'free' to just be themselves. Recent pop management books with titles like *Authentic Business: How to Make a Living by Being Yourself* (Crofts, 2005) and *Authenticity: What Consumers Really Want* (Gilmore and Pine, 2007) suggest that creating an aura of authenticity in the firm is the only way forward in these times of failed fakeness. A similar point is made by commentators like Kane (2004) pertaining to the 'play ethic' (also see Boyle, 2004). Contra the infamous self-sabotaging 'work ethic' whereby fun and play are driven out of the factory and office, the new corporate ethos is said to embrace frivolous light-heartedness. This will enhance work life quality and profitability since happy workers make for a healthy bottom line.

Much of this could be put down to ideological wishful thinking with little empirical credence or representativeness. This book aims to demonstrate, however, that apart from the growing use of words and phrases like 'freedom', 'authenticity', and 'just be yourself' in management discourse, it increasingly has practical purchase too (especially in the United States, United Kingdom, and Australasia). But it would be risky to impute complete novelty in this recent turn to authenticity in corporate discourse. In many ways, the 'just be yourself' method is a continuation of attempts to solve the problem of self-alienation and 'cure' the pathologies sustained by workers in the factory, the office, and the corporation. In the chapters that follow it will be argued that management has for many years been interested in reconciling the employee to the unpleasant reality of work. The neo-human relations doctrine of Mayo (1945) and Maslow (1954), for example, found the solution in rearranging the task environment so that self-actualization might occur. Consultation, satisfaction, and various forms of pseudo-therapy were at hand to square workers with their own subjugation, even if it was often practiced as a crude palliative to divert attention away from the continuing disenchantment on the shop floor or office (Hollway, 1991). Later on the high-commitment 'corporate cultures' that characterized the 1980s also attempted to recover the subjective experience of workers, hoping that they might 'find themselves' in the shared norms and values of the company.

There are also considerable discontinuities in the recent discourse around authenticity and the 'just be yourself' management approach. For example, it trades in a staunch individualism, evokes overt non-work associations, and flirts with a peculiar kind of anti-authoritarian chic. And it is not only the labour process that is the target of these authenticating techniques. In the area of branding, corporate reputation, and Corporate Social Responsibility (CSR), the notion of authenticity is a prime concern. As I will argue in Chapter 5, this has a number of features that influence how we understand the cultural structure of organizations today. The corporation is currently the focus of an immense critical gaze among the general population, consumers, and prospective workers. This means how the firm represents itself is of utmost importance. Value creation derives not only from the production of goods and services that extract surplus value from the labour process, but the manipulation of images that convince consumers of the firm's integrity. The sale of 'authentic' products in relation to organic foods, exotic holidays, and vegan sneakers, for example, are becoming more important for retailers as consumers desire something 'real' (Gilmore and Pine, 2007). CSR programmes not only present a 'friendly' image to consumers and government regulators but also focus on the motivations of an increasingly cynical employee base (especially in the professional workplace). The notoriously difficult generation-Y employee, who thinks capitalism 'sucks' but still wants to personally gain from it, is the target of a good deal of CSR initiatives (e.g. *pro bono* work). These exercises aim to placate both media-savvy generation-Y workers and those with a social conscience who want to gain from capitalism, whilst remaining 'true' to their own values.

The usual caveats apply here. The book will not argue that authenticity preoccupies all firms or that generation-Y employees are the only demographic of importance in the workforce. It may be the case that the 'just be yourself' ideology represents but a marginal sector in the corporate world. And for many others in the post-industrial non-spaces of itinerant and underpaid service work, such a focus on authenticity might seem insignificant or even indulgent. As I shall soon argue, however, there is an increasing body of evidence that demonstrates the growing practical and ideological diffusion of the 'just be yourself' ideology and its call for authentic expressions of identity at work. Additionally, if we are interested in how corporate capitalism justifies itself, it does appear that the trope of authenticity features prominently at this juncture. It thus warrants further critical scrutiny.

The Effort of Being One's Self

A central argument in this book is that authenticity becomes an issue when it is not present, pushed onto the corporate stage by the negative qualities of its absence (traumatic, boring, and inauthentic work). In other words, its importance is symptomatic of a more inveterate problem that has preoccupied managerial discourse and its desire for hard, fast, and smart work. This problem, as everyone knows, is the perennial contradiction between labour and capital; divergent interests, power relations, benefits, and privileges define the employment experience. This observation underscores the point made above that we must place the official pursuit of authenticity at work within a broader political economy of the corporation. The very slogan 'just be yourself', drawn from an empirical example that I will discuss in Chapter 1, is redolent of this political economy. The slogan is an encouragement but mostly a diktat. Like any other formal command it expects obedience even in a 'new-age' firm like Apple where a chic dissent pervades the corporate culture. Who issues this command on the one hand, and who is asked to be 'authentic' on the other? Despite the importance of self-managing work teams, autonomy, and empowerment programmes that have reconfigured the western workplace (see Delbridge [1998] for an excellent analysis of the 'new' factory system in the United Kingdom), a system of hierarchy is still present here.

If the call for authenticity is more indicative of a 'lack' that defines the work situation (since why else would it appear), what exactly might be lacking? This book wagers that it is a lack that goes to the heart of the employment relationship in profit-seeking firms, including the more liberal or humanized ones. It is a lack of power, lack of control, lack of choice, lack of dignity, lack of meaningful joy, a lack of community outside the commodity form; to put it rather telegraphically, a *lack of a life*. And this makes us unhappy. This book approaches the managerial edict to be authentic as an ideological attempt to suture this lack through a kind of false positivity. Why false? Because the 'just be yourself' business philosophy addresses this systemic lack of life in a manner that maintains its source. The corporatized 'truth of being' – encouraging superficial displays of difference, identity, and lifestyle – represents the transposition of authenticity into an instrumental discourse. Even if it packages itself in the lexicon of freedom, the 'just be yourself' discourse follows more the grammar of appropriation than redistribution or recognition.

This appropriation draws upon forms of social life that forever lie beyond capitalism, what I shall later call after Hardt and Negri (1994) *the commons*. This consists of a relatively autonomous and non-commodified stratum of cooperative effort that capitalism both needs to reproduce itself and simultaneously defers since it represents a dangerous counter-logic to its own axiomatic principles. Any act of appropriation always entails a profound uncertainty, but doubly so when the source of authenticity is something antithetical to the very machinery of the capitalist enterprise. The reader may tell by now that this book is not very optimistic about the recent freedoms to 'be yourself' in organizations. But the conceptual introduction of the commons does open a vista of positive possibilities regarding how authenticity might be practiced in the future. Given the unstable interface between the commons and the firm, the call for authentic selves at work might harbour a progressive kernel that could yet change the face of work for the better.

The shift in managerial rhetoric that I investigate indicates that the corporation is still very interested in what and how people 'feel' at work. An immense ideological apparatus is being deployed that aims to develop a 'dialogue' between capital and labour, work and life; and to harness

5

competitive, productive, and innovative energies required in the global economy. To use Delbridge's (1998) terms, the corporation certainly realizes that the worker is 'more than a pair of hands'. And as I have mentioned above, the entrance of authenticity into the vocabulary of mainstream managerial discourse is surely symptomatic of a constitutive lack that inherently defines labour vis-à-vis capital. But it might also be suggestive of some wider shifts in the cultural logic of late capitalism in which reflexivity is reaching almost crippling levels of intensity. According to Giddens (1991), for example, late modern individuals reflect on everything about their lives including their relationships, sexuality, childhood, life purposes, careers, and work experiences. Reflection is now a sited activity that folds the individual back on himself or herself. Accordingly, the self-help industry is sizable, catering to those who question 'the meaning of it all' and seek to discover the truth of oneself in a narcissistic dance between pleasure and anxiety. In institutional settings like the school, prison, or family, people are almost forced to confess their prospective life-paths and verbalize what is genuine about themselves in a world of strangers, con artists, and shallow pleasures. Amidst this insipid inwardness, it is an effort to be oneself (Ehrenberg, 1998). Authenticity in the workplace probably echoes these cultural tendencies too. Indeed, as McGee (2005) argues, life in the corporation is one of the main concerns of the self-help industry: 'Are you happy at work? Can you be yourself at work? Can you work somewhere else that makes you happy? Are you able to be all you can be at work?'

Within the horizon of this pervasive cultural malaise the middle-aged office worker looks to 'life' for something more than just their job. The downshifting movement is surely indicative of this change whereby the 'work at all costs' credo is declining in favour for a more 'spiritual' and 'fulfilling' engagement with organized employment (even if this is in the context an exponentially increasing, hyper-work milieu). As the thousands of weblogs also tell us, many are simply tired of the depressing world of corporate toil and have decided to reprioritize since 'life is short' and the firm will take everything if given half the chance. Perhaps more material forces are also responsible for this changing ethos. An increasingly self-satisfying and ultra-individualist understanding of labour and life might be more evident when work patterns consist of part-time, itinerant contractor employment (Kunda and Ailon-Souday, 2005).

Furthermore, the young employee that enters the corporate world today tends to be of a different ilk compared to previous generations. The generation-Y management consultant, for example, often arrives with a cavernous scepticism about capitalism (Costas and Fleming, 2008). They are nihilistic devotees of a countercultural chic that is prominent in popular culture, ardent watchers of cult films like *Office Space*, and fans of Radiohead. In this book I will particularly focus on how a certain ethos of criticism – manifested as an expressive radical chic – has entered into the halls of business. Authenticity here equates with being 'cool', thinking your job 'sucks', and wearing Che Guevara T-shirts to work (or at least to the company volleyball game; Liu, 2004). What I have referred to as 'designer resistance' (after Badham et al.'s [2003] notion of 'designer deviance') represents a largely aesthetic voicing of dissent, often involving little more than a fashion statement. It will be suggested in Chapter 5 that opportunities lie here too for taking this managerial scripted dissent in unintended directions, perhaps yielding socially progressive and democratic effects.

Just Be Yourself . . . or Else!

The language of emancipation and anti-capitalism seems decidedly out of place when enunciated in the official discourse of the capitalist enterprise. What happens to criticism when it is churned through this clumsy reflexive apparatus? It is the appeal to 'freedom' and 'liberation' in the 'just be yourself' management approach that most likely explains why pseudo-radical motifs are now popular in business ideology. More, the reliance on liberalist celebrations of self-expression and plural identities are also essential components. Some commentators go so far as to proclaim the end of traditional Fordist controls in light of the 'freedoms' now being enjoyed by large sectors of the workforce. Companies such as Southwest Airlines and Google, for example, trade in the sibylline of a frictionless capitalism in which the liberty to display a tattoo or confess one's sexual preference is tantamount to a social revolution.

As I will demonstrate in the forthcoming chapters, personal authenticity is encouraged by way of promoting those aspects of self that are more associative of the private or non-work realm. In a move that makes this corporate ideology quite distinct from past methods of management, signs of leisure, sexuality, ethnicity, alternative lifestyles, and consumption patterns are now welcomed into the sphere of production (or at least in a streamlined expressive form). This conspicuous reliance on extra-employment themes, gestures, and symbols is understandable given the cultural assumption that work is a place where we cannot be ourselves.

If freedom is historically and culturally associated with non-work, then it follows that the building blocks of authenticity must be sited there too. This is why its markers materialize in the organization to articulate what is different about the individual. But so much of this version of freedom depends on what non-work is presumed to stand for, involving abbreviations that transform it into something of a parody. Non-work becomes an exploitable reservoir, but also a screen upon which managerialism projects its only values.

Inside the organization, any hint of 'collective' or 'uniform' social processes is officially downplayed; homogeneous cultural values, Tayloristic standardization, and bureaucratic rationalization are jettisoned in favour of difference, uniqueness, and a private (yet visible) individualism. Indeed, many pop management commentators argue that conventional capitalist controls are synonymous with the loss of individuality since they smother what is different about us. The bureaucratic personality or inculcated devotee of the company visibly aspires to a collective norm. They tend to look the same. Liberation management and its call for authentic expressions of identity challenge this collectivism in the name of self-expression and the marketplace. This book will argue that it does this by manufacturing an even more insidious 'individualized conformism' – not only by constructing difference within very generalized stereotypes (the gay, the minority, the punk, etc.), but also by utilizing this difference to service the ultimate universal abstraction: the pursuit of profit. Difference beyond this universal rule is not permitted. 'Just be yourself', but only up to a point.

Even after we acknowledge these internal limits to the celebration of difference, the use of emancipatory language (including phrases wrapped in the countercultural garb of the late 1960s) still upsets typical assumptions about how management functions. Control, coercion, and compulsion are rhetorically sent out the door, and freedom of expression, lifestyle difference, and even 'resistance' enter as the corporation attempts to fill the fundamental 'lack' of organized work. Of course, if anything, both traditional and new controls intensify in such environments since freedom of self-expression is always delimited and can in no way be equated with freedom per se. Not only does the somewhat superficial expression of lifestyle choice in the workplace detract from existing controls connected to technology and bureaucracy, it also absorbs more of the employees' self into the regime of production.

In light of this more power-orientated view of the 'liberal organization', the book shall contend that, at the conceptual level at least, there is an interesting pull around the political significance of authenticity. The 'just be yourself' managerial approach draws upon many of the countercultural signifiers that were once the mainstay of anti-capitalist politics. Authenticity in the writings of Sartre (1943/1969) *inter alia* entails a formidable responsibility, a rejection of capitalist values resulting in a radical singularity foreign to the practico–inert rhythms of the corporation. I will explore some of the more interesting ironies that arise when such a discourse of authenticity arrives in the corporate boardroom. Important here is the analysis forwarded by Boltanski and Chiapello (2005). They suggest that humanist or 'artistic' challenges to capitalism feature in much pro-business rhetoric today. The 'new spirit of capitalism' endeavours to make good use of the lexicon of liberation that was forged from the crisis of everyday life in the 1960s. The sad remnants of a once vibrant anti-corporate stance are now key motivating slogans in executive coaching sessions and call centre Away Days. We thus arrive at a confusing situation in which control, freedom, managerialism, liberation, and capitalist values all tessellate into a single political montage. How are we to make sense of this knot of discursive confluences?

The Commons and Its Appropriation

To begin with, it would be short-sighted to accept the idea that the opportunity for self-expression results in freedom at work. There are obviously complex political processes functioning behind the scenes here, in which certain relations of power gain an even more strident grip over life and labour. This is evident in the way personal authenticity is defined and delimited in official discursive practices. In Chapter 1, I present an empirical example of this delimitation, which reveals the powerful normative edicts underlying the exhortation 'Just be yourself!'. My analysis views the corporate concern with authenticity as a further extension of control rather than liberation. Nevertheless, it would be a somewhat myopic to dismiss the partial freedoms that the 'just be yourself' management method affords some, especially when compared with the Fordist model of strict discipline and rationalization. The celebration of diversity and difference in relation to sexual identity cannot simply be rejected as artificial (also see Fleming, 2007). And the same could be said for workplace 'fun', especially in organizations where the point of production is dry, tiresome, and otherwise alienating. For sure, the discourse of freedom, as Žižek (2008) continuously highlights, is an important feature of domination in so-called post-modern societies, which is not to say that such freedoms are unreal. On the contrary, they are sometimes pleasurable and have effects. However, the explicit petition around emancipatory motifs in the corporate sphere (often swiped from the radical political movements of the 1960s) obviously raises suspicions about the structure and rationale calling for authenticity at work.

It is due to this suspicion that the book aims to position the 'just be yourself' managerial philosophy within a very political framework. Rather than signal a pure workers' paradise of self-determination, I instead read the celebration of authenticity as an articulation of domination. My analysis especially concentrates on the role of non-work in many of the 'authenticating' exercises that feature in the new workplace. As I mentioned above, this corporate interest in the extra-employment sphere could be explained by the widespread assumption that 'authenticity' is best borne outside of the rhythms of paid employment. When we are at work we feign commitment, tell the bosses what they want to hear, and forge self-presentations that have little relation to whom 'we really are' (and we do so for a number of reasons that have been discussed elsewhere; see Fleming and Spicer, 2003). For sure, following a tradition of political philosophy that begins with Rousseau, it is in the 'private' realm that we are truly ourselves and self-identity might be achieved.

The symbolic appearance of non-work inside the domain of production (as a way of prompting authentic displays of self) is significant for other reasons. This book develops a broader picture of the implications and rationale behind this fetishization of non-work by introducing the Italian autonomist ideas of Hardt and Negri (1994, 1999) and Tronti (1971), among others. They argue that capitalist development is not necessarily shaped by its own code of expansion, but by a proactive 'reaction' to the resistance it meets. This opposition flows from what Hardt and Negri (1994) call 'the commons' or sometimes the 'communism of capitalism'.[1] This can be described as those non-commodified associations, cooperative rituals, and gift-giving economies that form the underbelly of the capitalist system. It is the source of creativity and vibrancy that capital continuously attempts to valorize and draw into its own field: the gentrification process and the 'industrialization of bohemia' (Ross, 2004) whereby information technology (IT) firms relocate to more 'artsy' urban areas to exploit cultural capital is a good example. The commons is first and foremost a kind of non-commodified labour that exists outside the realm of capital (even though it is necessarily 'within' it since capitalism cannot reproduce itself). The creative commons is both the constant focus of the capitalist enterprise and a dangerous force since it develops from a basic distrust of exploitation. As Hardt and Negri (1994) put it,

the communism of capital can absorb all values within its movement, and can represent to the fullest the general social goal of development, but it can never expropriate that particularity of the working class that is its hatred of exploitation, its uncontainability at any given level of equilibrium. (Hardt and Negri, 1994: 51)

This syncretic union between the corporation and the non-work commons that capital parasitically feeds off properly explains why the corporation is currently so enamoured with non-work. While this book is not strictly a Marxian account of these developments in the instruments of corporate colonization, the autonomist theory of capitalism clarifies why personal authenticity is so closely associated with the sphere of non-work in contemporary corporate ideology. Moreover, if the commons is the wellspring of authentic expressions of self, then the 'just be yourself' discourse begins to look like a technology of co-optation rather than liberation. Each chapter probes this autonomist insight as a way for not only gaining a more nuanced understanding of what is happening in contemporary organizations, but also to place the corporate interest in authentic selves within a wider political economy.

The concept of 'the commons' allows for a more sanguine tone to emerge from the critique of corporatized authenticity. I will demonstrate how the co-optation process constantly fails given the recalcitrant nature of the commons. The appeal to non-work in the corporate sphere relies on a mimetic function in which 'play', 'sexuality', and 'fun', for example, are simulated in a figurative manner. The corporation appears to be constantly pointing to what it is not to justify itself and motivate workers, constructing simulacra imbued with the aura of uncommodified and non-market relationships (this is especially so in the case of Corporate Social Responsibility, which I discuss in Chapter 5). Such simulation can never replicate the commons with integrity given the inherently anti-capitalist values that underpin it. Hardt and Negri (1994) tell us why:

[T]he labour we affirm must be grasped on a different plane in a different time. Living labour produces life and constitutes society in a time that cuts across the division posed by the workday, inside and outside the prisons of capitalist work and its wage relation, in both the realm of work and that of nonwork. (Hardt and Negri, 1994: xiii)

The failure to faithfully map the commons inadvertently showcases the unavailable original, and thus places the corporation on shaky ground as workers begin to demand 'real' fun, sexuality, and cooperation in the workplace.

And finally, this approach to elucidating these recent managerial permutations could contain the seeds of a certain type of liberation. By inviting the commons into the corporation, albeit in a highly superficial and scripted manner, the call for personal authenticity might be an antechamber for introducing the commons *in toto*. Such an event would simultaneously see the significance of authenticity dramatically recede since the commons is ironically anathema to the version on offer in the corporation. If the commons suddenly burst through in lush positivity then the very antagonisms that made authenticity a problem in the first place would disappear. Correspondingly, the model of selfhood propped up by the modern corporation would dissolve since the 'authentic subject' would be de-subjectified in a somewhat radical manner. This part of the project resonates with Foucault's insistence that what is needed in order to circumvent the hyper-reflective flows of power today is *less* of the individual and not more. The whole idea of personal authenticity is built upon an experience of self shot through with the tools of its own neurotic self-domination. Perhaps abandoning it would make for the political statement par excellence: 'What is needed is to "de-individualize" by means of multiplication and displacement, diverse combinations. The group must not be the organic bond uniting hierarchized individuals, but a constant generator of de-individualization' (Foucault, 1983: xiii–xiv).

The commons too works on the same principle since its fullest realization would fill the political and subjective 'lack' that makes authenticity a problem in the first place. No doubt this book too is a symptom of our over-subjectified cultural moment that pervades so many spheres of life, including the corporation. But it does not aim to perpetuate this fetishization of the subject. On the contrary, it will probe the meaning of personal authenticity at work, move through it, and perhaps arrive on the other side without it.

Structure of the Book

The book proceeds in traditional analytical sequence, beginning with the phenomenon of authenticity and its management at work, unpacking its significance in each following chapter. Chapter 1 maps the emergence of the 'just be yourself' management approach. It does so in two ways. First it demonstrates the peculiarity of the exhortation to be authentic compared to traditional managerial methods, especially the neo-human relations movement and culture building in the 1980s. The emphasis placed on 'freedom' and 'identity' in the context of extant workplace controls is a defining feature of the 'just be yourself' management discourse. The meaning of authenticity – its historical antecedents and contemporary connotations in relation to private and individualized models of the subject – is also discussed. Second, the chapter gives an extended empirical example of this 'new' approach. The study is used to demonstrate this managerial discourse 'in action', but also reveal its connections to definite political flows of domination. In surveying the views, attitudes, and opinions of actual workers and managers in the liberal corporation, we are able to easily see how the 'just be yourself' approach represents an important articulation of power.

Chapter 2 discusses how the practice and discourse of authenticity evokes non-work, seemingly leading to the blurring of the typical boundary between labour and life (a process I aim to capture in the phrase 'the haemorrhaging organization'). The chapter maintains that the appearance of non-work in this managerial technique is important for two reasons. First, authenticity is considered to be 'at home' more outside the organization than inside. The evocation of non-work as the inspiration for authenticity relies upon a kind of simulation or mimesis whereby gestures connoting extra-employment activities (sexuality, fun, play, lifestyle, etc.) are reproduced inside the regime of production. I will later argue that this simulation is at the centre of the authenticity machine, unfolding in a contradictory manner since an inauthentic fabrication is required. Second, the image of non-work points to a broader political economy of which Italian Autonomism provides a number of useful insights. I unpack this perspective, especially underlining the notion of the 'social factory' and 'immaterial labour'. It will be suggested that the mimesis of non-work is an attempt to expropriate aspects of the commons and harness it to the production process in order to create capitalist value.

Chapter 3 concentrates on a particular empirical example indicative of the haemorrhaging organization: the managerial celebration of 'fun' in the workplace. Historically, fun and play have been officially chastised at work given the hegemonic dominance of rationality, time-discipline, formality, and depersonalization. As a result, playfulness was either consigned to the informal organization – relieving boredom and providing a conduit for anti-management sentiment – or pushed outside into the realm of leisure or the home. In the corporation that exhorts employees to 'just be themselves', fun makes a bombastic appearance in a whole number of ways, including games, exercises, 'fun' events, and everyday pranks. Again, mimesis is a crucial operating mechanism here since work is not much fun, and the commons of non-work value is generally its source of inspiration. Empirical data explored in this chapter particularly focuses on the failure of such mimetic processes, which is then theorized in terms of a more pervasive limit (and contradiction) of capitalism.

Chapter 4 extends the analysis of corporatized authenticity. Not only are non-work features of social life co-opted in the name of a more productive workplace, but so too are 'anti-managerial' discourses. This chapter unpacks the idea of 'designer resistance' *apropos* Boltanski and Chiapello's observation that a new ideology of capitalism has emerged. The contemporary spirit of the corporation has digested and defanged the criticisms of capitalism developed in the 1960s' counterculture, particularly with respect to the damaging psychological effects sustained by employees (e.g. alienation, depersonalization, disenchantment, etc.). The chapter builds on this argument to demonstrate how a specific notion of radical chic and 'cool' has come to be definitive of personal authenticity. Its evocation in the corporation requires resistance to be transposed into what I call 'designer resistance': an aestheticized and expressive display of dissent that is not too dangerous and actually fits nicely into the flexible, reflective regime of accumulation.

Chapter 5 discusses a particular variant of this 'designer resistance' in the form of current trends in CSR. CSR is discussed in the broader terms of marketing and branding since a burgeoning industry of consultants and marketing pundits has emerged to assist the corporation in giving its brand, reputation, and products an aura of authenticity. While consumers, government officials, and the general public are largely the target audience, this chapter argues that the CSR programmes also focus on the corporation's employees. For sure, generation-Y thinks that capitalism 'sucks' but still feels compelled to participate in some of its purest organizational forms. This chapter argues that CSR provides a means to placate the reservations arising among these employees and ameliorate workers who would otherwise adhere to socially progressive values. Again, CSR functions by pointing to what the corporation is not (and cannot be), the non-work sphere of the commons, the uncommodified flows of social life, and so forth. In this sense, CSR might become a radical force of change if taken 'too seriously', an intervention that would see the commons enjoy a full and positive presence.

Chapter 6 turns to the implications of the preceding argument for critical analysis itself. If the quest to engender personal expressions of authenticity in the 'just be yourself' corporation relies upon the appropriation of critique and anti-capitalist sentiments, then is there not a danger that the critical scholar remains one step behind the latest wave of managerial rhetoric (or even worse, unwittingly supports it)? This chapter centres on social critique generally, and more specifically the type of criticism developed within the business school called Critical Management Studies. The implications that a corporatized criticism has for CMS are unpacked. The chapter argues that we really must focus on the university as a site and space of politics (rather than simply the business world 'out there'). Moreover, if criticism is even primed for appropriation and co-optation, then we need to think about the demarcation of limits, or those modalities of criticism that could not be harnessed for the purpose of corporate managerialism. What might those limits look like?

In light of the terrain that the book has covered, Chapter 7 returns to the notion of authenticity. It begins by summarizing what personal authenticity is assumed to be in the 'just be yourself' management approach. Because of its compulsive emphasis on individualism, personal reflexivity, private sense of self, difference, and aesthetic expressivism, some arguments are made about why this mode of 'being authentic' is so useful to the corporation today. With the help of some empirical examples, authenticity is then rethought in relation to various kinds of freedom; namely, freedom in work, freedom around work, and freedom from work. Each articulation of authenticity and freedom has very important implications for how we might think about the political economy of the firm at the present juncture and the meaning of emancipation.

The concluding chapter focuses on the third of the aforementioned modes of freedom and its correspondent articulation of authenticity: *freedom from work*. This builds upon the logical conclusions of the Italian autonomist movement regarding what realistic emancipation might look like in a world overshadowed by corporate hegemony. Non-work and non-commodified values are being drawn into the sphere of production in order to meet capital's current needs. As intimated above, if the commons is the raw material for authentic expression at work (transposed as it is into something it is not), then a full and exuberant expression of this 'elemental communism' might transform the corporation into something infinitely more acceptable. And then would not the very ideal of 'being authentic' be rendered obsolete?

1

Towards a 'New' Cultural Politics of Work?

> Individuality is not just tolerated ... but actively encouraged – particularly when it comes to employees expressing the fun side of their personalities. ... All of this is based on the belief that when people are happy and have the freedom to be themselves, they are more productive and give more of themselves.
>
> (Bains, 2007: 241, on Southwest Airlines)

At first glance, there appears to be something qualitatively distinct in some corporate cultures emerging in Western economies. This became strikingly obvious from my own empirical research into call centres in Australia (see Fleming, 2005; Fleming and Sturdy, 2008). As is well recognized among the workers' movement and popular consciousness, call centres can be among the most oppressive organizations in which to work. Almost every aspect of the milieu signifies control, efficiency, and mechanization – from the physical environment, the standardized time regime, the technological cues, and emotional regulation. Union organizations (which find it very difficult to organize such workers given the fragmented and transient work patterns of this sector of employees) often refer to this type of work as 'assembly lines in the head' (satirizing the idea that call centre employment is 'knowledge work'). Not only is the labour alienating, boring, and bereft of autonomy and self-determination, workers must also deal with the daily humiliations of irate customers. 'Just another day in paradise' smiled one worker as he finished a call from a customer who screamed insulting expletives regarding the worker's relationship with his mother.

In organizations like this – and perhaps many others that have characterized the structure of industrial and post-industrial employment – the institutional logic of the firm is one that evacuates the 'human' from labour. As the concept of self-alienation has long highlighted, modern workplaces are zones of self-abnegation. One of the primary aims of the archetypical controls associated with technological pacing, bureaucratic formalization, and even cultural normalization is to nullify the idiosyncrasies and other immanently 'human' demeanours that are more likely to be expressed when we are free from control. As Tannenbaum (1967) argues in a classic definition of control:

Organization implies control. A social organization is an ordered arrangement of individual human interactions. Control processes help circumscribe idiosyncratic behaviours and keep them conformant to the rational plan of organization. . . . The co-ordination and order created out of the diverse interests and potentially diffuse behaviours of members is largely a function of control. (Tannenbaum, 1967: 3)

Employees (and managers for that matter) find themselves in that strange antinomian space of the 'inhuman' – still human for all intents and purposes, but in a manner that is devoid of what we often feel best characterizes human life. Marx's notion of alienation and Weber's concept of disenchantment both capture the inhuman preconditions of capitalist labour, especially when large-scale production and administrative coordination are involved.

If call centres are places where one cannot 'be yourself' (at least in the liberalist sense of enacting some kind of private uniqueness), then walking into Sunray Customer Service (a pseudonym) was surprising (also see Fleming and Sturdy, 2008). As opposed to the dull, standardized, and technologically oppressive environment that appears to be the norm in other call centres, the catchphrase at Sunray was 'just be yourself!'. Those aspects of self that define individuality should not be denied or proscribed in the name of rationality, but displayed and celebrated. Sunray can thus be considered a quintessential 'liberal organization' (Courpasson, 2006) since it formally challenges many of the conventional understandings of what it means to be a worker in a controlled environment.

The first impression one has upon entering Sunray are the bright colours, the youthful and 'cool' workers, and the extremely relaxed (even alternative) dress code. If the slogan 'just be yourself' is thought to facilitate the expression of personal authenticity (i.e. 'who I really am'), then the very idea of authentic selves is predetermined in specific ways. Emphasis is placed on play and fun, diversity, lifestyle, and difference. If workers are free to display attributes that were prohibited under previous management discourses, it is assumed, they will be more motivated and productive. In Sunray, the 'just be yourself' management philosophy is communicated to employees in the motto 'Remember the 3Fs: Fun, Focus, Fulfilment' and is disseminated in team training exercises, Away Days, recruitment documentation, and appraisal meetings. This discourse stresses input freedom with respect to workplace norms and invites employees to celebrate themselves, displaying a commitment to who they are rather than the company itself. According to the Chief Executive Officer (CEO), James Carr, Semler's *Maverick!* (1993) inspired this management style: '[T]he 3Fs philosophy delivers service excellence by simply allowing people to be themselves and communicate their uniqueness – we like different people here from all walks of life' (CEO introductory document for new recruits).

An important rhetorical component of this management approach is the open acknowledgement that call centre work is typically mechanized and routinized. Sunray seeks to do things differently by injecting an element of fun and life into the work climate. As the training manual states: 'At Sunray we try to make work fun – in fact we try to make it fun instead of work'.

Regarding the widely held belief that call centre work can be likened to being a battery hen, personal freedom and self-expression are underscored:

Forget lone rangers – at Sunray we have free-rangers! It's hard to have fun when you're confined to a workstation like a battery hen, so we encourage you to enjoy the freedom and latitude you need in order to fulfil your obligations to Sunray. (Training manual)

According to one employee, 'the idea is to get away from the boring office look and make things fun and happy like we are going out for the night'. This extended to 'fun' and 'cool' physical appearances among workers, including bright-orange-dyed hair, visible tattoos, and facial piercing; the official comparison to 'parties', 'raves', and 'clubbing' is justified in this sense.

In this chapter, I want to analyse the constituent components of the 'just be yourself' management ideology as it appears to be emerging in contemporary organizations. The chapter will propose that the ideal of personal authenticity among the workforce is an important aspiration of this method of management. An increasing number of pop (and academic) management commentators argue that free and authentic self-expression ('warts and all') in the corporation might provide an antidote to the dysfunctions of conventional controls. In this sense, we must place the managerial celebration of authenticity firmly within the cultural politics of the firm, especially in relation to the perennial labour–capital divide mentioned in the Introduction. What is fascinating about this discourse is the evocation of motifs connoting freedom, emancipation, and even various types of radicalism – some commentators call for managers to model their businesses after the 'joyous anarchy' of the 1968-era counterculture. I will analyse this aspect of the discourse of authenticity in more detail in Chapter 4 when the concept of 'designer resistance' is proposed.

The purpose of this chapter is to describe these shifts in managerial practice and demonstrate how personal authenticity is a key concern in the 'just be yourself' corporation. In the section that follows, we will unpack the 'just be yourself' managerial discourse in more detail and its relationship to self-identity and personal authenticity at work. Authenticity has traditionally been a guiding concern for radical politics given the way in which industrial labour processes have stripped work of its broader human element. We would therefore expect to associate the demand for authenticity more with Marcuse and Sartre than Tom Peters. How do we explain this expropriation of 'authenticity' and its transposition into a tool that serves the business firm rather than undermine it? Moreover, how does this turn to personal authenticity resonate with earlier managerial concepts such as self-actualization, autonomy, and task empowerment? To address these questions the chapter also explores the meaning of authenticity in Western thought and demonstrates how the 'just be yourself' management approach utilizes a very particular variant of it. An expressive and liberalist model of personhood underlies this permutation in corporate ideology. The final sections of the chapter link the celebration of authenticity to the long-standing corporate concern with control. While packaged in the verbiage of freedom and emancipation, I will show that the exhortation to 'just be yourself' is implicated with a deepening of corporate domination.

The 'Truth of Self' at Work

Many progressive organizations are adopting a new, seemingly more liberal approach to managing and motivating workers by de-emphasizing control and celebrating employees' freedom to just be themselves (in all their individual uniqueness and difference). Here, the focus is not so much on task discretion, but authentic displays of sexual identity, lifestyle, and 'fun' – aspects of self normally reserved for non-work.[1] Commentators like Bains (2007) argue, quoted at the opening of this chapter, that the

19

control-free organization is finally possible, where employees act as their own guardians without imposed constraints. Permitting employees to be themselves is presumed to result in higher motivation and productivity levels. Contra past controls that meticulously regulated the behaviour, values, and/or emotions of workers, 'liberation management' advocates freedom. Indeed, the approach is seen to be especially relevant in highly competitive and dynamic industries that rely upon employee trust, discretion, initiative, and creativity.

Freedom of self-expression is particularly cherished in this discourse and dovetails with the liberal mantra of being 'true to yourself'. What is important here is the opportunity to display lifestyle diversity, the fun side of selfhood, and authentic feelings ('warts and all') in the workplace. Even dissent and dissatisfaction are condoned up to a point (Ross, 2004). Among the more simplistic managerial celebrations of the 'just be yourself' discourse, this approach is considered anathema to archetypical controls like technological pacing, bureaucratic formalization, and cultural normalization. Indeed, much of the rhetoric presents control as an antediluvian force that stifles the quirky, wacky, and weird self-expressions now deemed crucial in firms like Google and Southwest Airlines.

Why would the corporation advocate such 'freedoms'? This managerial approach assumes that superior productivity and innovation can be harnessed if employees are freed from control (Bains, 2007). Following Mirvis (1994), it is the complete and idiosyncratic person that is desired by the corporation, with extra-employment themes such as lifestyle, sexuality, consumption, leisure, and so forth becoming salient. Conventional controls erode these attributes because they are founded on regimentation (technical control), standardization (bureaucratic control), and normalization (cultural controls). According to its most proud proponents, the new paradigm significantly displaces this keystone of traditional management: '[N]ow control is passé and a badge of incompetence. Now, you are free' (Semler, 1993: xiii). Likewise, Bains (2007: 35) avers that organizations have historically 'squeezed' their employees 'both psychologically and materially in a way they cannot continue to do'.

Tom Peters is also a particularly strong advocate of this view. Following long humanist traditions, Peters (2003) argues that workers are *naturally* inclined to be innovative, curious, risk-taking, imaginative, and excited. But Peters is not simply calling for renewed emphasis on self-actualization through job discretion (as the neo-human relations movement did), but for a challenge to outdated management controls that desire conformity. In direct contrast to his earlier views (Peters and Waterman, 1982), a laissez-faire approach to norms is the new imperative. The market metaphor is salient here. As opposed to the rhetoric of unitary values and extreme organizational identification, we instead find individualism, entrepreneurial risk-taking, and self-reliance as key signifiers (also Kunda and Ailon-Souday, 2005). Peters (1994) encourages a 'joyous anarchy' in which zanies, nutters, mavericks, and freaks are hired and celebrated (see also Fierman, 1995). Employee creativity derives not simply from job autonomy then, but from the freedom to be themselves and express their most private 'off the wall' desires. It is possible to highlight three elements of the 'be yourself' management approach in recent corporate discourse and practice.

Playful Expressions of Self

A significant way in which employees can 'be themselves' is by expressing their playful and fun nature. Popular writers like Deal and Key (1998) argue that sober productiveness – the cornerstone of technological and bureaucratic control – can undermine productivity and competitiveness given the boredom it engenders. Playful celebrations at work 'provide social support for being yourself and believing that you matter' (1998: 16). If employees are able simply to express themselves freely or, as Deal and Kennedy suggest, if the 'Fun Quotient' is high, everyone will benefit (1999: 234). Here, play and fun lead workers to love being *in the* company rather than love *the* company itself. Indeed, such instrumentality is implied in managerial efforts to become an 'employer of choice' or 'best place to work'. This type of fun is indicative of certain playful personality traits (mavericks, zanies, crazies, etc.) now celebrated in the market rationalist vision of employment.

While many of these 'guru' prescriptions can be treated sceptically in terms of their translation into organizational practice, there is considerable evidence that the management of fun has now become quite widespread, as Kane (2004) indicates in relation to the rise of the corporate 'play ethic'. Likewise, in popular surveys of 'best places to work' such as those in *Fortune* magazine and the *Sunday Times* (2005, 2006), fun is a prominent theme. Google, for example, explicitly draws on the image and social activities of a college campus (*New York Times*, 2006). Even in highly structured workplaces like call centres, employees are encouraged to engage in more or less organized fun (Kinnie et al., 2000). This also can impinge directly on work activity such as using their limited discretion – employees bring their own identity to the service encounter by evoking local accents and deviating from the service script (Frenkel et al., 1999).

It must be pointed out, of course, that employees have always found space and time to have fun. Outside the managerial gaze, the informal sphere of work provided ample opportunities for all sorts of mischief. The classic ethnographic studies of Roy (1952, 1958) and Burawoy (1979), for example, revealed workers joking and engaging in humorous rituals within the gaps and fissures of formal managerial authority. It is telling here that many of these fun games often resulted in the production process functioning even better since it provided a 'safety valve' for frustrations and an escape from the crippling boredom of industrial work. The 'just be yourself' advocation of fun can be framed as a kind of 'formalized informality' (Liu, 2004) in which these previous spaces of self-determination are captured as a productive resource. This is especially evident in the planned spontaneity of sponsored games and team-building exercises that we will further investigate in Chapter 3.

Difference and Diversity

According to Peters (1994), the standardized 'organizational man' (Whyte, 1956) is indicative of the controls that demanded conformity, homogeneity, and selves devoid of individuality or diversity. In keeping with the view that the market, rather than the clan, is becoming the guiding metaphor of workplace relations, Peters claims that 'chaos is with us . . . but the way to deal with it is pursue variation, not to manage (stifle) it' (1994: 51). If employees are to be motivated, innovative, and creative, they must be free to be themselves with respect to diverse lifestyles and identities. The celebration of diversity also has a moral dimension since it absorbs liberalist motifs pertaining to minority groups such as gays, ethnics, and others often disenfranchised in corporate settings (Florida, 2002). Difference along these dimensions should not be suppressed in favour of a singular white-male heterosexual norm, but openly encouraged and used by the firm for productive ends (Raeburn, 2004; Janssens and Zanoni, 2005). There is also an emphasis on celebrating different lifestyles, especially with reference to alternative and modish punk attitudes. This is why organizations, especially in the creative industries such as IT and advertising, allow employees to wear informal clothing and display visible tattoos and piercings.

Opposed to the 'rule of law' demanded by bureaucracy, the freedom to be yourself extends to difference of opinion, including voicing dissent. Accordingly, if management are to retain a role, they ought to hire and nurture employees who are troublemakers, insolent, uncomfortable with the norm, and willing to thumb their noses at authority (Sutton, 2001). For example, in his discussion of the 'industrialization of bohemia' in Silicon Alley dot-com companies, Ross (2004) observed firms actively recruiting employees with countercultural and anti-capitalist values (see also Liu, 2004). The Google way of running an organization requires radical variation and dissent to spark change and innovation. This is why the ethos of the unruly youngster is often drawn upon – 'go for youth' (Peters, 1994: 204) – even if this does conflict with liberal concerns over age discrimination.

Authentic Selves

As Sutton (2001) and Bains (2007) indicate, many of the exhortations to 'just be yourself' articulated above are captured by the term authenticity. Rather than hide, suppress, or deny those unique elements of self that make up the individual person at work, they ought to be communicated. As I shall soon explore, authenticity here refers to a particular kind of 'truth of oneself' and is an axiomatic virtue in Western currents of individualism (Guignon, 2004). Organizational control aims to generate conformity to a machine, bureaucracy, or cultural norm, smothering the so-called genuine identities of the individual worker. As we noted earlier, culture management is especially problematic in this regard, given the feelings of inauthenticity it can engender when employees engage in 'face work' that has little connection to those values, identities, or feelings which are felt to be true (Kunda, 1992).

In addition to play and difference, another method in which personal authenticity is encouraged is through blurring the symbolic distinction that traditionally separates home and paid work or, at least, the formal organization. The idea that employees must adopt an *organizational* persona at work, as Kunda (1992) found at *Tech*, is reversed. People can, and should, express their authentic selves at work rather than repress the intrinsic desire to be playful and curious (Peters, 2003). Likewise, Deal and Key (1998: 16) see a key barrier to fun at work as the 'tendency to partition life and work...only to recover our humanity once we return home'. While for Bains, the question is 'whether employees are able to bring their full selves into work...characteristics in their private lives that they could bring into play at work' (2007: 219). Peters (1994: 211) makes a similar point about the way office space and dress ought to be animated with individual quirkiness. Here, the plurality of strange and vibrant identities and tastes found in the marketplace are invited into work. Indeed, this may even make organizations more existentially meaningful than the traditional home, as Reeves (2001) suggests in *Happy Mondays*.

Many of these developments could be ignored if they remained empty prescriptions in cheap throwaways pedalled to tired in-transit managers at Los Angeles and London airports. Indeed, Liu (2004) has persuasively argued that many management ideologies ostensibly targeting the subjectivities of workers (in the guise of Taylorism, neo-human relations, culture management, humanistic motivation theories, etc.) were as much about securing the self-confidence of managers as achieving superior control over workers. However, there is now growing empirical evidence that the 'just be yourself' management approach is making practical inroads into large organizations from call centres in Australia (Fleming and Sturdy, 2008), IT firms in the United States (Ross, 2004), knowledge-intensive firms around the world (Liu, 2004), consulting organizations in London (Costas and Fleming, 2008), as well as the usual suspects identified in annual 'Best Companies to Work For' surveys (in *Fortune* magazine in the United States and the *Sunday Times* in the United Kingdom) that include Google and Southwest Airlines, among others.

Given its practical relevance, I want to suggest that like any managerial intervention in the space of production, it must intersect with the political currents of organizational life. But before I delineate the nature of these emergent cultural politics, we must first ascertain the distinct variant of authenticity and self-identity that underlies the 'just be yourself' ideology.

The Architecture of Authenticity

Over the course of the following chapters, this book will unpack the components of personal authenticity that is idealized in the 'just be yourself' management approach. Needless to say that the idea of authenticity often implies a number of essentialist connotations that have been heavily criticized. The post-structuralist stream of thought dismantled not only the notion of an essentialist core (which has long been discredited by Marx's historical critique of bourgeois economic/philosophic categories as well), but also the primacy of immediate experience. To be true to yourself, one has to know what that self is. This must assume a self-transparency that inherently brackets the historicity of the cogito. Adorno (1973) levelled perhaps one of the most vitriolic criticisms of authenticity as found in the existential thought of Heidegger and Buber. He argued that the 'jargon of authenticity' sold an untenable and (in the case of Heidegger) politically dubious form of humanism that surreptitiously dropped politics out of the subject. As Adorno (1973: 60) claims, this perpetrates a kind of 'cult of inwardness' in which immediate visibility is all there is.

Cultural Narcissism

Notwithstanding these criticisms of the philosophical ideal of personal authenticity, the concept remains to have huge empirical and popular purchase in Western societies today. Giddens (1991) points out how a kind of impulsive reflexivity now pervades everyday experiences in the late modern era. We are constantly thinking about the type of person we are, want to be, and could be, and most importantly, whether we are 'being true to ourselves' in our relationships, work roles, and everyday encounters. Playing on the technical meaning of the term, 'authenticity' provides a language for verifying the original as opposed to the counterfeit or fake. The dialectical underbelly of this quest for subjective verification is the nagging feeling of phoniness or being at odds with oneself. In this sense, authenticity only becomes a problem when we are lacking it. Giddens posits a number of causes for this extreme inwardness associated with late modernity such as the decline of community, traditional, and familial ties, and a rapid acceleration of mobility, risk (and its neurotic assessment), and precarious labour in a seesawing economic environment.

The prominence of the self-help culture nicely analysed by McGee (2005) is germane here. She suggests that the self-help movement emerges when the personal comes to be seen as the sole seat of responsibility for one's employment successes and failures. Authenticity is the driving aim of discovering oneself, expressing who one really is, and giving an account for one's position. The myriad books, DVDs, and manuals proffered by the self-help industry implies that if this inner reserve of truthfulness is tapped, then one cannot help but succeed in life. While the self-help quest for authenticity is not new (McGee traces it back to the nineteenth century, in the United States at least), she argues that it is no surprise its popularity waxes and wanes with economic booms and declines. According to Lasch (1979), this culture of narcissism ultimately becomes self-defeating since the use of self-help therapy reinforces a sense of inward isolation that is often the very cause of the angst one seeks to escape.

In the world of work too, many commentators have observed employees worried about their personal authenticity (and inauthenticity) in the office, call centre, or factory. Sennett's (1998) study of workers in the new knowledge-intensive economy found them bemoaning how they fell short of the ideals they aspired to. The constantly travelling consultant, Rico, for example, felt he was living a false life since he was not able to be the family man he thought he would become once the economic security he craved was achieved. Hoschchild (1983) demonstrated how airline assistants regulated their own emotions to display the right effect for customers. The net result was an ever-present feeling that they were losing touch with themselves, making it very difficult to actually pinpoint 'who they really were'. And the innumerable studies of 'strong' corporate cultures (a movement that perhaps reached its zenith in the late 1980s) have revealed the chronic sense of inauthenticity among workers who feel 'fake', 'phoney', and 'unreal' when feigning the corporate roles, rituals, and slogans (see Kunda, 1992; Willmott, 1993; Casey, 1995).

Individualism and the Original

This individualistic and inward notion of authenticity (or 'who I really am' behind the numerous veneers) has a definite history as a number of commentators have shown (see Berman, 1970; Taylor, 1992; Guignon, 2004). It coincides with the neo-romantic reconstitution of the individual as the unique site of immediate experience, an original self that cannot be reduced to abstract a priori categories. In his discourses, for example, Rousseau argued that the originality of individual experience risked being lost and corrupted by the falsities and manufactured desires of the dirty city. This aspect of his philosophy was born from a fascination with the metropolis and the one-dimensional rituals of petit bourgeois life. One must turn back to oneself, 'know thy self' apart from the hypocrisies of the metropolis. As Taylor (1992) points out, this romantic version of personal authenticity immediately pits us against other individuals: '[T]his is my unique self and it makes me different to everyone else.'

The intersection of the neo-romantic code of authenticity and the liberalist bourgeois model of self presents us with the building blocks of what passes for personal authenticity in current popular renditions. The liberal subject is one that has a sense of *privacy*, setting it apart from the public. In accordance with this individualization, selfhood becomes a marker of *difference* compared to others. This accounts for the fetishization of difference in the 'just be yourself' management ideology. Self-realization is about getting in touch with what makes me 'me' and not simply part of an anonymous crowd or mass (which distinguishes the liberal version of authenticity from Fascist approaches). As Ferrara (1998) notes, 'uniqueness is here the result of a metaphorical subtraction – uniqueness equals the sum total of our being minus what is shared in common with others' (Ferrara, 1998: 58). Following the liberalist axiom of freedom of self-expression, one must not only have an immediate experience of subjective difference, but also express it as an *identity* that is true to itself. Identity is a self that is identifiable to others and the subject himself or herself. Hence the paradox. What makes me personally authentic, for example, might be my race, sexuality, or political associations, but I must represent this to others as individuality. These sources of personal authenticity perhaps explain why extra-employment themes related to one's life outside the homogenizing influence of work are often drawn upon in the 'just be yourself' management approach. Finally, authenticity requires an audience and visibility. This gives it both an *expressive* or aesthetic quality that often removes it from collective politics.

Managing Authenticity in the Corporation

From this tradition of philosophical and cultural thought, a very individualistic and expressive version of authenticity is tapped by the 'just be yourself' management discourse. Employees are invited or encouraged to display what is unique, different, and distinguishable about their identities. This is often done by attempting to evoke various gestures and aspects of self traditionally associated with the private, extra-employment sphere (including sexuality, leisure, consumption, and so forth). Corporatized authenticity thus paradoxically relies upon a kind of mimesis or simulation in order to have the desired effect under conditions traditionally devoid of individual difference. I will follow this intriguing aspect of the 'just be yourself' management discourse in the chapters that follow.

There are undoubtedly many reasons why authenticity is now on the radar in many large corporations in Western economies, some of which we have already mentioned above. In some ways, it is a continuation of humanizing managerial discourses that can be traced back to the neo-human relations and culture management movements. They too make normative demands on employees in the name of adjusting them to the fundamental 'lack' at the heart of the employment relationship, softening the crunch of capitalist work (also see Bendix, 1956). What is different about this latest interest in authenticity is how it does not frame it in terms of self-realization via task empowerment (*namely* the neo-human relations movement) or see its realization in the identification with unitary values, beliefs, and emotions (*namely* culture management). Indeed, the fetishization of difference could well be a response to the failures of cultural control in relation to stifled innovation and creativity (see Foster and Kaplan, 2001). Moreover, with increasing scepticism in broader popular consciousness regarding the role of the corporation, an injection of liberalism into the sequestered realm of work might have useful motivational effects.[2] This accounts for the celebration of difference, diversity, and even a radical chic (e.g. wearing an anti-capitalist T-shirt in the corporation). Most importantly, I want to suggest that this latest reincarnation is closely linked to shifting techniques of power and control. The corporation achieves definite political gains from 'authenticizing' work in this manner, as more of the employee's personhood is linked (however vicariously) to the capital accumulation process.

The Politics of 'Just Being Yourself'

The corporate appreciation of personal authenticity prima facie appears to be a liberalizing gesture to erstwhile oppressive regimes of control and dated managerial ideologies. Some of the classic accounts of Fordist work-places demonstrated how employee lives were stringently circumscribed by the rhythms of work and rather draconian rules for how one ought to act and 'be'. These past prohibitions regarding identity and 'who one really is' seem needless and unwarranted today, perhaps indicative not so much of the necessities of production, but of a desire to simply exert authority. This observation is supported by the fact that even hard-nosed market rationalists today appear to advocate caution regarding the coun-terproductive effects of this gratuitous tendency in traditional manage-ment styles (see Kunda and Ailon-Souday, 2005). In this respect, even management today appears to be anti-management, at least conventional management with its egregious excesses that seem more self-satisfying than anything else.

Why should we view such managerial developments (packaged as they are in the discourse of free self-expression and emancipation) as a con-tinuation of the classic corporate objective to exact domination? I suggest we should do so for a number of reasons. The authenticity being recom-mended in the 'just be yourself' business philosophy represents a particu-larly invasive form of 'existential exposure' in which more and more of the workers' identities are prospected by the corporation and put to work. As I will demonstrate below, and in concurrence with recent criticisms of liberalist identity politics, such an exposure of self, seldom operates as a revelation of some more genuine substance (whatever that may be) but as a production of identity, fitted to a number of archetypical stereotypes. Also, as many critical observers did apropos the neo-human relations preoccupation with self-actualization (e.g. Braverman, 1974; Johnson and Gill, 1993), we ought to ask who exactly is being asked to be authentic and why. In light of that line of analysis, an obvious power structure is revealed since the sender and recipient of the message are not symmetrical. Senior managers are not subjected to the call to be authentic as much as the middle-level employee in an airline, a shop-floor worker in an electronics factory, or a junior consultant. Those who are most tightly controlled at work are more likely to be targeted by the 'just be yourself' discourse. This is so because it intimately connects with the perennial 'problem of control' that still persists even in ostensibly 'humanized' workplaces.

In order to unpack the complex relationships between power, control, and the 'just be yourself' version of personal authenticity, I will use an empirical example from my own research (as developed by Fleming and Sturdy, 2008) of the call centre mentioned at the beginning of this chapter. It can be recalled that Sunray Customer Service celebrated diverse employee identities that would have seemed alien to previous managerial systems. Encapsulated in the slogan 'Remember the 3Fs: Fun, Focus and Fulfilment', employees are encouraged to just be themselves: express lifestyle diversity (relating to gay sexuality, punk and alternative identities, sexualized expressions of self, etc.); consumerism (various dress codes, especially indicating a kind of youth 'slacker cool'); leisure (including partying and drinking); rituals of fun; and so forth. The idea here is that workers would be more motivated and engaged if they were free to express what made them unique individuals – both at and outside of work (hence the importance of expressions of lifestyle, sexuality, and leisure). I want to argue that the discourse presents a form of control in and of itself (given the way it exposes the workers' subjectivities in a particular manner) and also functions to detract attention from pre-existing controls.

Reinforcement of Subjective Categories

First, through both recruitment processes and the celebration of difference, Sunray reinforces broader societal constructions of identity in particular ways and forms. Identity is considered multifarious, in keeping with late modern constructions of society. Furthermore, and echoing the work of

Janssens and Zanoni (2005), diversity for both individuals and employees generally is constructed as particular variants of sexuality, ethnicity, consumerism, and playfulness rather than say occupational skills, familial roles, politics, and community. Social critics have challenged the practical implementation of multiculturalism and diversity as maintaining harmful stereotypes and validating only those characteristics that are useful to the system of production (see Chow, 2002).

Be Yourself . . . But Only Up to a Point

Second and most transparently, control is evident in the limits implicitly and explicitly imposed that contradict the rhetoric of a laissez-faire approach to norms, emotions, identities, and their expression, revealing managerial instrumentality and the manufacture of fun. For example, the numerous games and songs were largely prescribed and contained in time and space. Likewise emotional negativity, including that associated with problems at home, was proscribed or segregated into a counselling space. In other words, emotional labour prevailed and even extended to non-customer, non-work task contexts. There is no room for the non-fun, non-'different' person in the organized events. Similarly, Sunray was strictly non-union and explicit resistance was suppressed. There was no place either, then for a militant self or 'fun as sabotage'! Indeed, following the practice of bringing in homemade food for colleagues, one employee made cannabis cookies and was (unsurprisingly perhaps) dismissed for his efforts! In relation to visual aspects of identity however, there was greater tolerance, although this is likely to be a condition of the nature of the work with its lack of face-to-face customer contact. Indeed, more generally the instrumentality of the approach was clear. Fun and contained expressiveness were allowed in order to hide or counteract the otherwise constrained nature of the work – 'At Sunray we try to make work fun – in fact we try to make it fun instead of work' (training manual).

Existential Exposure

The 'just be yourself' regime was not just a managerial indulgence to compensate for hardship or even stimulate motivation. The third way in which it served as a control was in the appropriation (and partial construction) of identities and other unrewarded characteristics for productive ends. This is particularly evident in the recruitment and production of youthfulness, sexuality, and enthusiasm. By allowing people to 'be themselves' in ways that facilitate the customer service function (e.g. positive sentiments, flexibility, discretion, creativity, etc.), the 3Fs philosophy enlists the once private dimensions of the individual as a corporate resource. This functions as a kind of 'existential exposure' since it is those attributes that are thought to make up the individual – paradoxically defined through very generalized categories such as race, sexual preference, and so forth – that are now scrutinized by the managerial gaze in the name of championing freedom.

This type of control appears to utilize authenticity, difference, diversity, and lifestyle rather than the bland conformity recorded in earlier studies of culture engineering. Echoing a major theme in this book, the data suggest that Sunray does this by symbolically dissolving the private–public boundary. The motifs of fun, partying, and sex, usually associated with the private sphere, are discursively integrated into Sunray's team exercises, social events, and everyday interactions. And up to a point, employees were encouraged to challenge the way the organization operates, especially during new projects and the self-deprecating skits during the Away Day (the CEO was a particularly popular target).

Individualization and Responsibility at Work

While employees in a cultural control regime may have had 'private' reserves of identity from which they distanced work roles, and that allowed an internal preserve of genuineness distinct from the corporation, at Sunray, these very qualities were brought out into the open. And indeed, fourth, such a colonization of identities served as a form of self-disciplinary control in that individuals became accountable for their performance at an existential level. Because workers' real selves and identities were encouraged, more was visible to the managerial gaze in which certain attitudes were highlighted as problematic. Rather than motivational problems or insufficient correspondence with the company values, here, any failure is more personal. This was seen in the counselling dynamic of the 3Fs program where team members were policed on their own personal mental state: 'I will first recognize a difference in their attitude... and I will say "What has happened? Is it the job or something at home? What can I do to help you with that?"' Contrary to Peters' exhortations about promoting dissent then, Sunray unsurprisingly favoured only a certain type of authentic identity, as the cannabis cookie example above clearly indicates.

Detraction from Extant Controls

The fifth issue that links authenticity to control is the detraction it caused in the workplace. An obvious observation of the 'just be yourself' celebration of authenticity (via freedom from control) in the call centre was the continual presence of typical controls associated with technology, bureaucracy, and corporate culture (i.e. unitary values and commitment). In addition to this observation, accounts of the intentions of management and employees' various reactions suggest that the 'joyous anarchy' (Peters, 1994) prescribed by this management approach detracts from existing controls rather than precipitating their demise. In particular, the perennial dysfunctions associated with technological, bureaucratic, and cultural controls are a particular target for this detraction. In the Sunray call centre, a team development manager relayed a very telling rationale regarding the 'just be yourself' management approach:

Without the culture the place would be drab, and in most workplaces people can't wait to leave. But at Sunray they love to work and really get into it. You know, just the other day I heard someone say 'I can't believe they pay me to have fun!' and that is exactly what happens.

The mundane rhythms of technological control lead to boredom and alienation which is a key reason why Sunray attempted to impute a sense of fun and play in the roles (also see Kinnie et al., 2000). Likewise, the standardized and hierarchical formalities of bureaucratic control lead to feelings of disenchantment and sometimes anti-authoritarian sentiments. Sunray therefore focused on the importance of diversity, informality, and dissent as defining features of the employment experience. Similarly, culture management can result in employees having feelings of being fake, lacking individuality, and a cynical division between 'who they really are' and the prescribed corporate self. Sunray therefore galvanized its approach via an emphasis on individual differences, authenticity, and non-work selves in particular. The symbolic blurring of labour and the private realm was important for animating work with a sense of authenticity, something I will turn to in Chapter 2.

Overall, the dysfunctions of control that the 'just be yourself' discourse detracts from can be seen to derive primarily from the more general ills of collective conformity. Technology regiments, bureaucracy standardizes, and culture normalizes. This could explain the strong emphasis on individualism and idiosyncratic expressions of self in this discourse or what Tannenbaum (1967), cited earlier, argued are the central targets of organizational control.

The valorization of individual freedom and choice regarding how we define and express ourselves also resonates strongly with the way in which personal authenticity has been defined in liberal ideological thought (Taylor, 1992). Perhaps this is why the so-called liberal organization attempts to harness authentic expressions of self by drawing the private realm and its signifiers into the workplace, and thus making use of those aspects of employee selves that were previously barred by management or simply retained or protected by employees as a point of difference.

The 'just be yourself' approach detracts from the controls in the call centre by emphasizing a particular kind of freedom, which pertains to identity and expression of self rather than, say, job discretion or participation in decision making. The reduction of freedom to a question of self-expression and identity highlights important issues regarding what we might call the 'politics of detraction'. The 'just be yourself' management style did not free workers *from* control, but introduced freedoms *around* control. As practiced at Sunray, employees enjoyed liberties around the work task – displays of lifestyle choices, sexuality, private desires, and consumption patterns – rather than in the task itself, which remained tightly controlled. Visual aspects of identity in particular enjoyed greater tolerance although this is likely to be a condition of the nature of the work with its lack of face-to-face customer contact. Such freedom was especially noticeable in relation to technological control since this was the dominant mode of constraint in work tasks. Autonomy around the rules of bureaucracy – how one conducts him- or herself within a formally defined shift or mandatory social event – was also evident in the case. A similar process is inevitable with cultural control. Team-building exercises, for example, are imbued with an array of quirky idiosyncrasies such as an employee bringing in a surfboard to show peers 'who he really is'. There are however inevitable tensions here, given the contradiction between the requirement for collective identification and the celebration of individual difference and authenticity.

The difference between freedom *from* control and freedom *around* control gave rise to dysfunctions in and of itself. The demarcation between the two realms of freedom was sometimes unclear and ambiguous. For some workers, the newly legislated freedom to just be themselves did not sit well with the continued conformity to extant controls. It is easy to see why expectations were raised in this regard when one surveys the sensational claims about 'free-rangers' and the 'upside down organizational structure'. Indeed, for some employees, this identity-orientated detraction from control was experienced more as mystification, inspiring its own variants of resistance. They were cynical about the aims and legitimacy of the 'just be yourself' discourse since it did not afford practical freedoms in the concrete task of work and its organization. Charges of hypocrisy were common in relation to the culture programme: '[W]e are supposed to be individuals, but only on their terms'.

Conclusion

The tenuous relationship between freedom, control, and non-work that we see in the 'just be yourself' approach to personal authenticity constitutes the textual political economy of the firm that I will focus on in the forthcoming chapters. Authenticity in the rhetoric and practice of 'just be yourself' management perspective reflects the axioms of individual identity and market rationalism. Likewise, much of the recent practitioner-orientated literature simply equates authenticity with expressions of individual difference: the main 'reason why people have learned to be inauthentic in relating to others is the pressure to conform' (Bains, 2007: 249). Some employees at Sunray cynically challenged this notion of authenticity by highlighting commonality, solidarity, and uniformity – the labour process itself – as a sign for 'who they really were'. The focus was on the standardized nature of the work task itself (or outputs), undermining continual references to diverse identities and selves (or inputs) surrounding tasks. Perhaps such cynicism marks the return of the once derided 'organizational man' (Whyte, 1956) of bureaucratic corporations in which the communal and non-descript rhythms of public organizational life govern his or her identity at work while 'real' selves are downplayed. I will explore this reconfigured understanding of authenticity in more detail in Chapter 6 when it is linked to the politics of solidarity and contemporary workplace identities.

The 'just be yourself' approach resonates not only with contemporary liberalist themes such as diversity and market rationalism, but with what Sennett (1976) referred to over 30 years ago as the 'ideology of intimacy' in the drive to humanize work. This is the view that 'social relationships of all kinds are real, believable and authentic the closer they approach the inner psychological concerns of each person'. This, he argued, 'transmutes political categories into psychological categories' (Sennett, 1976: 259). In other words, employee performances are cast in terms of psychological characteristics and private identities rather than their structural position in a set of social relations. Moreover, as aspects of self become defined by the instrumental rationality of the economic realm, an unintended consequence may be a further loss of both individual and collective forms of authenticity and a renewed sense of self-alienation.

As Bendix (1956) shows in his classic history of industrial thought, managerial interest in humanization among the workforce is not entirely new. The neo-human relations and culture movements, for example, attempted to mitigate anomie and self-alienation through the appropriation of work group norms, organizational identification, and individual self-actualization through work tasks (Mayo, 1945; Ray, 1986). As indicated by Kunda (1992), however, the non-work realm was largely closed off from work for fear of contamination (also see O'Reilly and Chatman, 1996). The 'just be yourself' approach changes this in aiming to humanize work by appropriating (and therefore, partially constructing) a range of non-work identities and other unrewarded characteristics for productive ends. This is particularly evident in the recruitment and production of youthfulness, sexuality, and enthusiasm. It also echoes the, albeit largely informal, ways in which employers have long used gendered characteristics as well as indulgency patterns where a managerial 'blind eye' was turned for functional ends on non-work misbehaviour such as informal sports (Gouldner, 1955). A formalization of both these processes has been noted recently in the field of diversity legislation (Janssens and Zanoni, 2005) and in a case of 'negotiated leniency' by management in order to appropriate work-based occupational identities as a form of control (Anteby, 2008).

It is this interest in the traditionally non-work sphere, the connection between life and labour as Arendt (1958) might have put it, that is perhaps most striking about this management ideology. The aura of non-work appears to be useful in the 'just be yourself' discourse for providing the cultural scaffolding and inspiration for authenticity, almost in an attempt to make work seem as if it is not work at all. This would make it 'life' instead – but it never turns out this way. As I shall argue in the forthcoming chapters, this fetishization of non-work reveals an important political economy related to 'the commons' in which the source material of this truncated brand of authenticity is also the site of a counter-corporate mode of life.

2

Social Labour and the Haemorrhaging Organization

[T]he ideology of 'human resources' is preparing the ground for the instrumentalization of non-economic aspirations by economic rationality: the new type of enterprise will strive to take these aspirations into consideration but only because they are factors of productivity and 'competitiveness' of a particular kind. The question is whether this will lead to a greater exploitation and manipulation of workers or to an autonomization of non-quantifiable, extra-economic values.

(Gorz, 1988: 60)

There is something quite different about the 'Google-style' employee compared to what Whyte (1956) memorably called the archetypical 'organizational man'. The dull uniformity of the 'organizational man' was particularly definitive of the corporate bureaucratic office: he or she exuded a one-dimensional attitude and demeanour, and it was difficult to distinguish workers from one another. The generic homogenization of corporate life was transferred onto employees themselves as all those attributes that defined them as individuals were precluded in the name of bureaucratic efficiency and, later, corporate norms. Indeed, with respect to the so-called high-commitment organizational cultures of the 1980s and 1990s, it is no wonder that O'Reilly and Chatman (1996) see parallels between extremist cults and the modern corporation. Both represent 'greedy organizations' (Coser, 1974) that isolate the individual from the rest of their *lebenswelt*. Family, leisure, and other facets of the person indicating a life outside the firm are viewed by the prophets of culture as potential contaminants. Many insider accounts of life within the corporate clan found that management were particularly unwilling to acknowledge the private lives of workers since this was where the externalities of production were offloaded (see Kunda, 1992). The eventual ideological goal was internal coherency, uniformity, and homogenization whereby individual quirks and idiosyncrasies marking the private individual are kept to a minimum.

One of the more unusual features of the organizational types identified in Chapter 1 is the way the 'whole person' is included in the regime of the labour process. In accordance with the idealization of personal authenticity underlying the 'just be yourself' managerial approach, much of this 'whole person' is expressive or aesthetic, communicating a particular identity or lifestyle that is then celebrated inside the firm. The boundary of the corporation appears to be increasingly permeable as more aspects that constitute the 'authentic person' (in the liberalist tradition identified in Chapter 1) are evoked and voiced as a sign of originality and uniqueness. This shift in management ideology occurs in a number of organizational settings. Perhaps it is not surprising to observe punks with tattoos and facial piercing in the call centre situation mentioned earlier. High visibility within the confines of the firm is perhaps more likely to be condoned given the low physical visibility to customers. But we also see a version of this celebration of private lives in organizations more exposed to the customer gaze such as large multinational hotels (e.g. the Intercontinental) where the personal likes and dislikes of workers are included in 'worker of the week' lobby placards.

This aspect of the 'just be yourself' business ideology is interesting since authenticity or 'who I really am' is presumed to be something that is chiefly experienced *outside* the corporation (once the workday is done and life can begin again). There is thus an attempt to both practically and symbolically evoke the thematic lexicon of the private sphere associated with consumption, sex, leisure, lifestyle, and so forth. The assumption that we are more ourselves outside the confines of the factory or office reflects the continuing importance of a wider division between the public and private, life and labour that emerged with capitalism. I will suggest that the maintenance of this boundary was until recently politically useful in various ways (although not always successfully accomplished). The current invitation of private lives into the realm of work, where life has typically been officially denied, has important implications for how we understand the politics of authenticity. In particular, and developing the argument made in Chapter 1, I see this part of corporatized authenticity as a technique of power related to what I called existential exposure. By encouraging expressions of the 'whole person' (or that which makes workers individuals in the extra-employment sphere), more of the labouring subject is framed by the production process and put to work.

This existential exposure is unfalteringly peddled as a kind of freedom and perhaps it is exactly that in many ways. But to reiterate the central argument of this book, such developments need to be conceptualized as indicative of shifting political currents underlying the control of the corporate form today. With the exhortation to 'just be yourself' and express those facets of personhood that define one's life outside of work, a relationship of domination is established. There is nothing too mysterious occurring here. Take, for example, the way in which displays of personal authenticity are linked to the employment contract. Underlying the exhortation to 'just be yourself' is the coercive proviso, 'but only up to a point and only in the manner we deem appropriate' (Fleming and Sturdy, 2008). This immediately connects selfhood to the banalities of corporate domination in relation to motivation ('are you expressing the "right" attitude for this type of organization'), performance monitoring ('is something wrong at home?'), as well as branding to external parties such as consumers, contracting agents, and in the case of CSR initiatives, government and prospective employees.

This kind of domination of selfhood is very similar to the culture management paradigm of yesteryear. The crucial difference, however, is the way in which it seeks to exploit the 'life' of workers – a life that persists despite (and because of) the antisocial practices of the firm. A good example of this shifting dynamic of domination can be noted in the anti-management attitude of cynicism. In the halcyon days of high-commitment organizational cultures, workers were told to emotionally attach themselves to the corporation, its prefabricated vision, values, and beliefs. The corporate collective was everything. As many studies subsequently revealed, many workers did not really buy the culture. They secretly referred to the gauche trust exercises as 'California bath crap' (Kunda, 1992) and the newsletter 'Goebel's Gazette' (Collinson, 1992). Workers developed an undercurrent of 'authentic' feelings and definitions of selfhood through the classic backstage–front-of-stage demarcation, of which the non-work realm was a particularly important referent (involving class affiliations, family life, outside interests, etc.). The 'just be yourself' management approach, however, aims to expose and utilize these backstage spheres of selfhood by incorporating the whole person into the production matrix. Of course, only certain types of 'authentic' expressions of backstage identity are permitted, but the very strategy of exposing and prospecting this undercurrent of life (especially in relation to non-work) represents a significant development in the cultural politics of work.

I use the term *haemorrhaging organization* to somewhat colourfully describe some of the developments hastened by the 'just be yourself' management approach and its fetishization of personal authenticity. I will argue in this chapter that the symbolic boundary between work and non-work, life and labour, is an object of manipulation in the 'liberal organization' as it aspires to arrogate more of aspects of self to the datum of production. This disrupts the Fordist work–non-work boundary, a separation that, as Thompson (1967) argued some years ago, was always important for establishing work discipline. The current drive for expressions of personal authenticity symbolically invites the complete persona into the realm of work, including nominally private gestures associated with consumption, sex, and lifestyle. This completeness entails a paradox that reveals the limits of this managerial technique. It is only a partial kind of completeness that is welcome into the firm since there are many kinds of authentic expressions that remain impermissible. So, not only has the logic of production escaped the factory walls into all parts of society as many have argued (see Fleming and Spicer, 2007), but also the ideology of everyday life outside the firm has been transferred into the sphere of production. The chapter will demonstrate how this two-part movement has seen the boundaries of life and labour haemorrhage in significant ways.

How should we conceptualize this strategy to appropriate the life of the whole 'authentic' individual? For this task, the chapter will adapt the theoretical work of Hardt and Negri (1994, 1999), including the 'the social factory' and 'the commons' to argue that the quest for expressions of authenticity (via the symbolic dismantling of work and non-work) represents a moment of parasitic co-optation.[1] The undercurrent of life inspired by non-work associatives that the corporation seeks to mine for its own ends could be 'the commons' after the approach developed by Hardt and Negri (1994). For them, the commons are those non-work and uncommodified associations and creative labour that the corporation seeks to valorize within the productive sphere. The commons is the life-giving cooperative labour that occurs despite the domination of dead labour coagulated in the corporate form. I posit that under the commons is the raw source material for personal authenticity as it is prospected and objectified within the corporation.

The lack of life inside the sphere of production is ideologically sutured by bringing into the workplace a *life of sorts*, the remnant 'life' of the commons after it has been simulated and put to work. But the non-work that is evoked to represent such authenticity is of a very superficial, expressive, and staged kind since it has been processed through the machinery of appropriation. The theoretical approach that I develop in this chapter regarding the syncretic union between work and non-work in the name of a 'liberating' authenticity not only reveals how the logic of production has appropriated life, it also questions assumptions about where the moment of labour actually happens today. The term 'social labour', proposed by the Italian autonomist perspective, identifies how the corporation relies upon various nodes of productive and unproductive labour outside the formal organization as a source of innovation, dynamism, and cooperation. In the following section I want to explore the work and non-work boundary and its haemorrhaging in light of the 'just be yourself' management discourse. Then I will turn to the notion of 'social work' and the 'social factory' in order to link this corporate discourse to broader political flows of power within late capitalist societies.

Boundaries, Life, and Labour

It is no coincidence that the version of authenticity presumed in the 'just be yourself' discourse is one that privileges the non-work realm as a reference point. As we noted in the previous chapter, the split between the public and private is important in liberal political thought. The expressive individualism encouraged by organizations like Sunray, Southwest Airlines, and Google dovetails with the axiomatic notion that the authentic person can be found in the private, backstage 'truth' of the subject (usually expressed in leisure, consumption, lifestyle, and home life). Conversely, the workplace has traditionally been defined as a site of alienation and regimentation in which the individual quirks of the person are downplayed in favour of generic control systems. This is the 'lack of life' that many have argued necessarily pervades work, even if it offers limited enjoyments and pleasures occasionally. With the transformation of work into an end in itself, becoming a coercive chore bound to a fundamental antagonism rather than an expression of creativity and life, most of us would rather avoid work like the plague, to paraphrase Marx.

The 'just be yourself' organization attempts to put some life back into work by appropriating life itself. The so-called private individual is considered the prime site of this authentic life. The definition of authenticity as something private is shored up by two important historical achievements in Western societies. The first is the inauguration of the public–private division and the second is the material split between work (a place where we forego life) and non-work (where we hope to attain a life through sex, leisure, relationships, and so forth). We have already alluded to the public and private division, and it is a cornerstone feature of Western social–political thought (Arendt, 1958). It first emerges in the wake of the monumental advent of the nation state and public life where one engages in political dialogue and reflection. The *polis* provides the conditions for private life, but in liberalist thinking a kind of tense symbiosis emerges between the private individual and the public. As Sennett (1976) argues, the appearance of the liberal state co-emerges with the idea of a private person that is often set against the state or collective in relation to his or her views, feelings, and practices (the invention of the modern family was not far behind). Marx after Hegel saw this as a founding moment of alienation.

The second important historical achievement that underlies the equation of authenticity with private individualism relates to the establishment of the work and non-work division. The shift from feudalism to capitalism in Europe during the eighteenth and nineteenth centuries witnessed a major reorganization of both the physical and conceptual spatiality of working life (Braudel, 1961). Under feudalism, peasants and artisans were usually located in close proximity to home, family, and what today we might refer to as leisure; Mills (1956) calls this the 'craftsman' configuration of an integrated life. With the emergence of capitalism and factory production, however, the spatial characteristics of the 'putting-out' system in particular were unsuitable due to the lack of worker discipline and control (Thompson, 1967). Factories were fenced off like prisons, and the urbanization of the industrial proletariat created a new geography of work that was markedly different from previous ones. This division also involved important temporal and subjective elements. As time became the source of wealth under the aegis of capitalist production, the working day was dichotomized between company time and private time (Clegg and Dunkerly, 1980). And depending on whether one was at home or at work, quite different selves were exhibited (Nippert-Eng, 1996).

Although the division between work and non-work life was certainly not watertight, with the work ethic (Thompson, 1968) and industrial paternalism (Bendix, 1956), for example, playing a major role outside the factory gates, the spatial division did represent a significant shift from previous economic regimes. The phenomenological minutia of the effort required to maintain this boundary has been documented by Nippert-Eng (1996). Work and home connote different things to us regarding self-identity and the emotional geography we expect to occupy. In relation to the scientific-lab

41

workers she studied, Nippert-Eng summarizes the micro-management of this spatial division pertaining to one of the more 'life giving' activities, that of sex:

From the time they begin their apprenticeships, machinist folklore, contractual disputes, equipment requirements, and sexually homogeneous environments continually reinforce the idea that time and space is either dedicated to work or home, public or private pursuits. The lesson is that, ultimately, these cannot be the same. Because of its learned, exclusive mental association with one realm and not another, then, the more we are like Ed (a lab worker), the more even the thought of sex in the workplace is outrageous. (Nippert-Eng, 1996: 3)

Nippert-Eng (1996) points out that this boundary is, of course, imaginary, in that it is breached constantly during the vagaries of everyday working life. But as an associative imaginary (with strong masculine connotations regarding its connection with the home and family), it still organizes our lives in meaningful ways. The home is often romanticized, considered a kind of sanctuary, a place where intimacy, rest, and leisure are enjoyed outside the deadening rhythms of work. Non-work is a place of freedom and choice, and work is dominated by hierarchy and rule: 'As a private realm . . . home ideally is a place where we can "be ourselves", "put up our feet", "let down our hair" and relax among those who see us "warts and all"' (Nippert-Eng, 1996: 20). The imaginary boundary and its respective associations have for many years remained important for understanding 'who we are' in these different settings.

Managing the Private and Public at Work

Given the connotations outlined above it is not surprising that the boundary between work and non-work has been a perennial concern in management thought and practice. The associations noted by Nippert-Eng (1996) are certainly accurate for many, but she forgets that they arose from a long struggle between capital and labour that perhaps stretches back to the enclosure movement in the early phases of industrialism. Later, the factory sphere was clearly considered a zone of discipline and 'work' as opposed to leisure and freedom. As Weber (1948) also highlighted in his description of the bureaucratic office, depersonalization was a paramount objective in order to achieve efficiency. The office had to be evacuated of life and shaped after the image of a machine or army. Weber identified a process of 'eliminating from official business love, hatred and all purely personal, irrational, and emotional elements' (Weber, 1948: 216).

Moreover, in illustrating the 'rules of separation' in administrative bureaucracies, Weber states that there is usually a complete

separation of the property belonging to the organization, which is controlled
within the sphere of the office, and the personal property of the official, which is
available for his [sic] own private use. There is a corresponding separation of the
place in which official functions are carried out, the 'office' in the sense of premises,
from living quarters. (Weber, 1947: 331–2)

There are exceptions to this boundary maintenance behaviour in work
organizations – such as the activities of Ford's Sociological Department
and the interest shown in the influence of private attitudes on task performance by early Human Relations theorists (see Roethlisberger and
Dickson, 1939). But by and large the influence of non-work was considered something to be avoided.

This fear of 'contamination' was no more pronounced than in the
attempt in the 1980s and early 1990s to build 'strong' high-commitment
corporate cultures. As many commentators have observed (see Van Maanen, 1991; Casey, 1995; Barker, 1999), culture management aims to 'marry'
the employee emotionally and subjectively to the firm. Under the auspices
of unitary values, the organization becomes a community or collective in
which the 'old' divisions between capital and labour are outwardly super-
seded. The corporate solidarity that underpins cultural control is succinctly
explained by Barley and Kunda (1992: 382) – committed employees 'make
no distinction between their own welfare and the welfare of the firm'.
Kunda's (1992) analysis of cultural control at 'Tech' – a computer engineering firm – follows Goffman's (1959) classic dramaturgical front-of-stage
and backstage demarcation. Kunda depicted an organization in the throes
of a chronic struggle between *role embracement* and *role distancing*. Employees were constantly exhorted to absorb the designed membership role as
their own and become a 'company man or woman'. But at the same time,
they wanted to maintain a private reserve that was truly theirs and beyond
the corporate collective. Employees adopted a number of tactics to cope
with this, including depersonalization or distancing of self. As a result, 'the
emotions experienced as part of the organizational self are presented as
distinct from other aspects of emotional life and at some remove from one's
"authentic" sense of self' (1992: 183). According to Kunda, such depersonalization requires that

one control and even suppress personal and spontaneous reactions to the work
environment, thus purging them from the organizational self and leaving

only appropriate 'emotions'. Failure to do this is noticed by others. (Kunda, 1992: 184)

This purging process is no more evident than in the externalization of the emotional injuries incurred at Tech. Given the intense work effort that was required to signal loyalty to the company, marriage break-ups, burnout, alcohol abuse, and other pathologies were a common occurrence. However, there were limits to what Tech wanted to know about this more harmful side of its culture. An engineer speaks of a departed manager: 'One day he stood up and told us he was going to a detox center...he didn't have to tell us. Some people were quite upset. Keep that kind of shit to yourself.... He's gone now' (Kunda, 1992: 202–3). This managerial approach stands in direct contrast to a 'just be yourself' firm like Sunray that counselled employees on private problems and directly related them to attitude and work performance.

Authenticity and the Greedy Organization

It is against this backdrop that we need to understand the current evocation of non-work in the 'just be yourself' management approach. Notwithstanding the abiding importance of this boundary today, it is proposed that the current quest to authenticate the employee, in part at least, is characterized by the ideological displacement of this traditional symbolic boundary. This fetishization of the extra-employment sphere as a productive device to impute some 'life' into work and motivate employees was well underway before the arrival of liberation management. Earlier holistic approaches to human resource management (Heuberger and Nash, 1994) also mined imagery from the private realm, especially in relation to emotional labour where employees attempt to give customers a more homely and genuine service. Hochschild's (1983) ethnographic study of airline attendants recorded a striking application of this. In order to facilitate their emotional labour in the aeroplane cabin, employees were encouraged to use a 'living room analogy' and act 'as if' the aeroplane cabin was their home. Moreover, Kanter (1989: 286) also suggested that in the changing world of competitive markets that demand flexibility and creativity, the 'myth' that there ought to be a watertight division between work and non-work is increasingly untenable. This is demonstrated by the changing structure of professional employment (e.g. the office-less workplace, working from home, etc.) and emergent informal methods of management.

Despite these earlier manifestations, the idea of replicating the private inside the firm finds its fullest expression in the 'just be yourself' business philosophy and its concern with personal authenticity. The corporation can only give work some life by taking it from employees themselves. The appropriation methods of the 'greedy' corporation are different to that of, say, culture management simply encroaching upon the private lives of employees through overwork or stress (see Scase and Goffee, 1989; Watson, 1994; Perlow, 1998). Here, the inverse seems to be the case: experiences and emotions recognized to be associated with the non-work sphere (such as relaxation, recreation, fun, etc.) are actively evoked in the name of personal authenticity. It is important to note here that non-work is a kind of screen upon which the managerial gaze projects its own assumptions, desires, and images. This gaze sees in non-work a romanticized 'kingdom of individuals' that fits well with the hyper-individualized notion of authenticity discerned earlier. In the parlance of the latest managerial discourse, genuine selves are often identified within collective categories (race, sexual preference, consumption patterns, etc.) but firmly embodied at the monadic level of the unique person. Hence the importance of an expressive or aesthetic difference, diversity, and dissenting 'cool'.

An important mechanism for objectifying and utilizing 'life' inside the organization is by simulating themes, motifs, and activities that are mentally and symbolically associated with non-work and the private individual. Consumption, lifestyle factors, sexuality, and humour, for example, are not externalized in favour of a collective normative alignment nor barred from the organization in the bureaucratic tradition, but reified and put to work as an organizational resource. The title of Semler's (2004) latest book is telling in this regard: *The Seven-Day Weekend: Changing the Way Work Works*. The idea is that work can become a place of non-work (or a weekend in Semler's case) since the deadening uniformity of previous corporate regimes no longer meets the needs of a more dynamic and knowledge-hungry environment. Semler argues that by injecting into labour the authentic experiences and identities that we might enjoy outside the firm, more flexible and positive employees are likely to emerge.

There are some other emblematic themes of this version of authenticity that seem to appear quite regularly in companies that I have researched as well as those studied by others. Sexuality is an obvious 'source' of authenticity that I noted being reified in rather stereotypical ways in the Sunray call centre discussed in Chapter 1 (see also Fleming, 2007). As Nippert-Eng (1996) illustrated above, work and sex are conventionally considered mutually exclusive (although many also observe that sex was probably always secretly present in the form of games, flirtation, harassment, and so forth). The formal acceptance of sex and sexual identities associated with gay and/or lesbian identities is interesting. In the Sunray call centre firm, sexual fraternizing was condoned and promoted by the organization as a way of creating a more fun environment. In particular, Sunray celebrated gay sexuality, making it very different to the homophobic organizational structures in which gay workers have to hide their identities (Garbiel et al., 2000). For sure, many workplaces have approached diversity legislation as an opportunity for increased synergies rather than a restraint on effectiveness (Janssens and Zanoni, 2005). Raeburn's (2004) study of US organizations that embrace sexual diversity, for example, indicates that they generally benefit from more motivated and dynamic work environments.

Diverse lifestyles and identities are also a major source of perceived authenticity, attributes of self that would more likely be expressed outside of the organization. Management commentators suggest that this diversity ought to be harnessed and used to create more dynamic, creative, and enjoyable organizations. Deal and Key (1998: 25) argue that celebrations at work foster diversity and 'provide social support for being yourself and believing that you matter'. This celebration includes the expression of alternative lifestyles, different dress codes, and various ways of militating against 'the system'. In this regard, as Ross (2004) points out, chic 'slacker cool' is a favourite in the IT industry. This enables workers to feel that they are remaining true to their cyberpunk, do-it-yourself roots even if they are 'working for the man'. Fun and play in the workplace is also a major theme, going against the grain of much industrial ideology wedded to formal rationality. The transposition of fun inside the regime of work characteristic of the 'just be yourself' management approach is thus unsurprising. I will investigate this aspect of authenticity management in the next chapter.

Authenticity and the Social Factory

We can use the arguments presented in Chapter 1 to link this apparent 'haemorrhaging' of the corporate form to a political economy of control and power. That is to say, a twofold articulation of managerial power is operating when the organization attempts to utilize the non-work themes to facilitate expressions of personal authenticity. First is a kind of 'existential exposure' in which more of the employees' selfhood is made available to the managerial gaze in order to enhance motivation, sell the firm to the customer, and push the responsibilities of collective production onto the worker and so forth. In this sense, we must not take the symbolic blurring too seriously since there are obvious limits: employees can fulfil their personal authenticity and be themselves, but only up to a point (and that point represents the limits of the corporation). Second, the simulation underlying the attempt to foster non-work modes of 'life' in the organization detracts from the traditional controls already in place. I will argue in Chapter 3 that this simulation or mimesis often fails, becoming a locus of antagonism in and of itself.

What is this 'life' that the corporation now wants inside the firm? Answering this question will reveal not only the bio-politics of managed authenticity, but also a profound political economy of the corporation that is emerging today. Building on the ideas of the Italian autonomists such as Hardt and Negri, and Tronti (1971) we can surmise that this 'life' represents a kind of un-commodified labour (social work) that is primarily cooperative despite (and because of) the antisocial nature of the corporation (the commons), which the firm seeks to prospect and valorize in order to reproduce itself (the social factory). From this perspective, the haemorrhaging organization has a dual character. It externalizes the logic of production to the sphere of non-work as it parasitically internalizes the life of the commons for its own ends.

Italian autonomists or 'workerist' (*Operaismo*) thinkers such as Hardt and Negri remind us that the present juncture of capitalist development in the West is marked by the 'social factory' in which the logic of production and consumption has become a *social universal*. This bold conceptual proposition resonates with other commentators, such as the arguments of Deleuze (1992) and his notion of 'societies of control'. According to Deleuze, 'one is never finished with anything – the corporation, the educational system, the armed services being metastable states coexisting in one and the same modularity, like a universal system of deformation' (Deleuze, 1992: 5). The autonomists agree with this sentiment since (as is clearly obvious in the previous section) capital is parasitically turning to non-work – that which is formally outside the zone of production – in order to enhance the accumulation process. The autonomists, however, take the argument in a different direction by demonstrating how the 'social labour' the corporation wishes to valorize represents an autonomist 'other'. This stratum of social life formally outside the firm is increasingly required by capital to expand (a role once fulfilled by the social welfare state), and it is constantly attempting to seize it as social labour of productive value. The increasingly universal dimension of work–capital is therefore contradictory since the accumulation process can never reproduce itself alone. It requires life and the life of the commons persists *despite* (and *because* of) the corporation that has no life of its own. Autonomy derives from exactly this intersection of persistence: 'despite' because a huge amount of cooperative and unpaid labour has to occur before the corporation can become itself (it would cease to exist without it); and 'because' due to the commons only being able to generate life by antagonistically resisting the deadening effects of formalized work. This antagonism should not be considered a transcendental principle but simply a pragmatic necessity in the context of the corporate form (it would disappear with it).

The autonomist perspective demonstrates how the corporation therefore requires an outside point of cooperative and creative labour – a non-corporate commons – to sustain its own logic. The commons and the social labour proper to it is the undercurrent of capital, which the firm attempts to parasitically shift onto the plane of economic rationality (Virno, 2004). As we have already noted in the Introduction, the commons (or the communism of capital) is a constellation of communication, shelter, creativity, emotional frames, and mutual aid that we might call *life*. It is sometimes difficult to see clearly in the shadow of corporate rationality, but has to be posited for this corporate rationality to make any sense (much like the way astronomers suppose dark matter – for without it the observable universe would be nonsense): how else can we account for the wealth in society that is qualitatively above and beyond the surplus harnessed by life-draining financial markets, wage–labour relations, and private property (De Angelis, 2007)? While capitalism would stall without this autonomous other (the 'despite' vector of its persistence), it also exists 'because' of its resistance to capital – it needs resistance to have life; it *is* resistance. The commons therefore gives life to the corporation (which it mines, objectifies, and simulates), but this life is also a transformative hazard for the corporation.

An immediate implication here is that we move from a liberal understanding of the private non-work self (as the source of authenticity) to a radically socialized one. That is to say, sexuality, lifestyle, fun, play, and so forth are not individual characteristics of isolated subjects but aspects of an elemental communism (perhaps bolstered by networks of family, friends, spontaneous cooperation, etc.) that capital wants to use. The public–private dichotomy is eschewed for a radically social understanding of the working subject. The commons and social labour can now be clearly seen as the wellspring of personal authenticity. This understanding of capital and labour draws upon the early-nineteenth-century recognition of the centrality of labour for the development of capital. Rather than posit capital as an ontological 'first principle' and waged-work a reactive effect, the life of labour before work (the commons) including cooperation, communication, and antagonism, are what shape the contours of capitalist development. Especially since the commons is first and foremost resistant to the principles of capitalist domination for reasons we stated above. In this sense, capital is parasitical on the living labour that autonomously gathers around itself in the form of a commons:

> *Operaismo* builds on Marx's claim that capital reacts to the struggles of the working class; the working class is active and capital reactive. Technological development: Where there are strikes, machines will follow. 'It would be possible to write a whole history of the inventions made since 1830 for the sole purpose of providing capital with weapons against working-class revolt.' (*Capital*, Vol. 1, Chapter 15, Section 5). Political development: The factory legislation in England was a response to the working class struggle over the length of the working day. 'Their formulation, official recognition and proclamation by the State were the result of a long class struggle.' (*Capital*, Vol. 1, Chapter 10, Section 6). *Operaismo* takes this as its fundamental axiom: the struggles of the working class *precede* and *prefigure* the successive re-structurations of capital. (Hardt and Negri, 1999: 101)

Concentrating on a pivotal excerpt from Marx's *Grundrisse* and the chapter on cooperation in *Capital*, the notion of 'immaterial labour' (Lazzarato, 1996) captures the dimension of living labour within the commons that displays associative, creative, and often invisible elements of goodwill. The term 'immaterial labour' is certainly not a synonym for the rather tenuous categories of the 'service worker' or the 'symbolic analyst'. Instead it points to a dimension of labour that has probably always been present under capitalist conditions, even in its primitive formal sense inside and outside the corporation. Immaterial labour highlights the parasitical nature of capital and the importance of a kind of paradoxical autonomy. Since capital cannot reproduce itself and needs life, even as it aspires to be universal, it requires an outside point in order maintain the process, change and expand. The outside that is often appropriated is the so-called private identities that have been considered exogenous or antithetical to work in liberalist ideology. According to the autonomist conceptualization of the corporation, this is where the autonomy of the working class is pivotal for the production and reproduction of capital, otherwise labour becomes a mere reflection of capital and dead labour, and the whole process fails.

A crucial facet of autonomous immaterial labour is that of free association and cooperation – and hence the importance of non-work since the corporation traditionally represents servitude. According to Hardt and

Negri (1999) capital both produces and parasitically relies upon the creative initiative and cooperation of subjects within the very social body of universal capitalist order. These are the everyday spontaneous and non-commodified acts of collective life that must be posited in order to account for the corporate form. An analogy can be drawn with the classic studies of bureaucracy and its rule-laden milieu (see Blau, 1955). The best way to resist bureaucratic domination is to do exactly what it tells you, observe every rule to the letter, and quickly the system will short-circuit. The lesson being that discretion, gift-giving, creative initiative, and cooperation *despite the rules* are the dialectical requirement for bureaucracy to operate efficiently. Hanlon (2008) provides another example concerning the way human resource management (HRM) attempts to harness innovation revolving around endeavours to arrogate the commons already present in the firm (the informal zest and ingenuity of workers) and those facets of the broader social world embodied in the creative producer.

The Appropriation of Non-work as Immaterial Labour

In relation to the haemorrhaging organization and the replication/appropriation of the non-work commons within the orbit of the productive process, the notions of immaterial labour and the commons provides a useful frame for understanding what is going on. First is that aspect of capital accumulation that is pertinent today – the need for innovative, creative, and flexible work, in firms that range from IT start-ups and consultant firms, to the just-in-time factory and call centre. The immaterial labour here revolves around the evocation of those aspects of self that were once annulled by life-draining work. This feature of corporate valorization is most evident in the liberation management ideas espoused by Peters (2003) and others. When we think of the quest for authenticity via the replication/appropriation of non-work from this perspective, it is important to overcome the presumption of a private individual and the public organizational space. We must think of the 'private' and non-work themes – lifestyle, fun, sexuality, and so forth – as part of the commons that resides both inside the informal networks of the firm and outside the productive sphere. It is imminently social. This is why it is of such utility to the contemporary firm that wants subjects suitable for the demands of contemporary production as well as contain the antagonism inherent in the commons it seeks to use in simulated form.

For example, recall Hochschild's (1983) observation of how airline attendants were encouraged to use a 'living room analogy' and act 'as if' the aeroplane cabin was their home. The home space is directly evoked – including the family network, the feelings one has when relaxing in the living room, the polite rituals and kindness of entertaining guests, and other kinds of 'social labour' – funnily enough, the more negative aspects of the domicile are ignored in the analogy. It is not a coincidence that this kind of domestic work epitomizes an uncommodified relation that is mere parody when placed on the level of exchange. A particular assumption of cooperative work at home involving tacit knowledge and associative communicative rituals is being prospected for its symbolic worth. Such an appropriation of the commons and the creative immaterial labour that underpins it does a number of things. It individuates the commons as a productive skill through a mimetic function. Moreover, when it romanticizes domestic labour in this manner (also a site of struggle and hardship), the co-opting machinery completely misreads and depoliticizes the commons. The simulation is also a projective screen in this regard. Finally, it utilizes the already present cooperation among workers and customers mentioned earlier, objectifying it into an oppressive operational rule.

In his study of an IT firm that also aimed to interconnect productive work and play, labour and leisure, the public and private, Ross (2004) found very good incidences of what we might call immaterial labour and the appropriation of the commons. He observes that,

> in knowledge companies that trade in creative ideas, services and solutions, everything that employees do, think, or say in their waking moments is potential grist for the industrial mill. When elements of play in the office or at homesite/offsite are factored into creative output, then the work tempo is being recalibrated to incorporate activities, feelings and ideas that are normally pursued in employees' freetime. (Ross, 2004: 19)

The company that Ross studied also turned to anti-productive non-work source material to infuse work with a sense of personal authenticity and 'life'. Indeed, another good example is the way in which the anti-capitalist social movements of the post-Seattle period have been incorporated and utilized in the 'just be yourself' management approach. A growing number of management commentators argue that corporations need to absorb the spirit of resistance and revolt in a rapidly changing economic landscape. We therefore witness a somewhat counterintuitive celebration of resistance, anti-managerial and anti-corporate deviance in the face of an otherwise dehumanized social landscape. The message reads like this: "[T]urn management on its head", make organizations fun and subversive, and employees will be more motivated and engaged in their jobs. Peters speaks of "joyous anarchy"'. Bains (2007) suggests that employees ought to simply 'be them-selves', express their lifestyle difference, however *à rebours* they might be. Elsewhere, the 'tempered radical' (Meyerson, 2003) is celebrated as an important figure in the new corporation. More serious academic scholar-ship has similarly noted a shift in the employment practices and discourse of corporations. Ross (2004), mentioned above, observed, for example, the 'industrialization of bohemia' in Silicon Valley dot-com companies, in which anti-capitalist values and an underground counterculture are offi-cially endorsed. The key evaluative categories for team leaders are not obedience or complete uniformity, but authenticity, dissent, anti-hierarchy, and difference (see also Boltanski and Chiapello, 2005). The way in which this eviscerated and aestheticized 'designer resistance' utilizes the commons of non-commodified social life will be explored in more detail in Chapter 4.

Towards a 'Workers' Society'

If we think of the appropriation of the non-work sphere as a political tactic linked to the notion of immaterial and social labour and what Hardt and Negri (1999) call the social factory, we need to redefine what work 'is' and 'where' it is happening in contemporary capitalism. The boundary between life and labour changes in organizations that aim to facilitate expressions of personal authenticity among workers by allowing them to 'just be them-selves'. The mining and objectification of the commons 'outside' produc-tion displaces the imagined demarcation that once defined spaces of consumption, personal and family life, and the conventional workplace. With this displacement or even dissolution between life and labour in the 'just be yourself' discourse, the realm of non-work becomes marginalized (as it becomes functional) since more and more of the social landscape is constituted as a point of production. This occurs at both the individual and the collective level: individual insofar as more of the person is integrated into the discourse of labour as they get a 'life of sorts' at work; and collective in that every space of non-production for one person is invariably the space of production for another (take the leisure industry for example). Production becomes abstracted from a fixed and isolatable area to cover the entire social body. Indeed, Hardt and Negri (1994) capture this dynamic succinctly in their application of Deleuze's (1992) notion of societies of control in which it is argued that one is never done with anything when it comes to the contemporary logic of production:

[L]abouring processes have moved outside the factory walls to invest the entire society. In other words, the apparent decline of the factory as site of production does not mean a decline of the regime and discipline of factory production, but means that it is no longer limited to a particular site in society. It has insinuated itself throughout all social forms of production, spreading like a virus. (Hardt and Negri, 1994: 9–10)

This is the era of the social factory in which work is universal, but a deferred universal since autonomous 'living' labour is still a necessary prerequisite. This dependence on a non-commodified and resistant autonomy is risky for capital, since it is where its ultimate crisis lies.

Given these observations regarding the social factory and the popular definition of personal authenticity as something relating to non-work we can now identify three types of emergent work in the contemporary corporation. First is what we might call *conventional work*, those acts of industry that occur at what labour process theory scholars call 'the point of production': the call centre employee answering the phone, the consultant giving a power point presentation, etc. The second type of work is what Alvesson and Willmott (2002) phrase *identity work*. This is connected to the management of personhood within the corporations as they seek to become company men and women. This is especially associated with culture management and customer service discourse where workers must express a certain type of selfhood in order to be recruited, rewarded, and promoted. The idea of identity work extends the logic of production from manufacturing products and services, to that of self-production in those circumstances where employees are encouraged to work on themselves (i.e. become certain types of selves).

Echoing Hardt and Negri's (1994) argument, the third type of work might be called *social work* or social labour. Social work is inspired by living labour and objectified by the parasitical logic of the contemporary firm. The labour of 'elemental communism' (sexuality, rituals of fun, dissent, acting 'as if' the airline cabin is your living room, etc.) is the labour of the life-giving commons. It encompasses or frames the first two types of work by constituting a concrete universal, linking the conventional organizational space of labour to the social body as whole (cooperation, communication, affect, ingenuity, and mutual aid). It is also a point of instability since without it capital would become a mere dead reflection of itself, but if it subsumed complete dominion the corporation would become something very different.

I will argue in the remainder of this book that the commons and its appropriation through the rituals of social labour is the main inspiration and source material for 'personal authenticity' at work. Such an understanding of authenticity explains why the figure of non-work appears to be so important. Moreover, when the commons strolls into the corporation in this manner, new spaces of political potential arise since it could very well flip from its position of negativity (underlying the formal corporate valorization process) to one of plush positivity. If the appearance of authenticity is indicative of the managerial attempt to mollify the inherent *lack of life* in corporatized work by simulating the commons and arriving at a *life of sorts*, perhaps the fullest expression of life at work would implode the very notion of the corporation. The quest to facilitate personal authenticity in the workplace is not so simple or innocuous after all.

Conclusion

This chapter has identified a key mechanism driving the notion of authenticity and its creation within the 'just be yourself' management philosophy. This is the evocation of themes, experiences, and discourses that have strong mental and symbolic associations with the private sphere, non-work, and 'having a life'. The assumption seems to be that this is where 'real selves' reside, given the traditionally alienating environment of work. Attempts are made to give the impression that the corporation is actually a space of non-work, involving the fetishization of the things that define life outside the firm, especially lifestyle, sexuality, leisure, and so forth. I have used an autonomist perspective regarding the social factory and immaterial labour to place such managerial developments within a political economy. From this perspective, the so-called private domain celebrated in the name of difference, diversity, and idiosyncrasies is actually born from the commons – a reservoir of social networks, aptitudes, and initiatives that capital needs to put some life back into its deadening and antisocial structures. In doing so, the corporation individualizes the commons and transmogrifies it into an expressive poetic in the name of personal authenticity, with the outcome of enhancing control and power over the labour process in significant ways. This radically social understanding of work not only unsettles the liberalist understanding of the public and private subject, but also presents labour as a wider phenomenon that haemorrhages the conventional confines of the firm.

The chapter has focused on the 'horizontal' spread of the logic of production as it parasitically co-opts and transforms non-work life to provide the script around which authenticity might be played. But we also need to be attendant to what might be called the 'vertical' search for instances of common wealth when dissecting managed authenticity at work. For example, in the next chapter I will concentrate on humour and play, which have long been features of the informal organization, usually under the governance of workers themselves. As we shall see, self-valorized games and jokes among workers were often considered sources of disruption and points of possible contestation by a managerial gaze expecting strict subordination. The inclusion of fun in the 'just be yourself' organization is also inspired by non-work activities, but also parasitically commandeers what is already present in the subterranean interstices of the formal organization.

It is also interesting to note the contradiction underlying a version of authenticity that requires simulation and mimesis to aesthetically transform work into something that it is not. This is more than ironic. The mimetic machinery here represents a profound limit to this managerial ideology, as we shall demonstrate in Chapter 3. Moreover, with the assumption that authenticity is something primarily 'out there' in the world of non-work and life, the corporation overlooks an important insight from mainstream sociology: that work itself is a source of identity, dignity, and various other forms of 'psychological' and social needs. Hochschild (2003) remarks that for many female workers employment is an escape from the home, offering a temporary chance for self-affirmation that is otherwise denied them: 'one reason workers may feel more "at home" at work is that they feel more appreciated and more competent there' (Hochschild, 1997: 200). How do these workers feel when they see motifs reminding them of their private worlds appearing in the office? As it pertains to workplace 'fun', this question is unpacked in the next chapter since it flags an important internal limitation to the 'just be yourself' discourse and perhaps the corporation itself.

3

Mimesis and the Antinomies
of Corporate 'Fun'

> According to Max Weber, there is very little in mature capitalist society
> left to the irrational, but what is, is decisive.
>
> (Negri, 2003: 221)

The introduction of managed fun and play into the official discourse of
corporate life, traditionally a sphere of ultra-rationalization and bureaucratic regimentation, closely tracks many of the themes we have discussed
thus far. Fun is now serious business, and many corporations are staging
various types of funny and playful activities to enhance morale among
workers and cultivate experiences of personal authenticity. Some firms like
Sprint Paranet in the United States even have a 'Director of Fun' dedicated
to instilling play into the once dry work process. The idea is also very
popular in a recent wave of pop management commentators. They argue
that a colourful, fun, and engaged organizational environment is a prerequisite for satisfied and motivated employees. The nature of this corporatized fun takes a number of forms, ranging from funny paraphernalia
around the office (toys and posters), various types of contests (the best
Christmas costume or 'pyjama days' in which employees spend the day
dressed in their nightwear), and games and exercises at team-building
events. The idea is that workers and the organization as a whole are
more likely to be vibrant, creative, and productive when the environment
is imbued with lively fun and games.

One only has to look at the pop management publishing industry and
the remarkable number of e-consultants dedicated to corporatized fun to
gauge its recent attractiveness in the corporate world. Books such as *Fish: A
Remarkable Way to Boost Morale and Improve Results* (Lundin et al., 2000);

301 More Ways to Have Fun at Work (Hemserth and Sivasubramania, 2001); *The Play Ethic* (Kane, 2004) sell thousands of copies imploring managers to change their view of work. A plethora of consulting firms too now specialize in making the workplace somewhere fun to be. These 'fun-sultants' advise otherwise *quondam* and staid managers how to build cultures of fun (involving toys, games, jokes, etc.) as a quick method for motivating staff, gaining their full engagement with the labour process, and selling the firm to customers and/or contractors as a competitive advantage.[1]

The popularity of this attempt to generate experiences of fun and play in the corporate setting has significant implications for how we understand the cultural politics of work. First, as with many of these kinds of management initiatives, fun projects are a much easier way to adjust the worker to exploitive and otherwise alienating work processes. Instead of dealing with the root antagonisms of work by way of a modest modification to the institutional structures of the accumulation process (perhaps involving a different regime of profit distribution, access to strategic decision making, and so forth), injecting an element of fun into work is a much more palatable alternative. Fun psychologizes social categories quite nicely and thus draws attention away from the political foundations of the enterprise. Second, we must view these fun initiatives in the context of a more long-standing managerial concern with creating the 'happy worker'. As Donzelot (1991) argues in his essay on 'pleasure at work', the neo-human relations movement was very keen on crafting a more human and satisfying workplace to enhance the capitalist work process. And as many observers now suggest, the resulting success of job-enrichment programmes remains inconclusive. However, and as I also argued in Chapter 1, neo-human relations ideology focused on the organization of the task (autonomy, rotation, etc.). While inspired by the general ambitions of the neo-human relations school of management, the recent corporatization of fun would no doubt be viewed as gratuitous and frivolous from a conventional (even neo-human relations) management perspective. It largely targets the ambience and atmosphere inside the organization rather than the work task itself. Managed fun initiatives function *around* the point of production rather than *in* the labour process proper (which is not to say that such activities around the point of production are not also work, as we established in Chapter 2). Managed fun may detract employees' attention from the unerring datum of the capital accumulation (which every worker knows is generally un-fun) and might also be a form of labour itself, as the corporate 'social factory' extends its reach into most facets of society.

Another reason for the popularity of this most recent attempt to recompense the worker without altering the founding antagonism of the firm concerns the appropriation of a certain critical spirit in management discourse. As with the general theme of personal authenticity, fun and playfulness have been staple elements of radical attempts to criticize the logic of capitalism. The work of the Frankfurt School of Critical Theory, and in particular Herbert Marcuse (1955), saw pleasure and play as important sources of challenge to capitalist work regimes requiring self-abnegation and sober asceticism to reproduce itself. For Marcuse, capitalist authority relations were based upon the nullification of a deeper human playfulness that might endanger the rationality of the organization. It is therefore interesting to now witness a particular version of 'fun' – and it is very important to use inverted commas here as we shall soon demonstrate – being promoted in the firm to grease the wheels of exploitation. In light of Boltanski and Chiapello's *New Spirit of Capitalism* (2005), the managerial incorporation of 'fun' might well represent the internalization of an expressive or aesthetic critique of capitalism. In response to the younger, savvier, generation-Y employee housed in large firms, human resource managers realize that they have to be one step ahead and prefigure the prevalent scepticism about corporate life therein. As a 'fun-sultant' said in a recent newspaper report entitled, 'Forget Work, Have Fun':

Baby boomers are workaholics. Their attitude is that they are lucky to have a pay cheque. Generation-Y have seen their parents work themselves stiff and still get downsized. They have been latchkey kids who have watched the sacrifices their parents made and they are not about to make the same ones. For them a life–work balance is hugely important. (Rushe, 2007, *Sunday Times*)

This sentiment fits well with the general thrust of Boltanski and Chiapello's argument. They propose that the accumulation and legitimation crisis of capital was averted in the 1970s and 1980s by managerialism co-opting the artistic criticism found in the radical social thought of the 1960s. As opposed to structural questions of equality, exploitation, and ownership (or what Boltanski and Chiapello call 'social critique'), artistic radicalism was more interested in how capitalism impacted on our subjectivity: alienation, stultification, and boredom, for example, pervade the parlance of artistic criticism. Following this line of thought, perhaps the attractiveness of 'fun' in the context of a traditionally non-fun social environment can be explained by an attempt to respond to artistic grievance, and thus entice new generations of workers into the post-industrial workhouse. It is almost as if corporate capitalism has taken on board John Lennon's immortal anti-establishment mantra 'happiness is a good vibe for peace'; peace meaning here, of course, the absence of industrial unrest, overt recalcitrance, and worker agitation. I will explore Boltanski and Chiapello's arguments in more detail in the following chapters that discuss resistance and social criticism in the shadow of corporate hegemony.

In this chapter we will develop the arguments in the preceding chapters and attempt to not only politicize the corporatization of 'fun' as a managerial technique of power, but also place it within a broader political economy of the firm. Doing so will give some indication of the forces driving these initiatives. Much of the recent management and consultant literature promoting organizational fun links it to the broader notion of allowing employees to 'just be themselves' (in order to unleash personal authenticity at work). As the 'Director of Fun' at Sprint Paranet, Mona Cabler, once said: 'Fun and work are mutually reinforcing. When companies say they're employee-centred, they usually mean centred on helping employees achieve the company's goals. We emphasize helping individuals achieve their personal goals' (in Chadderdon, 1997). The rationale goes like this. Personal fulfilment and a sense of integrity at work can apparently harness a sense of authenticity regarding oneself in the context of corporate life. Because organizational forms have traditionally operated under the 'reality principle' of sober, serious, and alienating work devoid of much humanity, personal authenticity ought to be encouraged in relation to fun so that more life can be brought into work.

We note in the following sections that 'fun' is equated with liberating the 'child within' through various types of playful activities, and unleashing the curious side of ourselves. Of course, echoing the arguments made earlier, only certain types of fun are permitted, which must immediately arouse our political suspicions. Following the Marxist autonomist framework for framing the political economy of authenticity, we can understand the corporatization of fun as an attempt to absorb and co-opt features of the employee that have traditionally remained outside the conventional purview of work (i.e. the commons of social association). This occurs in two distinct, but related ways. First, there is the 'vertical' effort to tap the 'fun' that has always resided in the informal sphere of the organization. Innumerable studies, including what now must be considered some classic ethnographic studies of work (e.g. Roy, 1952, 1958; Burawoy, 1979) have revealed the importance of employee-initiated play, fun, and games that undermine the strict disciplinary control of the office, factory, store, showroom, etc. This type of self-authored fun was often at the expense of management and formed an important counterpoint of difference between them and workers. I will suggest that the corporatization of fun gains inspiration from this substratum of countercultural frolicking (a kind of internal commons) through a process that might be called formalized informality.

Second is the 'horizontal' haemorrhaging of the organization that we noted in the previous chapter. Since work has traditionally been considered un-fun and play something that can only really occur outside of the workplace, themes of non-work become salient in the 'fun' organization for obvious reasons. In its aim to trigger ideal–typical authentic expressions of personhood, fun-based management appropriates the outside sphere of organizational life by imitating what it considers to be 'fun' extra-employment activities. I suggest that following the logic of managed authenticity, this mimesis or simulation is an important technology for generating regimes of fun in the contemporary corporation. It must be recalled that such scripted 'fun' seldom disrupts the ground-zero principle of capital accumulation. It is not fun in work but fun around work, taking form at the expressive or ritualistic level (which is not to say 'fun in work' might not also enhance profitability in some cases). Here a kind of theatre of pleasure takes place in which non-work activities reminding employees of 'fun' are simulated in the hope of a more engaged and motivating workplace. The source material of this 'fun' is non-work, and as we have established in the previous chapter, this is namely the commons of free association and uncommodified labour that capitalism looks to exploit.

Such an appropriation of fun from the commons is fraught with tensions and contradictions. The antinomian relationship between replication (the unoriginal) and authenticity (literally the original) can merely highlight for workers the political predicament of their situation. In this chapter, I will relay empirical evidence of employees responding to this mimesis in a negative manner, since it undermines the dignity that they want to derive from enduring a horrible labour process. For them, ironically, the official discourse that made fun of their work actually undermined a sense of personal authenticity that they endeavour to piece together. This response in itself is revealing of how authenticity is defined in such a loaded and truncated manner: there is little room in the 'just be yourself' discourse for authenticity related to collective pain, solidarity, and hardship.

The chapter is organized as follows. First, I attempt to recreate the way in which work, labour, and organizations was understood in Fordist management thought. Work was (and for many still is) considered a place of serious, sober, and purposeful action that was not much fun. In the midst of such alienation, small freedoms could be forged, nevertheless, related to dignified achievement, long-standing social bonds, and what Sennett (2008) recently called a kind of learned 'craftsmanship'. In this section I will also demonstrate how workers informally did find room to express fun and play, even though the managerial gaze was worried about its disruptive influence on production. The chapter then turns to the recent corporatization of fun, and unpacks the various threads of this 'fun movement' that has developed over the last few years. I relay the empirical findings pertaining to the 'culture of fun' deployed at the Sunray call centre mentioned in previous chapters. The responses of employees to these managerial initiatives are suggestive for how we might understand the corporate concern with personal authenticity.

The Seriousness of Production

The move to imbue workplaces with fun, ebullience, and playfulness sharply contrasts with the way work has traditionally been formally conceived. In the pre-capitalist era, the peasant home was generally a place of both labour and leisure, with complex relationships of fealty and obligation tying them to the commons or manor. Since the inception of the industrial format for organizing labour in the pursuit of profit, work came to be associated with non-fun, toil, and various degrees of alienation. The reasons for this are obvious. As Pollard (1965) and Clegg and Dunkerly (1980) explain, with the advent of capitalism a new spatial politics emerged that demarcated the workplace, initially craft shops and then the factory, from the domicile sphere. Work is now a place of serious officiousness. This segregation was also temporal (Thompson, 1967; Perlow, 1998). The rationalization of time into calculable units marked a radical break with the seasonal calendar of feudalism, and particularly pronounced was the division between work time (owned and controlled by the company) and home time (devoted to more pleasurable pursuits of family, sexuality, leisure, consumption, sport, etc). In his classic essay 'Time, Work-Discipline and Industrial Capitalism', Thompson (1967) demonstrates how old habits that harked back to seasonal labour were difficult to break. The long-standing ritual of 'Saint Monday', for example, involved workers spontaneously vacating the factory to drink vast quantities of grog, just as generations had done before them in the putting-out shops and the commons:

The potters (in the 1830s and 1840s) 'had a devout regard for Saint Monday'. Although the custom of annual hiring prevailed, the actual weekly earnings were at piece-rates, the skilled male potters employing the children, and working, with little supervision, at their own pace. The children and women came to work on Monday and Tuesday, but a 'holiday feeling' prevailed and the day's work was shorter than usual, since the potters were away a good part of the time, drinking their earnings of the previous week. (Thompson, 1967: 75)

The use of time discipline and the strict separation of 'life' from 'labour' aimed to thwart such disruptive traditions. This simultaneously involved the formalization of the work process and its reconstitution as industry rather than life per se. Although by no means impermeable, the boundary between work and non-work life is exemplified by the development of the rational–legal bureaucracy, so incisively described by Weber (1947, 1948). As I indicated in Chapter 2, Weber's depiction of the 'rules of separation' in administrative bureaucracies underpins the rational–legal idea-type. This material division implied a concomitant normative code about how one should behave. The administrative organization is a domain dedicated to the objective discharge of business without regard to persons or personal interests. The resulting dehumanization that Weber regarded as a mixed blessing was viewed as a process of 'eliminating from official business love, hatred and all purely personal, irrational, and emotional elements' (Weber, 1948: 216). In the factory the same work ethic applied. In his renowned ethnography of the Ford Motor Company, Beynon (1980) quotes the Ford Philosophy prominently displayed on the shop floor: 'When we are at work, we ought to be at work. When we are at play we ought to be at play. There is no use trying to mix the two. When the work is done, then the play can come, but not before' (Beynon, 1980: 40). To repeat the caveat from Chapter 2, it is crucial not to exaggerate this division between work and non-work in industrial organizations. But we can nevertheless identify considerable effort to draw a symbolic boundary between work and life as it pertained to those 'human' qualities such as sex, fun, and so forth.

It is in this serious milieu that we can underline the significance of worker-initiated fun and games. Roy (1952, 1958) observed in a Chicago factory the way in which work groups attempted to relieve the boredom and undermine the managerial lead demand for rationalized performances through funny games. In his classic essay on 'Banana Time', Roy (1958) sets the scene by quoting the observation of Henri de Man (1927) regarding the need to make some fun out of even the most arduous and standardized work: '[C]ling to the remnants of joy in work . . . it is psychologically impossible to deprive any kind of work of all its positive emotional elements' (de Man, 1927: 80–1).

Roy goes on to observe the various ways in which workers did precisely that through different kinds of informal group games despite the protests of management. What were called 'times' usually revolved around a theme or piece of food and would informally interrupt work, so that playful verbal interaction could ensue among the group. The interaction was designed to entertain workers until the next interval, usually around an hour later. What come to be known as 'Banana Time' was particularly notable:

Banana time followed peach time by approximately an hour. Sammy again provided the refreshments, namely, one banana. There was, however, no four-way sharing of Sammy's banana. Ike would gulp it down by himself after surreptitiously extracting it from Sammy's lunch box, kept on a shelf behind Sammy's workstation. Each morning, after making the snatch, Ike would call out, 'Banana Time!' and proceed to down his prize while Sammy made futile protests and denunciations. (Roy, 1958: 162)

Similar informal games and fun were observed in the same factory years later in an ethnographic study that has also gained classic status in its own right, Burawoy's (1979) *Manufacturing Consent*. In order to leaven the boredom of industrial work, Burawoy observed employees playing 'making-out games' (competitions around the quantity of production) and 'goldbricking' in which manufactured parts were produced beyond sanctioned quotas and secretly stored for future use to provide informal rest breaks.

Such practices were once the leading hope of radical social theory that sought to understand how the rationalization of corporate domination might ultimately be transgressed through fun and play. In Marcuse's (1955) utopian approach to playful pleasure, this engagement with non-rationalized gratification formally diluted the 'performance principle' (Marcuse's historicized version of the 'reality principle') of regulated work. Building upon a Freudian Marxist analysis of labour, fun and play are for Marcuse primarily sexual categories (since the orgasm is the ideal form of all pleasure, including that derived from ostensibly non-sexual play). Marcuse argued that a new rationality of labour would emerge with the interaction of sexuality and Eros in the formal sphere. Upon such a merging, the arbitrarily imposed 'performance principle' would no longer be automatically equated with pain and desexualization, but a playfulness that would tear asunder the logic of capitalist production itself:

If work were accompanied by a reactivation of pre-genital polymorphous eroticism, it would tend to become gratifying in and of itself without losing its work content. Now it is precisely such a reactivation of polymorphous eroticisms which appeared as a consequence of the conquest of scarcity and alienation. The altered societal conditions would therefore create an instinctual basis for the transformation of work into play. (Marcuse, 1955: 196–7)

Notwithstanding this foray into the libidinal world of work, it is telling from the ethnographic studies of fun and play mentioned above (i.e. Roy and Burawoy) that capitalism was more than capable of co-opting the effects of such transgression. Indeed, the subtext in Roy's (1958) discussions and the overt message in Burawoy's (1979) argument is that given how self-initiated fun relieved workers of boredom and alienation, capitalism often benefited from their subversive games since they worked harder as a result. No wonder 'fun' seems to have moved from the informal underbelly of organizational life to the coercive formal rules engineered by laughing 'fun-sultants' such as FunCilitators.

Inside the Capitalist 'Fun House'

The seeming managerial U-turn from seriousness to fun might be explained by the vertical and horizontal corporate colonization of the commons. Under the mantra of 'just be yourself' as the path to personal authenticity, fun is transposed into a motivational (and perhaps palliative) resource that functions around the largely unchanged structural principles of accumulation. On the one hand, the always already existing informal sphere (including those transgressive interactions that actually make the organization function more effectively than if everyone followed the formally stated rules) is absorbed into the calculative logic of production. Second, and as I intimated in the last chapter, the promotion of fun relies upon a symbolic blurring between life and work since the aim is to make the act of production feel as if it is not work at all. As Kane (2004) puts it in relation to installing the 'play ethic' inside the firm:

[W]here do these new values and ideals come from? Surely not just from internally enlightened managers, fresh from their visionary workshops. Business should be seeking input from sources beyond the boundaries of the company or the corporation. (Kane, 2004: 275)

The under-labour of managed fun is the assumption that if employees are 'free' to express their authentic selves in the context of the corporation, then much of this would consist of fun, play, jokes, and lampooning each other (an assumption, of course, that is rather unimaginative as we shall soon see). And the inspirational source of such joviality is distinctly in the sphere of non-work.

As I briefly mentioned in the Introduction, the drive to corporatize fun is an extension of the neo-human relations project to cultivate satisfied and happy workers who accept the pain of labour. The adaptive logic of this sentiment was always something of an open secret, even among popular management theorists themselves, but especially among workers who never fully swallowed human relations ideology (Donzelot, 1991). A key difference is that the psychopathology of work inaugurated by the human relations movement aimed (and largely failed) to generate joy inside the task itself – quality circles, job enrichment, empowerment, and so forth. Later we can also see the culture-building trend isolate 'fun' as a positive motivating variable. According to the original culture 'gurus', including Peters and Waterman (1982), Pascale and Athos (1982), and Deal and Kennedy (1982), managers should revitalize employees by creating a climate conducive to fun, humorous, and playful experiences. Peters and Waterman (1982), for example, highlighted the productive energy that can be harnessed by promoting the playful 'messiness' usually associated with extra-employment activities. In a statement that is almost the exact obverse of the Weberian description noted earlier, it is maintained, 'all that stuff you have been dismissing for so long as the intractable, irrational, intuitive, informal organization can be managed' (Peters and Waterman, 1982: 11). What Deal and Kennedy (1982) called 'work hard/ play hard' cultures aim to supplant the traditional stereotype that assumes work is by definition severe, deadpan, and fun-less (also see Peters and Austrin, 1986; Kanter, 1989; Peters, 1989).

The Rationality of Fun

Given these historical antecedents and our political frame for understanding the corporatization of fun, how do the 'fun gurus' themselves understand 'fun' in the corporate context? Perhaps somewhat surprisingly, the notion of fun cultures appears to have outlasted the typically brief management fad life cycle (see Abrahamson, 1991), with much practitioner, consultancy, and scholarly interest in the topic presently growing. As the trend gained momentum in the 1990s, the message was much the same, but with the added emphasis on customer service, ingenuity, empowerment, and creativity (Peters, 1992; Barsoux, 1993; Deal and Key, 1998; Bolman and Deal, 2000). Through informal dress codes, office parties, games, humour, zany training camps, joking, etc., organizational members are encouraged to loosen up and find more pleasure in their roles (Green-wich, 2001). For others the approach has been used to diagnose and treat a diverse set of workplace ills, such as poor communication, sluggish innovation, absenteeism, anti-management sentiment, stress, conflict, lack of creativity, etc. Deal and Kennedy even suggest that if what they call the 'Fun Quotient' is high in a firm, then employees:

> will be more willing to commit themselves...people will pour their hearts and souls into what they do...it produces better results for everyone concerned – employers, employees, and society at large. (Deal and Kennedy, 1999: 234)

According to these authors, managing cultures that promote a childlike frivolity and playfulness is especially important today following the wave of downsizing that beleaguered corporate capitalism in the early-1990s. Perhaps echoing the recent attention on corporate spirituality and enchantment (Kline and Izzo, 1999; Casey, 2002), they claim that managers must now try to counter labour discontent by fundamentally changing the meaning of work among employees and managers alike. Companies such as IBM, Google, and Southwest Airlines and many more now all have regular meetings with 'fun-sultants' to imbue fun and life back into the work environment.

Fun and the Bottom Line

A whole raft of variables have been discussed in the practitioner and consultancy literature, including training, leadership, team dynamics, rituals, and communication, with most of the evidence being anecdotal in nature. For example, fun organizations have been causally linked to incidences of empowerment by Pickard (1997), Mariotti (1999), and Baughman (2001). They argue that empowered employees find their work more enjoyable because they experience their task activity as an extension of their own volition (see also Boczany, 1985). In this sense, the desire for agency that industrialism consigned to non-work pursuits can here be nurtured inside the workplace. Others have suggested that leadership is important for creating the conditions for pleasure at work (Hemsath and Sivasubramaniam, 2001). According to Peters (2003), managers should not only lead by example ('acting the goose', 'having a laugh', being humorous and zesty) but also be comfortable with employees expressing their cheeky selves rather than the cloistered ones indicative of drab work settings. Elsewhere, Peters (1992: 748) insists that the 'liberated manager' recognizes that 'pleasure is OK. But "fun" is even better' and she or he will use every opportunity to disseminate this attitude within their firms.

Lundin et al.'s (2000) widely read analysis of the Pike Place fishmongers in Seattle found a close-knit community of employees 'living their work' as an engrossing vocation rather than a mundane chore they would rather avoid. The extremely personal, intimate, and non-hierarchical system of management reportedly generated a sense of playfulness and enthusiastic 'fooling around' that eventually rubbed off on customers. Signs such as 'This is a playground – watch out for adult children' (Lundin et al., 2000: 88) were common features, as were other institutionalized rituals like 'joke-of-the-month' contests, bright colour schemes, and games.

As Collinson (1988, 2002) has demonstrated, *humour* appears to feature in a good deal of the 'cultures of fun' literature. While the significance of jocularity and play in relation to informal organizational processes was noted as far back as Roethlisberger and Dickson (1939) and Mayo (1945), interest in its encouragement represents a more recent trend. The instrumental potential of workplace humour has now been thoroughly explored in management scholarship (Malone, 1980; Duncan, 1982; Duncan et al., 1990; Holmes and Marra, 2002). It too has often been approached as a panacea for various organizational problems including subordinate–superordinate tension (Duncan et al., 1990), poor leadership (Miller, 1996; Avolio et al., 1999), resistance to change (Dwyer, 1991; Firth, 1998), communication failure (Clouse and Spurgeon, 1995), and stress-induced labour turnover (Kahn, 1989; Caudron, 1992). Perhaps the best-known proponent of staged corporate humour is Barsoux (1993, 1996). He maintains that management can use joking, laughter, and smiling in order to develop vibrant and creative organizations. In fact, its applicability is almost universal:

Humour plays a vital role in helping to close the communication gap between leader and followers, helping to extract information, which might not otherwise be volunteered. It also enhances trust, facilitates change and encourages plurality of vision . . . humour breaks down barriers between people and makes an organization more participative and responsive. It follows that an environment that is amenable to humour will also facilitate organizational learning and renewal. (Barsoux, 1996: 500)

The underlying paradox here, as in much of the prescriptive literature, is that humour is ultimately a serious business. It is unsurprisingly driven by very sober business motives. The obvious difficultly of institutionalizing an experience that is usually considered spontaneous is intimated by Hudson (2002), an executive for Brady Corporation. She observes that humour and fun can be developed through exercises that may feel spontaneous but are in fact well orchestrated through party events like 'Bradyfest' or the 'Lego Program' (in which employees play with Lego blocks like children). As will be discussed shortly, this institutionalized aspect of the fun discourse is of utmost importance for analysing worker perceptions of it.

'Fun' and the Antinomies of Mimesis

I now want to empirically explore the antinomies that arise when the quest to generate personal feelings of authenticity through 'fun management' is attempted by simulating presumably fun non-work experiences.[2] I have already mentioned the call centre Sunray Customer Service. It is a quintessential 'liberal organization' and places great emphasis on a fun environment. This is encapsulated by the slogan: 3Fs: fun, focus, and fulfilment. There are a number of facets to the corporatization of fun at Sunray. The most notable strategy used by management is the recreation of extra-employment motifs within the confines of the workplace. Significant effort is given to engendering relationships among people that are analogous to positive non-work social interactions. As a team development manager puts it: '[W]e remind telephone agents that their work time can be just as fun as their weekends, evenings or holidays because our philosophy is about being yourself and enjoyment'. Again it must be remembered that the non-work operates here as both a screen upon which managerial values are projected and an autonomous reservoir of creativity and non-commodified relationships (or the commons). The attempt to reproduce the 'fun' experiences of non-work in the organizational setting manifests in a number of forms.

School

Much of the 'fun culture' at Sunray attempts to emulate what managers believe to be the *esprit de corps* and playfulness displayed by good friends in a school setting. It is interesting to note that the average age of Sunray telephone agents is 21, a conscious recruitment strategy that selects people who have recently completed high school. The recruitment rationale here is: '[Y]oung people find our culture very, very attractive because they can be themselves and know how to have fun.' For example, 'Away Days' are held annually and consist of days where everyone travels to a 'party' destination to stage what a manager refers to as 'kind of school musical'. Other aspects of this school theme verge on the silly by imitating primary school and kindergarten themes. Training games involving mini-golf and quizzes are frequently employed for sales motivation purposes. In one induction session, workers stood and sang the Muppet's *The Rainbow Connection*. Following this training exercise, workers were asked to take home a rainbow-coloured pamphlet with a 'fill-in-the-blanks' word puzzle that reads: 'What are the 3Fs?', to complete in their own time.

This 'children at school' emphasis is also reflected in the physical space of the organization. The walls are painted yellow and red, the supporting pillars are purple, and the carpets are a vivid blue. These colours are designed to create a mood of verve and fun. Bright icons covering desks and pods proudly announce a team's client, accentuating the playfulness of working for this particular client firm. For example, the area designated for an Africa-based airline project is decorated with dazzling green cardboard cut-outs of jungle trees and photos of cheetahs and hyenas. In another area multicoloured building blocks spell out the name of a mobile phone company and rest beside figures of Big Bird and Grover from the children's television programme, *Sesame Street*. This gives the call centre what one employee called a 'playschool' or 'kindergarten' atmosphere because of the juvenile ambience it creates.

Partying

Management often say Sunray life is similar to a 'party' because of the energy and 'good times' that apparently distinguish this firm from other call centres. This party theme is literally evoked in recruitment advertisements as well as training and motivation exercises. During one team development session, various teams competed in a relay race in a nearby park – at the end of their sprint each team member had to quickly drink a large glass of beer. After the race, workers continued to drink and 'fool around', and when they returned to work, the effect of the alcohol was noticeable. And somewhat analogous to an 'actual' party, the expression of sexuality and flirting are openly encouraged at Sunray. The work environment is considered by a number of employees to be a fruitful place to proposition the opposite (or same) sex for a 'date'. As far as management are concerned, this is a healthy and innocent feature of the informal culture because it creates a less rigid and boring atmosphere. Some employees find this evocation of sexuality an enjoyable way to ward off the boredom inevitably associated with call centre employment. For other employees, however, the term 'meat market' (a bar or nightclub where people come to specifically 'pick up' dates) is used to designate this aspect of organizational life.

Dress Code

The relaxed dress code at Sunray is centred on the latest fashion labels and is promoted with the intention of creating a party-like atmosphere in the organization. This is designed to recalibrate the environment of a type of work often associated with uniformity and standardization. For sure, the ritual of consumption and shopping is a strong theme of the culture of fun. During the interviews I felt decidedly unfashionable and drab on many occasions because of the care employees had taken over their physical appearance. According to one employee, 'the idea is to get away from the boring office look and make things fun and happy like we are going out for the night'. This dress code also extends to 'fun' physical appearances among workers such as bright orange hair, visible tattoos, and facial piercings – the comparison to 'parties', 'raves', and 'clubbing' is justified in this sense. However, the Sunray dress sense often overlaps with the school theme. For example, teams have 'dress-up' days where employees must come dressed as their favourite superhero or in their pyjamas. Or, to take another example, sometimes employees are encouraged to wear clothing that reflects a particular theme, such as 'The Tropics' (floral shirts and sun hats) or 'Australian Capital Cities'.

While some Sunray employees interviewed found such 'fun' enjoyable, many were unsurprisingly sceptical and sometimes downright hostile. In accordance with the model of political power that I have developed regarding the parasitical colonization of the non-work common, the symbolic blurring of traditional boundaries appears to be an underlying thematic in the discontent expressed by employees. In particular, two dimensions of this relationship can be discerned.

Condescension

For a number of Sunray workers interviewed, being treated like a child was considered condescending, and the 'school' and 'kindergarten' environment particularly gave management a rather patronizing and mawkishly paternalistic flavour. Many of the cynical workers rejected the child–teacher roles implicit in the technologies of 'fun' because they wanted to be treated as rational, dignified adults. Sarah (a pseudonym), an agent for an airline company, says the thing she 'would love to yell at her team leader and project manager the most is [speaking to me as if I was a superior] I'm not a child and I won't be spoken to as one!'. In this sense, the presumption that the employment setting is akin to a schoolyard had the effect of undermining their sense of aplomb and they therefore actively dis-identified with the culture initiatives. Kim, a telephone agent for an insurance company, explains:

Working at Sunray is like working for Playschool [a popular and long-running children's television program in Australia]. It's so much like a kindergarten – a plastic, fake kindergarten. The murals on the wall, the telling off if I'm late and the patronising tone in which I'm spoken to all give it a very childish flavour.

The boundary between work and 'school' (especially for the younger workers) appeared to have important esteem and motivation implications. The company, through its use of the school and family narrative to instil fun into the work environment at Sunray, underestimated the way in which the traditional 'seriousness' of the employment situation is connected to feelings of integrity and dignity. Indeed, in light of the interview transcript, perhaps employees hold onto the boundary between work and non-work because the traditional employment situation (rational, relatively serious, unpretentious, etc.) is an important source of aplomb and self-respect – especially in an environment deemed pretentious and fake. In its most patronizing form, paternalism strips away this rational sense of self and endeavours to instigate a weak, dependent, and sometimes ignorant membership role that simultaneously positions management as benevolent caregivers.

The evocation of fun at work fails in this instance because it does not reflect pre-existing notions of what work means for employees in terms of their identities as rounded adults. Moreover, some employees felt that management did not consider the negative and unpleasant aspects of the outside institutions symbolically recreated in the workplace. For example, Sarah says she abhorred school, and much of the 'culture of fun' at Sunray simply reminds her of this past. In relation to the dress code and sexuality, this is what she said about waiting for her friend after work: 'When I go to meet Mark I wait a block down the road because if I wait outside I get looked at by the Sunray people to see what I'm wearing. I hate it; it's like being back at high school. They all must wear stylish clothes to [sarcastically and impersonating a subscriber] "fit in"'.

Failed Mimesis

An inadvertent effect of endeavouring to unleash authentic selves through the mimetic simulation of non-work was an enduring sense of inauthenticity among employees. The failure to faithfully reproduce the complete experiences of 'partying' or 'school' resulted in some employees viewing the 'fun' as pretentious, fake, shallow, and lacking honesty. This perhaps derives from both the rather one-sided depiction of school, weekends, bars, parties, etc., as maudlinly positive by the company, and also the perception that management are simply 'trying too hard' to recreate these feelings and experiences. In a focus group session with her cohort, Sarah said that almost every aspect of the culture initiative resembled a rather glib charade. Mark and Michael also agreed but were a little less abrasive in their evaluations. I asked the group about what they thought were the aims of the rituals of 'fun' and Kim said, 'its all the same thing – its all just an unreal image they're trying to present of the company and I wish they wouldn't say anything at all'. Kim seems to be saying that because the orchestrated 'fun' fails to successfully mimic the so-called fun experiences of extra-employment activities, management should not even try to make work fun in this manner, since it merely comes across as disingenuous.

Kim and Sarah tended to use words like 'plastic', 'fake', 'cheesy', and 'shallow' to describe the most prominent features of the Sunray culture, arguing that it lacks authenticity (or sincerity) and was intended to beguile them into subjectively conforming to the company's rules. It is not only management who are deemed pretentious. Employees who appear to enthusiastically subscribe to the culture – rancorously labelled 'Sunray people' by the cynics – are similarly spurned. Kim told me, for example, that the company encourages people to adopt 'shallow' personalities because these kinds of people do not notice the disparity between the Sunray rhetoric of family or parties, etc., and the actual reality of these social roles as they are enacted outside of work.

Sarah finds the pretentiousness of the 'culture of fun' offensive given the perceived 'creditability gap' between the dominant culture's representation of the organization (fun, egalitarian, empowering, etc.) and the reality of work and non-work experiences. This appears to translate into a poignant distrust of the intentions of management. She puts it in the following manner: 'I can't believe a lot of this stuff. I feel like saying, "how dare you stand up there and pretend to be something you are not". They pretend to be different but they aren't and in some ways are worse than other companies because they are not real'.

The Cultural Politics of Corporate Fun

Building on the previous argument about the corporate colonization of the commons (or that ostensibly non-work sphere that gives capitalism the material it needs to reproduce itself), I want to argue that managed fun involves an antinomian process of simulating or appropriating the commons: that is, reproducing non-work inside the organization (in an abbreviated form) in order to give workers the impression of being 'free', 'happy', and beyond the commodity form. This simulation fails in pretty obvious ways and the resistance from employees reveals the limits of the attempt to cultivate environments in the capitalist workplace that might provide personal authenticity.

One place to start to unpack this 'politics of fun' is to discuss whether 'fun' can simply be generated in a calculated and staged manner (by, say, imitating a weekend party or an enjoyable family experience). Can work really claim the associative energies of non-work fun and still adhere to the rules of the corporate regime? In much of the prescriptive and consultancy management literature, there is an assumption that organizational fun, joy, and ebullience can be managed in the same way as more concrete variables like absenteeism, recruitment, or efficiency. This was discussed earlier in relation to Barsoux's (1996) and Hudson's (2002) suggestions that fun can be institutionalized in rituals that resonate with experiences in the broader social world. But if we review the Sunray study, it is obvious that these workers still believe that corporate instigated 'fun' is very different to the fun experienced outside the organization. As far as the resistant employees at Sunray are concerned, there is something inexplicably 'unreal' about the silliness, merrymaking, and zaniness orchestrated by management in the corporate context. The parties, games, and rituals did not seem to be as authentic as an *actual* party.

There are probably a number of reasons for this enduring perception among workers interviewed. If we take a humanist stance, it could be argued that there is still an intractable element in humour, enchantment, and exhilaration that escapes the rationalization and calculative logic of corporate management systems. As Max Weber (1930) surmised, the sense of pre-rational frivolity and the calculative machinations of administrative bureaucracy are ultimately incommensurable. As constellations of meaning that structure the life worlds of social actors, neither can be entirely reduced to the other. This argument, of course, has been challenged by those proposing a return to 'spirituality' in corporate affairs, but the continuing persistence of employee cynicism in this context does beg the question of whether some kind of dissonance or tension will inevitably result from attempts to make rationalized work process enchanting or authentically fulfilling.

For Weber (1930), the ineffable element of pre-rational reason was linked to the uncanny and spontaneous. At Sunray, however, the inimitable feature of fun may be more related to control and agency. Outside of work, when employees do genuinely have fun and engage in various activities associated with joyful experiences, their sense of volition is undoubtedly high. They do it because they choose to – or perceive that they 'choose to' – which is no doubt a problematic perception encouraged by liberalist ideology. But when these experiences are transferred into the workplace, history cannot be so easily erased from the collective memory of workers. Just as before, the locus of control is still with the company. The paradox of 'fun as a serious business' was referred to earlier; employees are generally forced (often euphemistically termed 'encouraged') to participate in the silly rituals and office escapades and thus their self-perceptions of agency and autonomy are not that different to the traditional rule-bound workplace – except in the former, they are encouraged to 'make fools out of themselves', as one Sunray employee cynically put it.

It is not surprising then that much past research has demonstrated how some of the most authentically fun workplaces are ones that workers create themselves, independent of, and often *against*, management. The ethnographic accounts of life on the shop floor by Roy (1952, 1958) and Burawoy (1979), for example, point to the organic and self-authored nature of playfulness and light-heartedness in the workplace and the heightened sense of camaraderie that develops (see also Collinson, 1992). When fun is self-initiated in this way, however, management often finds it an affront to their authority and are quietly distrustful, even though it may actually lead to higher productivity, as Gouldner (1955) discovered in relation to 'indulgence patterns' (see also Mars, 1984). Indeed, it may even be interpreted as seditiousness and recalcitrance simply because it has not been officially sanctioned by management.

Conclusion

The mimesis of extra-employment enactments of fun that I have depicted here supports the overall argument of this book regarding the politics of authenticity and the analytical significance of what we have called after Hardt and Negri (1994) 'the commons'. Corporations now promote a more 'holistic' version of the employee for specific political reasons that are firmly linked to the demands of the capital accumulation process. While there is certainly a degree of humanization that flows from such initiatives, this current has long been an aspect of managerial thought and is specifically designed to integrate the worker better into the logic of capitalism. Even though the ideology of a 'frictionless capitalism' has a good deal of popular currency, work is still generally considered formally troubling by many, involving a 'lack of life' that the corporation seeks to suture and exploit by co-opting the external and internal commons to provide a *life of sorts*.

The failed mimesis of fun and the joy of the commons leads to renewed attempts by employees to seek a more 'authentic' and 'real' life in the corporation. Workers of all stripes – the office worker, the junior consultant, or the call centre employee – are finding their own ways to make their lives in the organization more dignified, crafting alcoves of self-authored fun in an otherwise dull and life-draining world. The feelings of alienation that are provoked even by techniques designed to reduce alienation (such as the fun schemes we have discussed here) are exacerbated, no doubt, by the popular cultural malaise regarding employment generally. The pervasive cynicism and distrust embedded in the consciousness of generation-Y workers and the multitude easily see through the rhetoric of 'fun-sultants'. Even generation-X-ers had no truck with this manufactured fun. In terms of this generation coming of age in the 1990s, who can forget the ludicrous and pitiful 'quality cat' described by Hamper (1992) in *Rivet Head*. The cat was named Howie Makem. To give quality management fun and playful connotations, Ford management dressed a hapless line-worker in a cat suit with a mute, permanent grin on its face. Hamper describes the 'quality cat' in laconic detail:

Howie Makem stood five feet nine. He had light brown fur, long synthetic whiskers and a head the size of a Datsun. He wore a long red cape emblazoned with the letter Q for Quality. A very magical cat, Howie walked everywhere on his hind paws. Cruelly, Howie was not entrusted with a dick. (Hamper, 1992: 113)

Workers viscously turned on the cat at every opportunity, making his life on the line a complete misery to the genuine joy of the shop floor. The fun that the quality cat represents was too artificial, too corporate and lifeless. As such, the ill-fated quality cat and the embarrassing performance of the 'Rainbow Connection' are experienced as coercive and humiliating simulacra. Life is attained precisely by opposing them. How workers engage with the failed mimesis of non-work (involving dreams of freedom and happiness) surfaces the political economy of fun in the corporate world today. The machine of mimesis, however, has not stopped at fun. More recent managerial discourse has ventured one step further into the commons and endeavoured to appropriate (by simulation) dissent and resistance too. For subversion and personal authenticity have always been intimately associated within our cultural imagination. How does the profit-seeking, hyper-commodified corporation use criticisms of capitalism to further its business objectives? This we turn to next.

4

Cobain as Management Consultant? 'Designer Resistance' and the Corporate Subversive

> Beginning in 1991–1992 (when *Nevermind* ascended the Billboard charts and Tom Peters *Liberation Management* appeared), American popular culture and corporate culture veered off together on a spree of radical sounding bluster that mirrored the events of the 1960s so closely as to make them seem almost unremarkable in retrospect. Caught up in what appeared to be an unprecedented prosperity driven by the 'revolutionary' forces of globalization and cyber-culture, the nation became obsessed with youth culture and the march of generations. . . . In business literature, dreams of chaos and ceaseless undulation routed the 1980s dreams of order and 'excellence'.
>
> (Frank, 1998: ix–x, *The Conquest of Cool*)

Authenticity and subversion have been closely linked in radical social theory. At no other time did personal authenticity and transgression resonate with each other in progressive politics than in the 1960s and 1970s. The nature of this connection was drawn long before, especially in the existentialist philosophy of Jean Paul Sartre. He, of course, exuded a subversive cool that has forever endeared existentialism to the fashionably chic, remaining unsurpassed in this regard by any other radical philosophical movements. Sartre, of course, was notoriously uncompromising in his philosophical views and praxis, a reputation difficult to call into question since it was earned at the harrowing coalface of Nazi brutality. As we noted in the Introduction to the book, authenticity for Sartre was about owning up to oneself, living the life one has chosen, and accepting the abysmal ontological freedom that defines us within the sticky bounds of social facticity. In the 1960s and 1970s radical views of authenticity and selfhood took on various guises. Humanist Marxism, for example, was interested in the stultification and eventual expression of real desires in the face of a commodified social universe. Freudian Marxists such as Herbert Marcuse called for a de-sublimated desire that would inject the 'human' back into the human. Even facets of Foucault's pessimism found a kind of authenticity in transgression for those experiences of self that find its own limits (Foucault, 1963/1998). For sure, 1960s' and 1970s' radicalism, especially during the events of May 1968, had a lasting impact on our cultural understandings of authenticity. As the laconic and counterintuitive observations of Frank (1998) intimate above, this is certainly evident in the mass media where the heroes of subversion – such as Kurt Cobain – are romantically assumed to pay the price for living an authentic life.

Given this cultural backdrop that connects personal authenticity and resistance, it is no wonder that corporations come under special fire for being quintessentially inauthentic places. The modern corporate form exemplifies uniformity, homogenization, and ascetic rationalization in which the conforming 'organizational man' (Whyte, 1956) holds the marker of success. Social criticism portrays the corporate world as essentially dehumanized environments in which we must suspend those things that make us unique individuals. As mentioned above, such a depiction of corporate life is especially evident in the popular media where employees are likened to drones, robots, or sheep that enjoy very little differentiation or difference (think of the opening scenes of Charlie Chaplin's *Modern Times*, for example). It would be no less difficult to imagine the paragon of authenticity, Jean Paul Sartre, working as a finance executive for a large real estate agency or corporate law firm than it would to envisage Kurt Cobain as a management consultant.

Life in the corporation might also be inauthentic because it represents everything that democracy is not. When one enters the firm it almost goes without saying that basic freedoms are forsaken until the workday is over. Organizations demand conformity, obedience, and identification with the objectives of the business. The *Umwelt* of production elicits an expectation that instructions be followed and the job carried out as specified by superiors. While employees have always broken the rules in some manner or form, structural recalcitrance and overt subversion have no place in the organization. In this sense, corporations are ultimately authoritarian situations. This is so not only for the disciplinary organizational forms of yesteryear, the Fordist factory, or the Weberian bureaucracy, but also those funky high-commitment firms (in which various forms of luxuries and perks are showered on core employees if not on periphery workers). As Peters and Waterman (1982) put it with respect to organizations with strong corporate cultures: 'you either buy into their norms or you get out' (1982: 77).

Now let us examine two examples from the management literature indicating a peculiar sea change that might scramble our conventional understandings of how subversion is appreciated in organizations. The first is in a gushing appraisal of the Starbucks coffee chain called *The Starbucks Experience* (Michelli, 2007). The book contains the usual harangue about how wonderful Starbucks is, being a leading-edge firm in relation to service efficiency, corporate branding, customer satisfaction, and so forth. However, as anyone knows, Starbucks has received fierce criticism for its exploitative supply chains, oppressive management practices, and predatory competition. It is the target of so much rancour, in fact, that police automatically barricade outlets (along with McDonalds) wherever anti-globalization and anti-capitalist protestors are in town. In Michelli's discussion of what defines Starbuck's business strategy it is very curious to discover that Principle 4 is 'Embrace Resistance'. What does he mean? 'Whereas many corporate executives dread dealing with complaints, Starbucks management actually invites dissenters into problem solving discussions' (Michelli, 2007: 118). It is important to be perceived to be dealing with complaints since visibility is paramount: 'When employees see that management actually cares about feedback – positive and negative – they are more likely to care as well' (p. 113). In endeavouring to counter the inimical effects of dissent from community groups and local councils, Starbucks apparently has an open policy by listening to the criticism, negotiating with dissenters and using the information in various pre-emptive ways. Such openness to resistance, according to Michelli, is also important for generating a specific type of culture in the organization. Employees and managers can use the criticism of Starbucks in proactive and developmental ways:

While the path of an elephant may not easily be diverted, most other forms of resistance can be resolved through active listening and a commitment to use feedback for long-term growth. Great leaders drop the defensiveness and open their ears and minds to the input of others, accepting resistance as a valuable developmental tool. (Michelli, 2007: 149)

The second example that might indicate a shift in how corporations approach resistance can be found in Meyerson's (2003) *Tempered Radicals*. This book studies the different ways ordinary employees become 'leaders' that challenge their work environments in order to integrate personal authenticity and integrity into their corporate roles. She defines the tempered radical as:

people who want to succeed in their organizations yet want to live by their values or identities, even if they are somehow at odds with the dominant culture of their organizations. Tempered radicals want to fit in *and* they want to retain what makes them different. They want to rock the boat, and they want to stay in it. (Meyerson, 2003: xi)

Authenticity and difference are key motivators for the tempered radical. They are opposed to traditional radical collectivity – this annuls difference – and ultimately find something redeemable in the corporation and capitalism more generally. This persona resists because they want to express their unique identities in terms of race, sexuality, ethnicity, and so forth (class does not seem to feature in the *de rigueur* list of what makes us different). Meyerson goes on to consider the activities of the tempered radical as 'resisting quietly and staying true to one's self, which includes acts that quietly express peoples different selves' (Meyerson, 2003: 8). If we recall the discussion in Chapter 1 of the 'just be yourself' management approach, many of the hallmarks of an expressive liberalism are embodied by the tempered radical as well. Moreover, the book makes a strong case for considering the managerial benefits of encouraging this tempered dissent in terms of innovation, morale, and creativity. For sure, perhaps the idea that Kurt Cobain might have found a place in the corporate world today is not so whimsical after all.

The two examples presented above reveal something quite interesting that oscillates with significant elements of corporatized authenticity as discussed in preceding chapters. Rather than subversion (as an expression of personal authenticity) being considered purely illegitimate and dangerous, it now enters the official discourse of management as an ally of capitalism. Similar to the rise of the 'just be yourself' business ideology, the reasons for this counterintuitive managerial foray into the parlance of emancipation and transgression are obviously complex. Many senior human resource executives are worried about how to approach the army of nonchalant and sulky generation-Y employees joining their ranks. Unlike earlier generations of workers, they are less willing to forget their countercultural attitudes in the workplace. Overlaying this disposition are ideological changes in the organizational form marked by the transposition of liberalist values into the sphere of work: life, liberty, and happiness ought to be found at work too and not only at the weekends or when one finally escapes into the leisure industry. The pervasive scepticism about the legitimacy of the Anglo-US corporate model must feature in this managerial shift as well. The modern corporation has suffered a legitimation crisis in relation to its politically regressive impact on the environment, markets, employees in the Third World, etc. (Parker, 2002). Managerial discourse has regrouped to try and justify itself not only to the outside world but also to the multitude of workers it needs to reproduce itself.

In this chapter, I intend to analyse this advocacy of a specific modality of dissent in relation to corporatized authenticity and the autonomist framework developed in preceding chapters. The first observation that directs us towards this line of analysis is the fact that only certain forms of resistance are permitted in the politically correct firm. It needs to mainly be aesthetic and visual in which difference and designer Che Guevara T-shirts come to the fore more than, say, unionizing the store or calling a wildcat strike (or even insisting on higher wages). As I shall demonstrate below, the sort of resistance sponsored in the ideal–typical dot-com IT firms is acutely expressive and trades in a slacker underground cool reminiscent of college radicalism and counterculture motifs. I will propose that fostering such 'designer resistance' serves two purposes. It motivates (and ameliorates) generation-Y workers who think the corporation 'sucks' but would nevertheless like to cash in (this ethos is captured by Liu [2004: 76] in the expression, 'we work here, but we are cool'). Second, many prescriptive management porte-paroles now realize that work organizations seldom function very well when strict adherence to the rules is enforced. Sociologists have known about the importance of indulgency patters for years. Now liberation management and the 'just be yourself' business approach also recognize that 'slack in the system' is a prerequisite not only for creativity and innovation, but simple day-to-day functionality. And to reinforce an earlier point, the initiative, self-organization, and cooperation that this discretion calls for is the commons that capitalism parasitically bleeds in order to reproduce its fundamentally anti-social nature.

The formalization of 'designer resistance' supports the assertion that corporations now rely upon, it co-opts and transmutes into its own image the 'other' that lies beyond the formal sphere of production. In this case it is not simply non-work that is being utilized to facilitate personal authenticity in the domain of production, but anti-work, which certainly indicates a fascinating shift in management ideology given the authoritarianism that has conventionally sustained it. Building on the analytical framework developed in the last few chapters, I aim to demonstrate how the corporate interest in resistance and dissent represents a noteworthy political strategy. In the next section I will use Boltanski and Chiapello's (2005) idea regarding the 'new spirit of capitalism' to explain why capital is now espousing a form of self-critique to sustain itself. Then following the postulates of the autonomist argument about the way capital co-opts the commons, we will demonstrate how the mechanisms of designer resistance involve two processes that have already been mentioned in Chapter 2. First, the attempt to simulate gestures conventionally relegated to non-work inside the sphere of production, thus blurring the traditional public–private division. And, second, this simulation of subversion inside the corporation relies upon a mimetic deformation that eviscerates what it mimics. Resistance is transmuted into a subversive 'expressivism'. In the concluding section of the chapter I plan to trace the limits of this co-optation and rethink the idea of personal authenticity in light of such limitations.

It is important to state from the outset that this analysis of 'designer resistance' does not necessarily aim to perpetuate the rather tired dispute about what counts as real and false resistance. These debates concerned labour process theory in the 1970s and 1980s, and although they remain enlightening, it will not be our intention to unpack them here. The objective is more to understand exactly why intimations of 'subversion' appear in corporate ideology today and explain the function that it might play.

The Corporate Rebel

To be just a little cheeky, it could be argued that one of the most 'critical' texts dissecting the rhetoric of contemporary management is not inspired by Marx or Deleuze, but a Tom Peters (2003) pulp production. According to Peters, contemporary workers are deeply attuned to anti-hierarchy, anti-authoritarian views that were once the sole bastion of underground culture. As Harney and Oswick (2006: 105) nicely put it, '[M]anagement itself is today against management'. Rather than exhorting employees to subjectively conform to a unitary set of values, for example cultures of commitment, they are invited to simply 'be themselves' in all its subversive truthfulness. Here, in addition to task empowerment, recruits ought to be existentially empowered and do not necessarily need to share the organization's values. They might even oppose them. In Tom Peter's latest works, for example, he argues that managers should hire the young, imaginative, underground type, who despise outdated managerial hierarchies, display a generation-Y cool, and follow individualist portfolio careers. It is fascinating to note the way Peters looks for transgressive kudos in the nomenclature of counterculture. Take these slogans about how to lead from his online lecture slides (see http://www.tompeters.com):

Those Who 'Made' the Tenth-Grade History Books

- Made lots of people mad
- Flouted the chain of command
- Were creative/quirky/peculiar/rebels/irreverent
- Were masters of improv/thrived on chaos
- Exploited chaos

For Peters, of course, this celebration of resistance embodies a very conservative message. The idea is not to undermine the for-profit model of accumulation, but make it function better by bypassing the inefficiencies and counterproductive impediments of conventional management wisdom that is hell-bent on direct control. With the failure of the mono corporate cultures of the 1980s and 1990s, managerialism is increasingly mobilizing reflective technologies in the name of authentic individuality. Business commentators now argue that 'liberated firms' can add value by employing free radicals, dissenters, and freaks. As Sanbonmatsu (2004: 50) amusingly puts it, the once radical 'Yippie cry "Do it!" has been transformed by the Nike Corporation's *detourement* into "Just do it!"'.

While some may cite such developments as evidence of the humanization of work and an attempt to finally bring about a frictionless capitalism free of draconian controls, I suggest that the corporate rebel is actually congruent with the conservative demands of the contemporary corporate form. This discourse of radical chic is symptomatic of what Boltanski and Chiapello (2005) call the 'new spirit of capitalism'. They argue that 1960s' radical humanism has been partially processed by management thought in relation to authenticity, expressions of difference, autonomy, and so forth (see also Latour, 2004). Although it is risky to suggest that there might be something 'new' about capitalism, their argument is interesting in relation to the 'designer resistance' we can observe in several sectors of the economy. Fair-trade branding in consulting firms, open sexuality in call centres, and generation-Y attitudes in IT start-ups all incorporate various aspects of the radical values once considered anathema to the firm.

Of course, such radicalism is neither unconditional nor unbounded since it is encouraged only to the point where it might undermine productivity.

The New Spirit of Capitalism

Boltanski and Chiapello's 2005 study surveys an archive of French management literature over the last twenty years. They demonstrate how European capitalism successfully recovered from the 1970s' legitimation crisis by developing a new 'spirit' (in the Weberian sense) or 'ideology'. By ideology they mean 'reasons for participating in the accumulation process that are rooted in the quotidian reality, and attuned to the values and concerns of those who need to be actively involved' (Boltanski and Chiapello, 2005: 21). Mapping shifts in managerial ideology against the economic vicissitudes of Western economies, the authors observe that artistic (or humanist) critiques prevalent in late 1960s have been co-opted and repackaged by managerial thought. This modifies the criticism (reducing critique to a managerial ideographic horizon using terms like empowerment, self-management, etc.) as well as management practice (tokenistically adjusting the managerial imperative to negate the effects of an injurious labour process). In this sense then, rather than criticism (and the types of activities with which criticism sympathizes, such as resistance) being purely antithetical to the social structure it targets, a certain type of energy is gained that sustains the very object of radicalism: '[I]n our construction we are going to assign critique the role of motor in changes in the spirit of capitalism' (Boltanski and Chiapello, 2005: 27).

When clarifying the vast movement against capital in the late 1960s and early 1970s, Boltanski and Chiapello distinguish artistic critique from social critique. The former has roots in the Baudelaireian contempt for petit bourgeois values and the vertiginous hurry of modernity. Questions of alienation, dehumanization, disenchantment, and the banality of everyday life are keystones here. They maintain

[artistic critique]...is rooted in the invention of the bohemian lifestyle, draws above all upon the first two sources of indignation that we mentioned briefly above: on the one hand the disenchantment and inauthenticity, and on the other the oppression, which characterizes the bourgeois world associated with the rise of capitalism. (Boltanski and Chiapello, 2005: 38)

Social critique, on the other hand, is more derived from a Marxian political economy with the structural features of capitalism coming to the fore including exploitation, real subsumption, and class position. This dichotomy is undoubtedly problematic. One can find overlap between artistic and social critique in the work of Debord or Sartre, and it constructs something of a straw-man version of 1960s' radicalism. Notwithstanding the limitations, Boltanski and Chiapello's analysis usefully demonstrates the supple tactics of co-optation in new management discourse. They argue that artistic critique has been especially susceptible to colonization since it does not necessarily reconfigure the structural arrangements of the prevailing accumulation process. In other words, artistic critique is ideologically caricatured in a manner that makes the production process a nicer place to be, without challenging the fundamental axioms of private property and the expropriation of surplus value:

> The pinpointing ... of the four sources of indignation of which critiques of capitalism draw will help us to identify the demands satisfied by the new spirit. It thus seems to us fairly obvious that the neo-management aims to respond to the demands for authenticity and freedom, which have historically been articulated in interrelated fashion by what we have called 'artistic critique'; and that it sets to one side the issues of egoism and inequalities traditionally combined in 'social critique'. (Boltanski and Chiapello, 2005: 97)

The new 'spirit of capitalism' thesis is compelling and surprising since it makes us rethink our assumptions about radicalism that have long been key features of critical thought. In particular, it allows us to explain why the corporate subversive (no doubt embodying an ethic of criticism that is transmogrified into a conservative and pro-business praxis) might now be the darling of pop management authors and human resource executives in many large firms.

As an illustrative example of what I mean, we can find an exposition of this new spirit of capitalism in the neoconservative writings of David Brooks (2004). His discussion captures how the new corporate subversive has quickly become the handmaiden of a more 'funky', freestyle variant of capitalist life. Brookes explores the rise of what he calls Bobos or bourgeois bohemians and celebrates the contributions they make to business, academia, government, and elsewhere. What exactly is a Bobo? According to Brookes, in business and industry Bobos are 'countercultural capitalists'. They display the cool acumen and finesse of the countercultural militants prominent in the 1960s and are exceedingly good business people because of it – they can turn their transgressive ethical values into good business practices and entrepreneurial zeal:

If you want to find a place where the Age of Aquarius radicalism is in full force, you have to go higher up the corporate ladder into the realm of companies listed on the New York Stock Exchange. Thirty years after Woodstock and all the peace rallies, the people who talk most relentlessly about smashing the status quo and crushing the establishment are management gurus and corporate executives. (Brooks, 2004: 110)

The turn to 1960s' radicalism is not only occurring in the marketing projects of large companies – what Frank (1998) calls the conquest of cool by the capitalist enterprise (think of William S. Burroughs's advertisement for Nike), but also among the personal expressions of staff inside the corporation. True to the new spirit of capitalism, the Bobo is not averse to being radical in terms of his or her identity – buying organic food, being part of a transgressive social movement – and can quickly don a power suit to still play in the corporate fun-house. Brooks goes on to say:

Especially in business sectors dominated by information elites – high technology, the media, advertising, design, Hollywood – business leaders have embraced an official ideology that would look very familiar to radicals and bohemians: constant change, maximum freedom, youthful enthusiasm, radical experimentation, repudiation of convention and hunger for the new. (Brooks, 2004: 112)

The hypocrisy in the Bobo ethos and business ideology that embodies the new spirit of capitalism is fairly straightforward. All the exhortations listed above are defined in very specific ways that reinforce the dominant economic logic: only a certain kind of change, a certain type of freedom, a certain form of youthful enthusiasm, racial experimentation, repudiation of convention, and hunger for the new. All these descriptors could be defined in fundamentally different ways that would confound the rhythms of accumulation at their root. In this sense, the radicalism involved in the new spirit of capitalism (and the mentality of the Bobo) contains a number of important definitive features. The transgressive labels are empty signifiers that do not mean a great deal in practical terms – freedom, novelty, and change are all inane icons of a resistance geared more to conserve the corporation than undermine it. They become expressive tools that convey a lifestyle or ethic, which has expressive import but is bound to the continuing whirr of profit accumulation, efficiency imperatives, private ownership, financial buoyancy, and so forth (all of which in ideal form at least have not changed very much since capitalism was invented).

The kind of corporate subversive that Brooks claims has resolved the contradictions of capitalism sounds much like the character-type Slavoj

Žižek (2008) recently lampooned as the 'liberal communist'. Žižek is targeting not only middle-class eco-warriors and participants of anti-capitalist rallies, but also elite personifications of the Bobo such as Bill Gates, George Soros, and the insipidly self-righteous Bono (I would also include Enron's Jeff Skilling who liked to come to work in a leather motorcycle jacket). He writes about these types of business leaders:

> Some of them, at least, went to Davos. What increasingly gives a predominant tone to Davos meetings is the group of entrepreneurs, some of whom refer to themselves as 'liberal communists', who no longer accept the opposition between Davos (global capitalism) and Porto Alegre (the new social movements alternative to global capitalism). Their claim is that we can have the global capitalist cake, i.e., thrive as profitable entrepreneurs, and eat it too, endorse the anti-capitalist causes of social responsibility and ecological concern. (Žižek, 2008: 14)

According to Žižek we must see the people who work and manage companies like Google and IBM, as well as big executive names like Gates and Soros, as 'personifications of the inherent self-negation of the capitalist process itself' (Žižek, 2008: 20). This is because capitalism finds it difficult to reproduce itself without some mitigating exogenous point that provides resources and absorbs costs. As Žižek portrays him or her, the liberal communist is a peculiar figure in that the elementals of capitalism are nourished under a veneer of liberal vitriol against the excesses of profit-making. Such a response, to paraphrase Walter Benjamin, sustains the very flows of excess given that the capitalist norm is defined by excess (which is often mistaken for balance and equilibrium in functionalist thought). Thus the corporate rebel that sustains the new spirit of capitalism entails an emptiness in light of the 'radical' signifiers to which he or she subscribes and a flexibility that is required if 'freedom' is not to be defined in a way that actually undermines the system. Moreover, with perhaps a nod to aspects of 1960s' artistic rebellion, designer resistance entails an aesthetic expressivism that requires 'style', visibility, and thus an audience – subversive cool has to be displayed.

Slack in the System

As the 'trager' of the new spirit of capitalism, the corporate subversive is someone who radiates an expressive 'cool' and has a penchant for breaking the rules. Especially in the context of knowledge-intensive work, the cool slacker likes to navigate between the formal edicts of the corporation, teasing authority, and forging a quietly subversive trail through the maze of organizational life. The type of 'cool' that gives the corporate rebel a valuable aura among peers derives from the ability to simultaneously poke fun at management and be very good at their job. This makes it difficult for authority figures to complain, especially if the subversive uses the very rhetoric of 'empowerment' against management itself. While corporate slackers believe that they engage in all sorts of elicit naughtiness, it is unsurprising that analysts of work have long known about the efficiency gains that can accrue when the rules are not followed. Gouldner's (1955) classic study of a gypsum plant found that management frequently turned a blind eye to worker pilfering, non-observance of safety rules, and other kinds of 'misbehaviour' since such minor infringements forestalled the articulation of more serious grievances. The power of these 'indulgency patterns' was observed in the obverse by Blau (1955). When workers actually wanted to disrupt the system of production they simply worked-to-rule, obeyed the orders of superiors to the letter, and the organization came to abrupt halt.

The corporate subversive not only enacts minor practical infringements but also what might be called 'subjective resistance' in which the so-called thought rules of cultural domination are undermined by dis-iden-tification. In the heyday of culture management and its insistence that workers identify with unitary values – epitomized by Peters and Water-man's (1982) classic authoritarian warning to slackers that 'you either buy into their norms or you get out' (1982: 77) – cynical disbelief operated as the required 'slack' in the system for the organization to function prop-erly. Žižek's (1989) fascinating analysis of 'cynical ideology' is important for understanding the relationship between cynicism and domination. He uses the example of the characters in *MASH*. A typical interpretation of the movie suggests that the doctors in the mobile field hospital are critical of the war (which they are), and the cynicism and ideological 'rule breaking' contains a subversive core that the authorities find dangerous and undesirable. Žižek gives an alternative explanation:

Contrary to its misleading appearance, Robert Altman's *MASH* is a perfectly con-formist film – for all their mockery of authority, practical jokes and sexual escap-ades, the members of the *MASH* crew *perform their jobs exemplarily*, and thus present no threat to the smooth running of the military machine. In other words, the cliché which regards *MASH* as an anti-militarist film, depicting the horrors and meaningless military slaughter which can only be endured by a healthy measure of cynicism, practical jokes, laughing at pompous official rituals, and so on, misses the point – this very distance *is* ideology. (Žižek, 1997*a*: 20)

A like-minded cynicism with similar self-defeating effects also functioned in the contradictory spaces of the high-commitment cultures indicative of 1980s managerialism. Cynicism was both 'prohibited' and necessary for the corporation to function. In the 'just be yourself' business philosophy, on the other hand, cynical cool comes into the open and connects with the official 'anti-managerial' sentiment of contemporary corporate ideology. Unlike the *MASH* scenario above, managers themselves poke fun at the organization as well and ask this from staff since an inbuilt 'false reflexivity' softens the ground for team exercises of the most puerile kind ('none of us take it that seriously'). On this topic, Liu (2004) identifies an important overlap of 'slacker cool' and the structural need for 'slack in the system'. That is to say, slackers not only express a type of aesthetic subversion that motivates the workforce, they also enable a systemic slack that is very useful, especially when creativity and innovation is the source of wealth, even in extremely mechanized and boring knowledge jobs (which he suggests makes up most of the work in the so-called knowledge economy). The nature of this slack is ambiguous. It does not belong to the organization at all, but the initiative, creativity, and discretion of the workers themselves as they endeavour to be 'cool' in a decisively 'uncool' environment: 'Slack, then, is not just a resource useful for optimising knowledge work but also a hidden reserve that insinuates itself into each of the stray and informal intervals of work... "I work here, but I'm cool"' (Liu, 2004: 299).

The Transposition of Subversion

The new spirit of capitalism forwards a particular variant of authenticity and is perhaps most apparent in the 'just be yourself' work environment where employees are encouraged to express their unique individuality (up to a point). This expressivism must, however, rest upon a structural political economy of the firm for it to be congruent with the accumulation process. As I suggested in earlier chapters, the Italian autonomist perspective regarding the social factory, social labour, and the commons is very useful in this respect because it demonstrates how capitalism today relies upon an immaterial labour formally outside itself. The commons is a substratum of uncommodified associative labour, self-initiated acts of cooperation, and anti-corporate gift-giving that resides in the sphere of non-work. This sub-economy must take place before the corporation can even become what it is, given the fundamentally antisocial nature of the firm. It is thus useful to the corporation for its reproductive cycle in both an economic and symbolic sense. The commons, as Hardt and Negri (1999) argue, is no more evidenced than in the forms of life antagonistic to capitalist forms of life (also see de Angelis, 2007). It is this negative–positive quality vis-à-vis capital that results in a dynamism the corporation wishes to formalize into a palatable resource. The recalcitrance of the commons can be harnessed to the organization in a number of ways, coupled to the ever-growing regime of work that Hardt and Negri (1999) call 'social labour'. As with the example of 'fun' explored in the last chapter, this is done by (*a*) haemorrhaging the organizational form to transplant symbolic non-work associatives inside the world of production; and (*b*) deploying a mimetic mapping that aims to transpose the commons into a productive gesture. The mimetic function is especially important for politically abbreviating and stylising resistance, cultivating a corporate ambience that 'feels' as if one is not working at all. In relation to 'fun', of course, such mimesis fails miserably, generating feelings of inauthenticity among many workers. Can the same be said for 'designer resistance' and the corporate subversive? Let us explore its mechanical properties in more detail.

Parasitizing the Countercultural Ethic

In terms of its historical development, the capitalist enterprise (in the West at least) has traditionally been a site of radicalism in relation to organized and collective resistance. The research of Edwards (1979) and others have tracked the importance of collective action in defining what we now call the contemporary organizational form. This variant of resistance is certainly not the kind of 'challenge' that Tom Peters has in mind when promoting the benefits of liberation management. In order to tap into the slacker chic of the counterculture, the 'just be yourself' approach turns to specific motifs that have traditionally lay outside the sphere of production. In his book *The Laws of Cool*, Liu (2004) provides an excellent example of this process *apropos* the emergence of the computerized office and the prominent ethic of 'cool' among workers employed in the IT industry. What makes an individual 'cool' in this regard? The archetypical web designer or IT hack is someone who is disenchanted with capitalism, exudes an 'outsider' attitude, and holds relatively anti-capitalist views (here one thinks of the famous *Hacker Manifesto*). Free access, shareware, and non-regulated spaces of intellectual freedom are at the centre of the web ethos. And for sure, this would be the kind of employee that Tom Peters argues is the true source of value in an economy increasingly built around ideas, innovation, and creativity. In this regard, the slacker occupies an ambivalent space. They are against the firm, but this 'againstness' is now part and parcel of an official ideology that seeks to consolidate corporate power. Liu's catchphrase for this pseudo-transgressive outlook is the following: 'We work here, but we are cool'.

Importantly, Liu suggests that this corporate subversive ethic giving sustenance to the knowledge-intensive firm is no doubt animated by significant grievances within the workplace. With the emergence of post-Fordist employment practices that are high-tech, precarious, and exploitive all at the same time, only certain modes of opposition are available. He writes:

> [T]here are only two equivocal ways that the archaic and unreasonable can protest their submission to the new rationalization. One is to quit and move to another job . . . the other is just as conflicting: to express in lifestyle and, increasingly, in what I have called 'workstyle' the enormous reserve of petty kink that *Processed World* called 'bad attitude' but that now appears with mind-numbing regularity in popular culture, the media, and the Web as 'cool'. Cool is the protest of our contemporary 'society without politics'. It is the gesture that has no voice of its own. (Liu, 2004: 294)

The promotion of this 'cool' ethos inside the firm is a concession on the side of the corporation in face of growing despondency among these types of generation-Y workers (they used to be 'authentic hackers' but are now working for 'the man'). But it is also a manoeuvre to extract more effort from the worker since the motivational values of distancing and dis-identification have been well documented (see Fleming and Spicer, 2003). Moreover, echoing my previous analysis of authenticity and expressivism, the 'cool' corporate subversive enacts their bad attitude as a 'gesture' or 'style' that individuates rather than collectivizes the organizational body. The question Liu asks in this regard is:

> what ethical foundation enables identities to live an un-networked and counter-informational fantasy within the spirit of informationalism? What room might there be for a counter-ethos *within* the dominant ethos of informationalism that spends its days and nights locked within the cubicles of post-industrialism but 'gestures' all the while that it is something else? (Liu, 2004: 71)

To answer these questions, Liu takes his cue from Frank's *The Conquest of Cool* (1998), which investigates the appropriation of counterculture by the mainstream advertising industry. In a similar manner, Liu argues that the instigation of a slacker cool inside the corporation developed from an important interplay between work and non-work, work and leisure. In the halcyon days of Fordist employment, the leisure industry functions as a subventing counterbalance to alienated work. This explanation of leisure is well established in the sociological histories of industrial labour (e.g. see Gorz, 1988). While leisure absorbed the privations exacted inside the factory gates, it nevertheless felt mainstream and somehow still part of the system of a production society – it was not a place of protest or resistance, but a kind of anaesthetization from work. This is where consumerist-oriented subculture and counterculture developed. Cold production turned to 'hot' consumption in order to vent against the system whist still remaining 'inside' it, as various types of music, film stars (Marlon Brando), and fashions came to be deemed as 'outside', 'excluded', and 'against' the dead zone of work. As Liu puts it: '[W]hite collars displaced the very experience of alienation onto outsiders who could do the heavy lifting of being alienated for them' (Liu, 2004: 100). Subculture on the other hand turned to 'cold' production to consolidate its anti-establishment ethos: gangsters wearing business suits, for example, and musicians utilizing cold rationality such as the reggae sound system.

Hence, according to Liu, the birth of cool. But how did this subversive 'outside' later come to feature so prominently in the office? There are a number of factors. First is the continuing attempt by workers to make sense of themselves in a manner that retains personal authenticity and integrity; no one wants to think of themself as a 'sell-out'. Moreover, the computer hacker has always traded in the founding myth of being against the grain of corporate capitalism, reared as they are on ideals of free access, anarchism, shareware, and unregulated networking. The evocation of an outsider cool inside the firm allows one to maintain this positive identity whilst making perverse profits for its private owners. The appearance of the 'outsider' and extra-employment motifs inside the firm also must palliate the alienating aspects of work more generally. The hot counterculture was transferred into the cold realm of work, generating a 'slacker' and 'playful' outlook that is especially useful in the networked, high-flexibility environment of emerging organizational forms. The ideological fantasy of being outside the firm appeals to a version of authenticity that not only satisfies employees by appeasing the bad faith of their position, but also caters to a more precarious paradigm of work in the so-called digital era.

Simulating Subversion

The mimetic function that transposes subversion from the outside realm of counterculture into the gesture of work itself is crucial to note. Such a process of simulation and re-representation would not be necessary if work actually did become non-work. This is not to say that 'fun' or 'lifestyle' inside the firm is any less real for being a simulation. It is very real, and indeed has important political implications for being so. In the case of 'designer resistance', however, the simulation process requires dissent to be made into something far away from itself, something actually useful to the production process. The transposition process of simulated resistance streamlines dissent into a harmless theatre that is entertaining to its actors and audience. For sure, in the same way simulated 'fun' was received as inherently inauthentic by some workers, the antinomy of designer resistance as a path to personal authenticity might also render the subject into a self-conscious parody of itself.

One of the most interesting examples of this process of simulated subversion can be found in Ross's (2004) *No Collar*, an exceptional ethnographic study of a 'permissive company', the IT company called Razor Fish (situated in a bohemian urban district of Boston). According to Ross, the permissive firm attempts to manufacture a transgressive culture, hiring anti-conformist employees for many of the reasons that Liu (2004) suggests above. The no-collar worker resists labelling, exudes transgressive attitudes about capitalism and the corporate world, and re-enacts lifestyle diversity and tastes in the realm of work. At Razor Fish this 'mentality is called no-collar... because of their self-conscious rejection of labels, not to mention status-consciousness work uniforms and attitudes' (Ross, 2004: 10). Along with sexual and ethic diversity, the promotion of this ethos of subversion (supporting anti-capitalist causes, for example) suited the firm for very distinct reasons. It connected with the pre-existing attitudes of workers regarding the 'hacker' ethic mentioned earlier and its anti-capitalist values. Moreover, it played to the more general popular scepticism regarding the corporation (and the ills it precipitates) among generation-Y employees. As Ross puts it: '[G]iving the finger to corporate America might not always be good for business, but the sites were a big boost for recruitment and employee morale' (Ross, 2004: 141).

Authenticity at the individual and corporate level was said to derive from approximating the bohemian countercultural values, those conventionally external to the sentiments of production – something Ross calls 'the industrialization of bohemia'. An important element of this business strategy was to locate the company outside the typical suburban or central business districts of large cities. Razor Fish was set up in a very alternative and bohemian area of Boston where creative workers and the artistic poor resided. Such a strategy of appropriation – often called 'gentrification' – has been noted as an important turn in the post-industrial pursuit of accumulation (see Harvey's [2002] study of Barcelona and Berlin). Moreover, in creating a vibrant and transgressive flavour in the firm, Razor Fish also dismantled the work–non-work boundary in important ways. As Ross observes, hedonistic partying, play, sexuality, consumerism, lifestyle, and ethnicity were all promoted during work hours as fitting for no-collar expressions of selfhood. 'Neo-leisure' was actively staged to motivate workers and make work seem like it was not really linked to the capital accumulation process at all.

Missed in Ross's analysis is the immense importance of mimesis in order to recreate and transpose the subversive components of non-work inside the office and render it into a profitable platform. How was this done? An important replication was of the bohemian 'hacker' environment in which long hours in darkened rooms was thought to represent a sense of being against the norms of middle-class conformity. Some Razor Fish sites put much effort into designing office decor and workspace that mimicked this type of atmosphere. In one case, warehouse space was rented and left partially unrenovated to convey an ambience of countercultural cool – an atmosphere that is the direct opposite of the plastic golden facades that characterized corporate life in the 1980s and early 1990s. Even details such as bare plaster walls and exposed overhead cables in the ceiling were intended to achieve this effect. The attempt was to regenerate the bohemian artist's lifestyle inside the capitalist organization. The college ethos too was simulated through spatial design. This was accomplished by the windowless spaces in the office 'warehouse', endless supplies of coffee, and anti-globalization protest posters on the wall to ensure the corporate subversive's political views were visible. In effect, the transgressive doctrine of 'first-generation' websters became a thin caricature of itself.

These mechanisms of appropriating the commons and the immaterial labour of the employees that persist *despite* corporatized work faced the same limitations noted in Chapter 3 exploring 'fun'. While providing some relief and personal authenticity in the context of the for-profit environment, the objective of making work into non-work or even anti-work continuously bumped up against the realities of the corporation. At Razor Fish this was evident when the economy dipped and cutbacks and layoffs loomed. Moreover, even within the official counterculture, an employee-led *unofficial counterculture* developed in order to maintain a note of realism among workers who enjoyed the 'permissive company' but still aimed to retain something for themselves.

It is difficult to say whether the co-optation of subversive non-work motifs through the mimetic function has more purchase in some occupations, industries, and companies than in others. The examples I have recounted from Lui and Ross above are from IT, knowledge, and creative-oriented firms. The same managerial strategy has, however, also been noted in other more mechanized environments such as call centres (Fleming, 2005). But what would the corporate subversive look like in the medical or law industry? Authenticity might mean something very different to a nurse or a lawyer. In addition to the limitations of mimesis internal to capital, perhaps there are some very practical occupational limitations to this approach of 'authenticating' employees within the corporate infrastructure.

Conclusion

Since the corporation has traditionally signified conformity, domination, authoritarianism, and hierarchy, it is certainly curious to observe managers now endorsing a discourse of subversion and emancipation. In the 1980s, management gurus like Tom Peters told workers that they either 'buy into the norms or get out'. Today it is these same 'outsiders' who are considered to be the vanguards of value-added productivity. This chapter has attempted to explain this inversion by suggesting that corporations are still very conformist places. Designer resistance and the 'new spirit of capitalism' that informs it can be seen as a kind of corporate manufacture that conserves rather than undermines. With the aim of harnessing a specific brand of personal authenticity, it draws inspiration from the genuinely subversive reservoir of non-work that we have called the commons after Hardt and Negri (1999). The commons is a space of immaterial labour that collects at the borders of non-work and work, commodification, and cooperation. In this sense, then, the corporate subversive is not a complete mirror image of capital since the commons lies partially inside and outside the production–consumption cycle. The motivations for this attempt to reify the more antagonistic elements of the commons have also been highlighted. They pertain to detracting from the enduring alienation that work engenders, connecting with pre-existing anti-corporate values in certain occupations and motivating generation-Y employees who think the corporation 'sucks' (but still want to buy stuff). It is important not to exaggerate the pervasiveness of this corporatized variant of subversion. Many contemporary corporations are undoubtedly intolerant of any hint of employee dissent, but the tendency described above deserves explanation, especially from a political economy perspective.

In proposing a term like 'designer resistance' we do not want to fall into the trap of positing an authentic kind of subversion, a space of purity untainted by power and oppression. Much research now demonstrates how organizational resistance uses the instruments of power in a tactical manner, reproducing aspects of the governing hegemony at the same time. As Laclau (1996) puts it, 'there is no clear-cut solution to the paradox of radically negating a system of power while remaining in secret dependency on it' (p. 30). In an abstract sense, a degree of co-optation probably defines every social relation. However, the concept of 'designer resistance' highlights how certain expressions of recalcitrance can be exploited to serve pro-business objectives. My particular take on co-optation has been significant here. It refers to the way in which opportunities of resistance are forcibly repositioned away from the commons as a serviceable gesture for the business process, including ostensibly anti-management criticism. In firms like Sunray (mentioned in Chapter 3) and Razor Fish, this is mainly done by confining protest to an *expression* – a display akin to an individual consumer choice, and hence the importance of authentic lifestyles, or what Health and Potter (2005: 69) consider 'a set of dramatic gestures' and not much else.

While it is certainly tempting to get into an ontological debate about what is real and false resistance, this would lead to the usual cul-de-sac. Instead we should turn the usual question on its head and ask about boundaries instead. What type of resistance *could not* be accommodated, commodified, and co-opted by these recent trends in management practice? What are the limits to the modern corporation, and how are they being tested by political intercessions that cannot be simply enlisted to enhance business as usual? This boundary can be found in all the motifs of the new spirit of capitalism itself since employees can only 'transgress' or have 'fun' up to a point (and only a particular type of fun at that). Such limits might also be surfaced by some quite 'old' interventions around collective action, be it 'joyous' union agitation (which Sunray management despised and undermined at every turn), strike action over wages and gender discrimination, social movements that damage corporate reputation, and so forth. These forms of resistance remain inscrutable to the corporate gaze and cannot easily be absorbed within its own frame by making them 'cool'. To include such inscrutability would challenge the axiomatic principles of the firm. Such protests are occurring today as much as any other time, but they are unlikely to feature in the management guru's glorification of the corporate subversive. 'Trotsky at Saatchi's?' (Kane, 2004: 228). I doubt it.

5

Authenticating the Firm: Corporate Social Responsibility as Parasite

The rats, the country- and the city-dweller, have shown us that the system of parasites in stepladder formation is not very different from an ordinary system. Who will ever know if parasitism is an obstacle to its proper functioning or is its very dynamics?

(Serres, 1982: 27)

In some of the poorer districts of London, one can see a strange collection of people that is almost reminiscent of a Lars Von Trier film. The author came across such a tragi-comic gathering a few months ago in East London. A group of smiling young men and women dressed in matching T-shirts were leading another group of decidedly anxious blind people through a park. Nearby the encroaching business district was hastening the gentrification process of the East. The strange crowd bustled along, white canes tapping erratically and the young T-shirted chaperones dragging them along, creating a spectacle in which passers-by (such as myself) either stopped to watch or stole a brief glance as the show moved on. From a distance, most of the audience to this little theatre of the blind would have surely assumed it was the work of a Christian group attempting to provide services to the less fortune (and overtly letting others know about their *caritas* by putting on such a noisy display). Upon closer inspection, however, it was not a crucifix or local parish insignia that could be seen on the T-shirts – instead could be seen the brand name of a very well-known management consultancy.

These young men and women of the corporate world were engaged in a popular Corporate Social Responsibility (CSR) exercise in which employees with social progressive values are able to 'give back to the community' on company time. Such CSR exercises are common in the city of London, sometimes involving community street tours with mentally ill patients, as well as services for the elderly. For sceptics and cynics alike, such activities, brazenly branded as they are with the company logo, are but clumsily organized publicity stunts. From this stance, the exercise represents an attempt to signal to the community that a ruthless management consultancy does have 'heart and soul' despite brutally rightsizing yet another government office. Sceptics with a more nuanced understanding of such public relations (PR) exercises might look to employees themselves to uncover the corporate rationale behind these curious congregations on the streets of East London. Perhaps it is a way of ameliorating or prefiguring dissatisfaction among those workers with a social conscience, providing a sort of safety valve in which a 'feel-good' glow can be nurtured, whilst one is exploited (and exploits). Given that the corporate sector hires not only from business schools but also from the humanities and arts, *pro bono* allotments of time dedicated to charities might enable some consultants to align their personal values with the otherwise frosty pursuit of profit.

The incisive question we need to ask here is why the corporate world would bother to invest people and money in CSR at all. While various forms of corporate social responsibility initiatives have been a keen aspect of industrial capitalism from its nascent years (especially in the form of charities, philanthropy, and so forth), today it has developed into a full-blown and cogent corporate discourse involving marketing, recruitment, employee motivation, governmental regulation, and a keen awareness of shifting consumer values. In its contemporary guise, CSR is defined in fairly consistent ways in various quarters of the business world. For example, here are some definitions that Blowfield and Murray (2008: 13) summon to capture the phenomenon:

CSR is a concept whereby companies integrate social and environmental concerns in their business operations and in their interactions with their stakeholders on a voluntary basis. (European Commission, Directorate General for Employment and Social Affairs)

CSR is the proposition that companies are responsible not only for maximizing profits, but also for recognizing the needs of such stakeholders as employees, customers, demographic groups, and even the regions they serve. (Pricewaterhouse-Coopers)

In much of the business literature, a thorny question lies at the centre of these definitions and is quietly put aside: Can the business enterprise 'do good for society' as well as make profits for itself? Is the age-old contradiction between public good and private gain surmountable? Addressing this question successfully, of course, depends on the firm under investigation, and, more importantly, it needs to tap into a deeper ideological framework regarding the way in which capitalism is thought to function (Heilbroner, 1986). Many governments and big business think tanks, for example, believe that there is little contradiction at all since the goals of business and other stakeholders can be allied. Groups more critical of the corporate model argue that the profit motif is directly and necessarily antithetical to the broader goals of social justice (think of Shell Nigeria, for example). Notwithstanding these tensions, it is safe to say that not even the quint-essential philanthropist, Andrew Carnegie, would have envisaged a CSR campaign in which employees ventured into the poor areas of the metropolis with cane-tapping blind people in tow. Why is the business world suddenly so interested in being seen as an agent of community ethics and social justice? Is it simply a case of a new corporate ideology being developed to obfuscate the truth of an uncaring capitalism or is something else happening here?

I will argue in this chapter that authenticity appears to be a key element of this turn to ethics in the corporation. It will be suggested that CSR (and its related family of discourses such as social accounting, social auditing, the triple bottom line, and sustainability) resonates with the broader concern with authenticity (especially as it has been defined in the previous chapters) in a number of ways. Since employees now search for a sense of personal authenticity at work, the so-called tempered radical might find this amidst the *pro bono* exercises like the one mentioned above (Costas and Fleming, 2008). More and more consumers are demanding so-called authentic products and services, as opposed to the fake and superficial goods that abound in the wasteland of post-industrial society (Boyle, 2004). And consumers want to feel that the 'ethical companies' they support are authentically following their espoused principles of responsibility. Large multinational firms like British Petroleum and Shell struggle to anticipate consumer cynicism regarding their intricate CSR programmes, no mean feat given their respective horrendous human rights and environmental track records. Intersecting with these concerns is the power of the 'authentic brand' and the importance of marketing and the spectacle. A large industry of advisors and consultants has grown around the notion of 'authentic marketing'. In the current era of organic vegetables, reality TV, and a default consumer disbelief, the corporation endeavours to be perceived as genuine, something which often calls for creative self-interpretations, since how does one, for example, make a tobacco company (which kills millions of consumers every year) look like a purveyor of social justice and public good? And yet again the familiar contradiction manifests, in which the quest for authenticity is often self-defeating since it requires branding, simulation, and dissimulation in order to convey a message of integrity. Surely our hapless and socially progressive young management consultants mentioned above might feel a twinge of 'fakeness' when fulfilling their values in such a contrived way?

How should we understand the intersection of manufactured ethics – such as the *pro bono* exercise noted above – and the pursuit of authenticity by the firm and those employees who are troubled by the logic of the corporation even while they seek to gain from it? In this chapter I will argue that we can make sense of CSR and the ideals of authenticity underlying it in a number of different ways. In the first section we will position CSR in the context of a reflective capitalism whereby automatic employee–consumer disbelief is prefigured in managerial discourse. Then I turn to the way in which CSR functions inside the firm. Most of the criticisms of CSR and business ethics tend to focus on how they aim to validate the corporation to an outside audience. In this section, I suggest that we also need to think of CSR in the context of what I earlier called the 'haemorrhaging organizational form' in which the values, practices, and rituals of non-work (including the political views of employees sometimes associated with counter-capitalist values) are increasingly included in the rhetoric of business. The firm is very interested in the problem of attracting and motivating distrustful generation-Y employees who often find capitalism and corporate life antithetical to their own values.

I then discuss CSR and authenticity from two sometimes conflicting theoretical perspectives, those of 'ideological legitimation' and 'parasitical appropriation'. Both perspectives place CSR and its claims to authenticity firmly within a political economy framework. This section particularly highlights how CSR might represent a technology of appropriation (or co-optation) by drawing upon the Italian autonomist movement. We have already discussed this approach in relation to the overt non-work associa-tives in the 'just be yourself' management discourse. The chapter con-cludes by theorizing the limits of CSR as an engine for corporatizing authenticity. As I argued in Chapter 4, the limits of capital can be found in the very structures of capitalism itself. In the same fashion, the limits of CSR (and its appropriation of the commons to manufacture an aura of authenticity) are CSR itself. If it is taken at all seriously and made into a reality, it would definitely spell the demise of corporate capitalism as we know it today.

CSR and the 'Reflective Moment'

CSR now represents a large and relatively prominent aspect of management practice and scholarship. In the realm of academic research, CSR is usually studied from a business ethics point of view, and generally takes two forms. The CSR framework can be used as a criterion to dissect various business activities, usually in a critical mode (see Banerjee, 2007). The second take on CSR is more managerialist and attempts to identify the value-added potential for firms that adopt CSR initiatives (here CSR has largely been subsumed by strategic management). In the corporate world, CSR has a long and somewhat variegated history. Industrial capitalists (especially the exceedingly wealthy ones from the United States including Carnegie, Ford, Rockefeller, and Gates) established philanthropic subsidiaries to enhance the reputation of their firms. In the United States, much of the debate was around the meaning of corporate capitalism in the context of private ownership and the politics of redistribution in the face of market forces. For some, including Leavitt (1958), and, most notoriously, Milton Friedman (1970), social responsibility fell outside the remit of managerial expertise and actually undermined the broadening of social wealth via the market mechanism. The considerable difference in the economic–ideological climate of the era in which Friedman was taken seriously and the current juncture in which CSR discourse is bandied everywhere is telling of the broader cultural shifts that have occurred in late capitalist societies. For sure, Hanlon (2007) also demonstrates that we see CSR entering into the mainstream discourse of large corporations and governmental policy with the end of the Fordist regime of accumulation. As the welfare state is dismantled and the corporate crisis of the late 1970s averted through the marketization of everyday life (shifting the costs of production to the consumer or worker), CSR mysteriously appears to fill the legitimation breach left in the wake of a reconfigured state apparatus. As Hanlon points out, this is not to say that state has disappeared as some erroneously assume in the CSR and business ethics field, but rather it has been rebooted to be more supportive of the transnational corporation.

The Corporate Spectacle and Persuasion

The legitimation crisis that follows the dismantling of Fordism and the rise of 'new' corporate forms coincides with certain changes in the cultural logic of capitalism. Many commentators have recognized the poignant irony (Jameson, 1991), cynicism (Sloterdijk, 1988), and diffuse criticism

(Boltanski and Chiapello, 2005) of capitalism pervading important parts of contemporary experience. The CSR discourse and practice, in which 'social' goals and needs are figured into the official principles of corporate strategy, can be seen as an important facet of this kaleidoscopic cultural shift. A useful marker for the change to which I am referring can be found in the popular advertising industry. Frank (1998) notes this in relation to the corporate conquest of 'cool' in US advertising. There are three elements of this conquest that reveal the emergence of a 'reflective turn' more generally regarding the tastes and concerns of consumers and the parallel pre-emptive manoeuvres of the corporation. First of all, advertising from the 1960s and 1970s for home products, for example, displayed an expectation of consumer earnestness. The marketing of washing machines and detergents seems so unsophisticatedly ideological to us today because we see them from such a jaded perspective. There is a different logic of seeing functioning here. Contemporary eyes are more inclined to disbelieve and view the typical sales pitch with a measure of incredulity. As Latour (2004) also implies, it is almost as if the de-masking strategy of traditional 'ideology critique' has filtered into popular consciousness (perhaps coagulating into what Žižek [1989] refers to as an even more insidious ideology of cynicism).[1]

The second element of contemporary advertising that is of note compared to previous generations is a sense of irony and self-parody. Like the inbuilt reflexivity of the corporate 'fun' exercises in the 'just be yourself' management discourse noted in previous chapters, an inoculating self-criticism is evident in a good deal of advertising, especially that which is geared towards the young. Much of this advertising actively draws upon the preceding 'fake' generation of adverts to heighten the effect. A great example is the anti-acne cream advertisement that tells the viewer the product will not magically transform the consumer into a super model but simply into their true selves. This reflective turn imbues other advertisements by conveying the message with a tongue-in-cheek aloofness, while some still directly tap into the critical ethos of the generation-Y consumer, which thinks capitalism sucks. As Boyle (2004) puts it in relation to brands and consumerism:

High-pressure marketing to young people – probably the critical audience – tends to mean developing a rebellious atmosphere around your product. That means sports players who break the rules, former terrorists, reformed criminals and mild Mafiosi are in demand. (Boyle, 2004: 106)

In connection to authenticity, this observation regarding contemporary marketing and advertising resonates with Liu's (2004) point about the corporatization of 'cool' mentioned in Chapter 4. Authenticity and 'staying real' is the product of a dialectical tension between work and non-work, where the frustrations of alienation are displaced onto 'rebels' who burn a path outside the market and often against the stuffy bourgeois strictures of capital (what Gilmore and Pine, 2007 call 'anti- as authenticity').

The third aspect of the reflective turn that can be gauged by observing shifts in advertising is the way in which the critique of capitalism (and the cost externalization it frequently entails) is surreptitiously incorporated into the selling mechanism itself. This is sometimes taken to the extreme in which an anti-commodification ethic is included in the packaging of the commodity as evidenced in the music industry (grunge rock, e.g. Nirvana, and alternative rock, e.g. Radiohead) are good examples). This marketing approach utilizes counterculture to make the commodity seem more authentic, involving what Heath and Potter (2005) call the 'rebel sell'. This is also where we see many CSR tropes coming to the fore in advertising and the commodification process. The branding visibility of green issues, social auditing, the influence on the Third World, and developing countries reflects a certain mood among a good segment of consumers. While not all consumers, advertisers, or corporations engage in such a discourse, compared to branding in previous generations, the inclusion of such 'social criticism' is markedly significant.

The Aura 'Beyond' the Commodity Form

It is doubtful the firm would have put such emphasis on CSR issues on its own. What has therefore changed? Much of it relates to the crisis of the capitalist enterprise itself and its renewed framing of those failures as yet another opportunity to exploit new markets. The market and private enterprise are constantly failing in both their own terms (economic crisis and corruption) and in broader social terms of worker and consumer rights, the natural environment, and poverty. A distinct and profound distrust rightly exists among many citizens of the West regarding the corporation (even though they participate and support them now more, perhaps, than ever). Consumers are decidedly more unwilling to accept visible profiteering. A good example is the way Nike and Gap radically changed their marketing strategy following the discovery of child labour and sweatshops in their supply chains. The consumer boycott of Nestle after the powdered baby milk scandal in Africa similarly had a major impact on the firm's operating practices (also represented in changes in governmental regulation). These systemic (rather than aberrational) failures of capitalism have *inter alia* contributed to a reflexive moment among many consumers, whereby the contents and production process of the commodity are increasingly scrutinized. This is especially so for the middle classes who are more wracked with an objectless guilt than other groups. The reflective consumer that CSR programmes seek to engage also represents an opportunity to make money above and beyond the mere legitimation of 'business as usual'. We shall study this process of 'appropriation' and the exploitation of self-failure in more detail later in this chapter.

The intersection of CSR and the reflective moment transforms authenticity into a powerful signifier on three levels. The first is what might be called the consumer-led demand for so-called genuine goods and services (see Gilmore and Pine, 2007). While this sounds simple, it does connect with a specific definition of authenticity – there are many 'real' commodities that would not meet the criteria of authenticity. And it is this very bracketing and truncated version of authenticity that echoes the arguments in the previous chapters. In a similar manner to how the 'just be yourself' business philosophy ultimately attempted (and failed) to transmute work into a non-work zone through mimesis, the authentic commodity also attempts to exude something beyond the commodity form. As Crofts (2005), a popular management writer calling for 'authentic business' puts it: 'purpose beyond profit is the key for authentic businesses' (Crofts, 2005: 1). The authentic good and service aims to be more than it actually is, usually by way of referencing something beyond the commodity form. An authentic holiday package may attempt to resonate with social justice claims of the poor by allowing tourists to spend money unmediated by the middleman. An operator might whisk the tourist in Brazil away from the beach (a blatant and obviously commodified space) into the impoverished and crime-ridden *Favelas* (or local slums) in order to experience the city as it really is. This tourist experience points to something considered to be beyond the logic of the commodity, even though such a tour represents an even more problematic commodification process. In a similar way, fair trade, organic vegetables, and tobacco companies concerned with biodiversity all aim to foster authenticity by (*a*) weaving an uncommodified aura around the product and (*b*) then cashing in on this aura by using it to package the good as more genuine than its fake rivals. The best example of this outside 'x' that is beyond but still vital to the product is British Petroleum's (BP's) re-branding of itself as 'Beyond Petroleum'.

The second element of authenticity that is important here in relation to CSR is proper to the marketing process itself. A double authenticity is evident. Not only does the product itself need to exude an authentic aura – which the CSR process can help since it speciously points to a space beyond profits and cold cash – but also the marketing process must similarly be considered 'authentic' and truthful. In marketing more generally, there is a considerable authentic marketing movement in which consulting firms and branding advisers aver that the corporation must avoid looking 'fake', 'superficial', or 'phoney'. Online consulting depositories like 'Authentic Business' and 'Authentic Marketing Services' and texts such as *The Authentic Brand* (Rosica, 2007) attest to this new fad. As Trosclair (2008) argues in an online blurb regarding the virtues of branding authentically:

The premise is simple: Today's consumers are 'longing' for authenticity because they find so many fakes and phonies in their lives. If people believe a company, product or service is authentic, they will buy and support it. If they think the company, its products and/or services are inauthentic, the firm is labelled a fake and is headed for failure. (www.advertising.suite101.com/article.cfm/authentic_ marketing_strategy)

And third, this objective of generating a brand that drips with authenticity is now also a major concern for those responsible for devising CSR programmes in large corporations. The inbuilt reflexivity and cynicism that marketers are faced with – and as we shall soon argue, get many of their ideas from – makes for quite a challenge for CSR spin doctors. Imagine being given the task of drawing up a CSR branding programme for a petroleum or tobacco company, or any corporation (and industry) that has been criticized for misconduct and unethical behaviour. Yet again the consultants are never far away who offer their assistance. Generating a sense of unforced and sincere authenticity via a CSR policy is treated as an art form requiring expertise, experience, and cunning. In relation to the use of youth empowerment programmes to bolster the firm's brand value, one consultant advises the following techniques:

Generation-Y are the future consumers and employers across the private and public sectors. The need to create an authentic experience to this market is paramount. . . . The authenticity of your CSR initiatives depends ultimately on the people you choose to leverage. In the areas of youth and ethnic diversity – you must engage those who have strong reputations in their communities and who have the ability to connect to these audiences. (Dockery, 2008: 2)

There are several aspects of this advice that will inform the investigation in the remainder of the chapter. The first relates to the importance of creating a sense of authenticity not only to an external audience but also to those who work inside it. The 'war for talent' depends upon developing CSR initiatives that allow employees to feel a degree of personal integrity with respect to their broader participation within the firm. Generation-Y employees ask for something more than the previous generations of workers since they insist (and are encouraged) to 'just be themselves'. But the advice also hints at the political economy underlining CSR and the authenticity claims that legitimate it. This involves the parasitical appropriation of the commons we have referred to in previous chapters. For CSR to be authentic, it must not only point to something that is disingenuously outside the commodity form (an event that instantly draws this self-styled aura into a tenuous relationship with economic rationality) but also it must utilize it, and parasitically feed on its connections and networks (as the advice states above, 'engage those with who have strong reputations'). I now turn to the employee and CSR, and then to the importance of appropriation and the commons as the political economy backdrop of CSR programmes and their attempt to authenticate the firm.

CSR and the 'Authentic' Employee

When Google founders Sergey Brin and Larry Page began their company, they had from the start a clear idea of the people they wished to hire given their corporate strategy and market focus. Following Conway's law, the much-revered adage among IT professionals that suggests technological systems (software, communications supports, etc.) tend to mirror the pre-existing organizational structure, Google's vision of a rhizomatic interface needed a specific culture and, most importantly, the kinds of people that would complement the technological systems they inspired to design (Vise, 2005). The company already had many of the cultural ingredients that would see a particular type of flexi-techno system emerge: youth, adherence to political autonomy, a do-it-yourself ethic reminiscent of the anonymous *Hacker Manifesto*, and so forth. The Google search engine aimed to reflect these qualities since it was modelled on the ostensible democratic freedoms of the World Wide Web. The company's culture has subsequently become famous for the way it encourages individual freedom of expression. Indeed, the Google approach has become the pin-up case for the advantages gained when employees can 'just be themselves' within the confines of the for-profit firm. Vitally important in their suite of socially progressive employment practices is the CSR policy that defines much of what the company stands for. Google tells itself and its users that it has aimed to develop a search engine that avoids the heavy and exploitive advertising of rivals like Yahoo and AOL, as well as the predatory competitive practices of the colossal Microsoft. While this policy was geared to woo customers, Google blurred its consumers and employees into one figure, following the principle that many IT geeks are most attracted to companies from which they purchase products (and vice versa). As Vise (2005) points out:

Engineers who once longed to work for Microsoft came to see it as the Darth Vader of software, the dark force, the one who didn't play fairly. By contrast, Google presented itself as a fresh new enterprise with a halo, the motto Don't Be Evil, and a pair of youthful founders with reputations as nice guys. (Vise, 2005: 96)

The religious connotations aside, Google's CSR policy builds upon a number of axiomatic features of the ideal socially progressive company that flirts with left-wing ideology in order to create a certain internal atmosphere. The kind of 'good' that Google is pursuing is not necessarily the squeaky-clean kind but closer to the countercultural ambition of 'making a difference' in an over-commodified world. 'Evil' is considered to be those large corporations that are simply out to make a quick profit at the expense of the consumer and worker. Again, given that Google is operating within the medium of a capitalist market and labour process, it needs to point to something outside of itself, and this is where the importance of CSR comes into play. According to Vise (2005), the founders of Google and their top management view the company as more of a social movement that can make a difference and transform the world into a better place. This plays into the 'cyber-utopianism' often surrounding the IT ethos, especially among the left-leaning CEOs and hackers who feel that computer technology and the Internet are tantamount to a revolutionary democratizing process.

The Inward Gaze of CSR

But Google is, of course, a capitalist enterprise that has a major hold over the technological medium of search engine interfaces. While there are varieties of capitalism within the broader frame of profit and rent-seeking behaviour (that allow, say, Google to distinguish itself from dark overlords like Microsoft), it still must adhere to the same principles that any other firm does in order to generate returns. Like other politically correct organizations, the 'outside' utilized as a reference point by the CSR policy is the social movements that are contrary to the more brutal facets of the capitalist marketplace such as the Indy Media movement. As an aside, it is interesting to note that Google's principle of free access and pro-democratic rights crumbled miserably in the face of the gargantuan communist capitalism of China when it refused to comment on the Party's censorship of certain Google-provided web sites.

That a publicly listed firm views itself as a progressive social movement advancing social justice and human rights reveals many of the contradictions at the heart of CSR. We will turn to unpack the generative function of this contradiction in the next part of the chapter, but it is important to outline here the significance of 'the worker' regarding CSR in the current corporate context. As many commentators have argued, the so-called business case for companies adopting a CSR policy requiring resources above and beyond the regulatory minimum is manifold. It enhances reputation among consumers and lobby groups, forestalls government intervention, and so on. Often downplayed in the literature is the function that CSR plays in attracting, motivating, and retaining workers, especially those employees who are more inclined to identify with socially progressive causes outside of the official remit of corporate life (as is frequently the case of many IT, advertising, and consulting firms).

CSR consulting firms are increasingly selling programmes and strategies to companies as a tool to manage classic human resource problems in the face of changing worker demographics characterized by the so-called unmanageable generation-Y group and a pervasive anti-corporate cynicism. CSR assumes the role not only of a branding exercise for luring consumers, but an instrument for tapping the otherwise extra-employment concerns of workers. It may even smooth over experiential dissonance regarding the potentially harmful corporate effects on the community (petroleum, arms, alcohol, and tobacco companies are good examples here). British and American Tobacco (BAT), for example, have articulated a charter highlighting the importance of human capital. The company openly acknowledges that its products are somewhat 'controversial' and has developed a very elaborate CSR programme that points to the importance of biodiversity, human rights, and fair wages for workers down the supply chain (amazingly enough, BAT has consistently ranked very well in the Dow Jones Sustainability Index). Given the pervasive antipathy towards cigarette smoking and the damage it causes, recruitment is a challenge in the tobacco industry. This is doubly important given the perception among professionals that working in controversial industries might jeopardize future job prospects. BAT's charter called 'Employment Principles' emphasizes the importance of its CSR initiatives, its commitment to 'diversity', giving back to the community (e.g. being against exploitation, child labour, etc.), and guaranteeing a job for life.

'Why Am I Here?'

According to Bhattacharya et al. (2008), companies can 'win the war for talent' when they employ a CSR policy that makes it seem as if the firm is more attractive and socially embedded than other more distant and 'uncaring' organizations. This is not only the case for policies geared towards humanizing the workplace (such as work–life balance initiatives, childcare facilities, and payroll contributions), but also for broader commitments to biodiversity, fair trade, and community volunteering, which perceptively extend the firm's influence beyond its traditional operating ambit. The significance of individual and personal authenticity is paramount in this regard. Dissonance between one's personal values and corporate activities can engender a poignant sense of inauthenticity (Costas and Fleming, 2008). CSR polices are an important mechanism for reducing such apprehension, providing an inoculating pocket of authenticity that allows one to participate in an environment that would otherwise seem foreign and alienating. This is the case in both 'controversial' industries, where most people might feel at least a modicum of anxiety, and mainstream enterprises since the reflective movement among the workforce is just as likely to frame an ordinary firm in negative terms. Blowfield and Murray (2008) put it thus in discussing the findings of Hemingway and Maclagan:

Hemingway and Maclagan (2004) argue that the commercial imperative is only part of effective corporate responsibility management and that it should also be linked to the personal values of individual managers. They point out that individual discretion allows personnel to introduce their values into corporate responsibility policies, whether through officially sanctioned actions, the unintended consequences of an individual resolving a problem by drawing people beliefs, or an individual's entrepreneurship in bringing values into the workplace. (Blowfield and Murray, 2005: 110)

There is a lot happening here that brings personal authenticity into the fray of the firm's CSR initiatives. A key idea is that individual integrity and values need not be completely compromised when entering the corporate sphere. This highlights, of course, the contradictory nature of the generation-Y employee that we have already mentioned. They are anti-corporate in their sentiments and values, but fanatically capitalist in their deeds. The corporate pay-off for a CSR policy (such as community volunteering) is that a sense of personal integrity can be preserved as one participates in the cut-throat world of high finance, consulting, and so forth. If organizations are increasingly staffed by the silent, yet influential, 'tempered radicals' as Meyerson (2003) suggests, then a CSR policy demonstrating a commitment to diversity and community both fosters a conciliatory atmosphere for those who want to 'make a difference' and provides a pre-emptive conduit to channel frustration in functional ways. And the concern employees must have with the values plays to their narcissistic inwardness. In the context of the reflective turn in which we increasingly ask ourselves 'what is it all for?', the corporate milieu begins to cater to the broader values of professional employees.

Most striking about the excerpt by Blowfield and Murray, however, is the importance placed on the personal, non-work values and extra-employment attachments of workers. It is this parasitical concern with what the firm is not (and perhaps can never be) that gives CSR its peculiar modus operandi and allows the corporation to pretend it is otherwise. But is this merely a case of superficial legitimation, a rosy facade concealing the truth of capitalism in order to placate workers and consumers?

CSR as Legitimation and Appropriation

It is only sensible to view the vast majority of CSR initiatives and programmes with scepticism. This is not to say that the capitalist enterprise and more or less 'ethical' firms will always be something of a ruse. There are numerous examples where this is not the case, in which people make money in a manner that is relatively harmless compared to the vast industrial institutions that dominate the city today. But when we observe companies like Shell, BAT, McDonalds, Nike, and those in the arms industry develop, rehearse, and communicate elaborate CSR polices, alarm bells go off for most of us. One of the best instances of a CSR discourse being espoused by an organization that kills is Royal Dutch Shell. In the 1990s, its Nigerian drilling activities were linked to the oppressive governmental polices of the Nigerian government and its thugs who perpetrated gross human rights violations. The Ogoni tribe's protest against Shell and its audacious profiteering reached its zenith when the government executed the activist poet Ken Saro-Wiwa. Shell, of course, has had what only could be described as a horrible history in Nigeria, involving environmental and human rights abuses on an impressive scale.

With mounting criticism of its dubious business practices still continuing in Nigeria, especially in relation to flaring, where oilfield emissions are burnt off, creating considerable health hazards (95 per cent of emissions are flared in Ogoniland compared to 0.6 per cent in the United States), Shell Nigeria has crafted a cheery CSR campaign. One only has to visit the Shell Nigeria web site to observe some fascinating damage control tactics – with photographs of fresh fruit and happy local people. In many respects, CSR is operating here to ideologically legitimate the organization. How so? It is patently proffering a ridiculously positive image of the firm aimed to justify its activities by showing how ethical they are (or will be). In this sense, CSR initiatives detract from the organization's nefarious operations by functioning as a kind of 'smokescreen' to consumers and regulators. Shell Nigeria executives probably think that although the hypocrisy is glaringly obvious to most, orchestrating a colourful CSR veneer is better than doing nothing.

There are many positive things to be said for this criticism of CSR. But it does frame the firm as a rather static institution, reacting to the demands of society by inventing cunning PR campaigns to obscure its activities. Contra to this view, some analysts have argued that we ought to see CSR not only as a thinly veiled ideology that diverts attention away from the underlying truth of the enterprise, but also as more of an aggressive and parasitical venture into the world of social protest. This would be the autonomist view of CSR, a theoretical perspective we have already discussed in this book. Appeals to social responsibility involve the corporation mining the extra-corporate sphere in order to fabricate an authentic brand that enlists the personal values of employees who feel inauthentic in the enterprise. It is the non-commodified and militating practices of the commons that CSR seeks to appropriate for its own purposes. For example, we noted earlier Dockery's (2008) advice for CSR youth empowerment programmes. He recommended utilizing the networks linked to the most influential gang members. They no doubt hate the corporate man and everything he stands for. And as Blowfield and Murray (2005) point out, for CSR to reap increases in motivation and retention, the personal values of employees need to be engaged and harnessed to the production process (even if this means, in the case of Ross' [2004] Razor Fish that those values might be prima facie anathema to the conventional logic of profit-seeking).

Building on an autonomist understanding of the firm, Hanlon (2007) argues that we can theorize CSR as a parasitic manoeuvre by late capitalism, especially if we place it in a post-Fordist context. Legitimacy is still important to his argument given the widespread reflexive turn among the stakeholders mentioned above. But it is more of an appropriating legitimacy that seeks to take over the non-corporate 'other' as a resource for promoting justification. Hanlon interprets CSR as symptomatic of an emerging social structure of accumulation whereby the state has cast aside a number of its 'social welfare' functions, including the maintenance of a formally autonomous civil society. Following the autonomist contention that capital follows a parasitical dynamic that attempts to suck the commons back into the accumulation process, Hanlon suggests that CSR is an entrepreneurial exploitation of the bio-sociality left vacant by the departing Keynesian state apparatus. He quotes an excerpt from advocates of the business case for CSR to give a flavour of what he means:

> [T]his [CSR] spending may well be a source of growth, since many of today's most exciting opportunities lie in the controversial areas such as gene therapy, the private provision of pensions, and products and services targeted at low income consumers in poor countries. These opportunities are largely and mostly untapped, and many companies want to open them up. (Cogman and Oppenheim, 2002: 1, quoted in Hanlon, 2007: 160)

From an autonomist viewpoint, CSR can be approached as a 'pro-reactive' appropriation of a commons that persists despite of the corporation. In this sense, CSR is not merely ideological window dressing. Hanlon particularly protests against the naive view that CSR represents a business world finally discovering its ethical compass, reining in its excessive and damaging elements to accord with the values of society. CSR is not the humanization of the corporation for consumers or workers, but a colonial project that effectively further entrenches the logic of profit within the social body:

> CSR represents a further embedding of capitalist social relations and a deeper opening up of social life to the dictates of the marketplace.... CSR is not a driving force for change but the result of a shift from a Fordist to a post-Fordist regime of accumulation at the heart of which is both an expansion and a deepening of wage relations. (Hanlon, 2007: 157)

One of the most explicit examples of what Hanlon is referring to is the way in which fair trade branding has been exploited by multinationals like Nestle. The company continues to sell its usual products, but also positions its brand on the shelves of more 'ethical' goods with the hope of enhancing its otherwise tarnished brand reputation. What does all of this mean for personal authenticity at work? Following Hanlon's (2007) description of CSR and its logic of appropriation, our unease with the corporation is ideologically appeased by the jargon of CSR and simultaneously exploited through a parasitical prospecting. In this way, CSR cannot be considered as simply another piece of ideological mystification because the media savvy corporate persona is one step ahead of such inept justifications. And it is this 'one-step-aheadness' that is tapped to give the corporation an 'ethical' front. We can thus see a congruent link between

CRS and the resistant integrity of employees and also the protesting vocabulary of 'authentic' figures within the community – be it the impoverished blind, charismatic members of various youth networks, or indigenous landowners (in the case of BP's anticipatory CSR move to secure the Baku–Tbilisi–Ceyhan pipeline; see Crane and Matten, 2007).

Conclusion

The interpretation of CSR as sheer ideological legitimation intuitively makes sense in light of the superficiality of many such initiatives in large corporations around the world today. But it is this very superficiality that raises doubt about how far this analytical explanation can be pursued. If it represents an ideological mask that no one really accepts, being something of a 'public secret', then it would be difficult to explain the frenetic energy that corporations currently expend in this area. Moreover, this explanation does not sit well with the corporate preoccupation with authenticity. What people think and feel obviously matters here. The alignment of personal values among consumers and employees and the economy of 'subjective identification' in CSR policies testify to this. We need to take CSR more seriously than the explanation of mere legitimation allows.

The 'pro-reactive' legitimation-by-appropriation perspective forwarded by Hanlon (2007) is useful in this respect. If anything, CRS represents a fuller extension of capitalist values into 'the commons' both inside and outside the corporation. According to the autonomist understanding of the political economy of the firm, it is the non-work and even anti-work zone of cooperative association that is key to appreciating CSR's claim to authenticity. It targets and exploits various social movements and transforms them into a corporate resource (i.e. creativity, motivation, innovation, personal integrity, etc.). In view of this approach to CSR, is there any potential for it to create a platform for social change in the business world? If authenticity and the commons share a close syncretic association, a similar point of reference that somehow lies beyond the commodity form and the dominant economic logic, then it might also be a site of struggle that can easily flip the corporation on its head. As Costas and Fleming (2008) note, the non-work aspect of CSR can be elevated by some to forge an emancipatory praxis that frees people from the corporation altogether. From my own experience with ex-students in the business world this seems a common enough occurrence. *Pro bono* schemes, for example, slowly take on more significance, overshadowing the corporate world as this particular lifeline to personal authenticity results in exit.

The most obvious weakness of CSR can be found in the discourse itself and the vision of society that it contains. Although CSR discourse must take our subjective processes very seriously in order to function (and cannot simply be dismissed as an unengaging sham), it still seeks to dissuade an overly enthusiastic adherence. The reflexive distance discussed above that questions the authenticity of the firm in the first place also provides an ironic distance in which the precepts of CSR ought not to be taken too seriously. This is very different to disbelieving in CSR. If the principles of CSR in Shell Nigeria, for example, were practiced to the letter, enacted evangelically in every facet of the firm, the company would simply cease to exist in its current form. Similar to the work-to-rule strategy of unionized resistance, the corporate structure would bend and buckle under its own weight. It may be recalled that the discourse of CSR must look to a reference point outside itself, a certain 'x' that it is not. This is the multitudinous social (flows of peace, minority grievances, and the disenfranchised) and non-market associations that persist despite the corporation. Taking CSR seriously, to the letter, without ironic or cynical distance, insisting on its realization down the literal core or impossible 'x', might see the very source of authenticity (that sub-world of free association) breakthrough as the guiding principle of a new economic order.

6

Critique, Co-optation, and the Limits of the Corporation

Even Horkheimer could not have foreseen that by century's end, 'critical' theory itself – an emancipatory discourse rooted in the French Revolution – would come to mimic the logic of the commodity.

(Sanbonmatsu, 2004: 55)

When a subversive theatre production aping the consulting firm McKinsey recently opened in Berlin, it was not just the usual left-leaning city dwellers who turned out to see it. Local newspapers reported the strange event of McKinsey senior management having themselves booked an entire night for their employees. The play was a critical attack on the growing over-reliance on consultants and the ruthless activities of the large banks for whom they work. It is fascinating to think of the kind of reasoning that would prompt McKinsey to attend this production. Perhaps their attendance was a kind of pre-emptive inoculation against the expected criticism in the press. Perhaps senior partners wanted to promote both an internal climate and an external appearance of 'openness' and tolerance. Maybe they even wanted to learn about the nature of the criticism aimed at them and to gain a better understanding of why the consulting industry is one of the most disliked industries in Europe.

What is striking here is the propinquity with which the corporation now engages with its own criticism. Critique of a certain type becomes a developmental tool, something along the same lines discussed in Chapter 4 regarding the importance of 'designer resistance' as an instrument of innovation, creativity, and so forth. Social criticism of capitalism (in an abbreviated and designer form) appears to feature increasingly often in the official discourse of the corporation. Along with claims to humanist authenticity, empowerment, and flexibility, the politically correct and sometimes 'permissive corporation' (Ross, 2004) arms its justifications with prose and tropes that were once the exclusive preserve of the left-wing intelligentsia. Closely aligned with the encouragement of an expressive radical aesthetic touched upon in Chapter 4, criticism (of a particular kind, of course) has itself been reconfigured into its opposite and put to work in the sphere of the corporation. Take this excerpt from a management consultant text the author purchased in the departure lounge of a large airport, which is worth quoting at length:

Have the confidence to let people be themselves. Tolerating different approaches and expressions of individuality can make life much more complicated and disrupted for leaders. Of course, gaining immediate agreement to decisions from everyone or going with the first idea rather than inviting challenge is infinitely more efficient. Yet, compliance and conformity are less likely to help leaders come up with groundbreaking ideas than conflict and challenge. Involving people in decision making, and letting them express their views and their individuality freely are key determinants of building an authentic and meaningful environment. The upcoming X and Y generations certainly expect it. (Bains, 2007: 251)

The tenor of this advice to the 'leader' captures almost every aspect of the 'just be yourself' discourse that aims to gain better work performances via a certain kind of personal authenticity. As we have argued in previous chapters, this version of authenticity is expressive, individualized, and reduced to a gesture of subjective, visible difference. We have also indicated how such expressivism often entails a faux dissent ('designer resistance') and intimations of social awareness (CSR) by appropriating the kudos of the 'other', the substantive commons that is both a point of hazard and of productiveness for the enterprise. For sure, as Žižek points out, even 'leaders' are now reinventing their style in the image of the subversive, reinventing criticisms of capital into a tag of 'cool':

A crucial feature of [Bill] Gates is that he is perceived as the ex-hacker who made it. One needs to confer on the term 'hacker' all its subversive/marginal/anti-establishment connotations. Hackers want to disturb the smooth functioning of large bureaucratic corporations. At the fantasmatic level, the underlying notion here is that Gates is a subversive, marginal hooligan who has taken over and dressed himself up as a respectable chairman. (Žižek, 2008: 15)

If the leaders of industry are themselves semi-against the system, then the system cannot be too bad can it? In this sense, the 'new spirit of capitalism' (Boltanksi and Chiapello, 2005) plays on an essential liberalist ruse that justifies the corporation and its mode of domination. The 'liberal communist' simultaneously condones the system by denouncing its excesses (overt poverty in Africa, corruptive practices in the banking industry, etc.), drawing attention away from the fact that egregious excess is the norm. Bono-styled criticism targets corporate surfeit as erstwhile 'subversives' take up important management roles in large firms and humanize this runaway norm by allowing workers to 'just be themselves'.

In this chapter I want to build on the argument developed so far regarding the political utility of authenticity in contemporary management practice and discourse, and to turn to the thorny question of criticism itself. Until now we have charted the various ways in which the corporatization of personal authenticity has been manifested in organizations today. We have argued that the expressive and individualized variant of authenticity currently prominent in contemporary business ideology takes its cue from the realm of social life that is ostensibly 'external' to the whirr of accumulation. Examples include personal fun, play, leisure, lifestyle, and other so-called private social activities. This exogenous point also features in organizational dissent which too has been utilized in a truncated form. While resistance to managerialism and the corporation has always entailed a dimension of immanence – as the dialectical analyses of industry have reminded us (see Ramsay, 1977; Edwards, 1979) – dissent usually gathers itself around a point outside the existing conditions in which it is embedded. In other words, resistant activities are frequently inspired by a *possibility* that has not yet arrived (even if only a nothingness weighty with hope and the stains of the present). And it is this imaginary outsideness that capital relies upon to sustain its own rhythms. We previously noted this in relation to the way in which managerialism has co-opted variants of 1960s' counterculture, more recent movements involve underground slacker cool (in the IT industry), anti-capitalist cynicism, and consumer politics (fair trade advocated in consulting firms). It is this facet that makes the co-optation of the radical ethos so troubling, since resistance is transposed into an aesthetic or spectacle contrived to oil the accumulation process at a time when the corporate workforce is increasingly reflective.

While we might accept that aspects of resistance have now been safely defanged and turned into a caricature in order to enhance production and consolidate corporate hierarchies, we now must turn to the question of critique itself. This is especially so in light of the developments noted above in which past radical interventions now feature prominently in business ideology. Building on Latour (2004), Boltanski and Chiapello's *New Spirit of Capitalism* (2005), and our framework pertaining to authenticity and the commons, this chapter will investigate the protocols of critique. Given the discursive and practical shifts in managerial discourse, in which 'designer resistance' is celebrated in the name of innovation and freedom, it is perhaps germane to ask some questions about the role of criticism: How are we to make sense of 'critique' when even Tom Peters is celebrating anti-managerialism, 1968-inspired subversion (around cynicism, irony, sexuality, and parody), and expressions of anti-bourgeois chic? It is well known that the flexibility and innovative nature of capitalism leads to an ability to incorporate its own criticisms, but where does this leave the scholarly and pedagogical labour of criticism today? With the co-optation of resistance or criticism via a debasing mimesis, how does one critically engage the corporation without partially perpetuating it? Along with the problem of resistance and those forms of dissent that cannot be enlisted and remain inscrutable to control, perhaps the real issue here is discovering the ideological limits of capitalism. What types of criticism cannot be absorbed and repackaged into a motivational slogan at the next business Away Day? At what point does criticism go too far for even Bono to espouse?

These questions are especially important for the academic field of criticism that has grown in the business school, CMS. The author himself has been using CMS in his curriculum in the business school environment for a number of years. Many times when teaching organization theory and society from a CMS perspective, I have the uneasy feeling that my course is one step behind emergent corporate values. I don't just mean this in an instrumental sense – say, the panopticon materializing in the Birmingham branch of some faceless multinational, I also mean in a more general sense of imparting a certain brand of critical awareness that suits the 'new spirit of capitalism' in terms of creativity, cynicism, innovation, and political aptitude – indeed, expressing oneself with authentic difference. I once mentioned this concern to a colleague and she told me a story regarding one of her students she had hoped would embark on doctoral studies. The student had become enthralled with critical theory and had mastered its subversive lexicon superbly, but had later landed a job in a major consulting firm renowned for its neo-liberal yet permissive stance. We could put this down to necessity, pragmatism, or plain inconsistency, all of which are part of modern life (or of an articulatory politics, as Laclau and Mouffe [1985] might say). But what are we expecting to change by teaching a CMS curriculum? After comparing the new spirit of capitalism to the pedagogical values of the CMS movement, it is worth revisiting the relationship between critical pedagogy and domination (as Freire [1970] did in another context).

Similarly to the earlier analysis of resistance, this chapter will not get into a discussion about what is 'truly critical' or what the 'real' mission of

CMS ought to be. But when this scholarly movement enters the classroom, is there not a danger that it might nourish an ethos wedded to the designer radicalism currently being encouraged by large corporations? Perhaps Latour (2004) is correct when he suggests that popular modes of scholarly critique (he mainly targets neo-Marxist and post-structuralist theory) are now behind the times, using the wrong tools to confront the ideological under-labour currently supporting the corporation. To explore these assertions further, the chapter is organized as follows. First, I discuss in greater detail the idea of critique and especially the variant of criticism that typically characterizes the CMS project. Then I tease out the connections between criticism and the new spirit of capitalism, and the appropriation of a specific rendering of radicalism from what we might call the sub-commons. Having traced the points of reinforcement and resonance between contemporary critique and the mechanisms of corporate self-maintenance, I will 'test' the limits of absorption by discussing those lines of criticism that perhaps could not be enlisted. Here we shall discuss the role of business school pedagogy in more depth and, following Harney's (2007) recent autonomist argument, we shall reject the socialization image of the university for a more situated and immediate politics. This line of analysis brings us to the simple formula that has long been the starting point of critical inquiry: the limits of capital are capital itself.

Critique and the CMS Project

While undoubtedly consisting of many strands, influences, and trajectories, according to Alex Callinicos (2006), social criticism began as a form of left-wing scholarly analysis seeking to understand and change the relations of power and oppression underlying capitalism. If we accept this brief, telegraphic definition, some elements can be isolated for further scrutiny. As a form of scholarly analysis, critique involves the dual process of abstraction and normativity: Abstraction in that it suggests that all is not what it seems, and hence there is the need to 'get to the root of the matter' (especially in Marxian thought); normativity because criticism is traditionally articulated in a manner that poses socially progressive alternatives in which existing conditions are improved either *in toto* or in piecemeal fashion. The left-wing aspect of criticism generally outlines some coordinates for an alternative situation since, as Sartre (1948: 55) said, 'man is all the time outside himself'. But with the arrival of a more poeticized post-structuralist criticism, few alternatives posited in concrete or abstract form bar the very notion of possibility, which, of course, equates to no possibility at all but only more of the same. Another element of criticism in the introductory definition stated above is the object of criticism: Traditionally this is capitalism, the capitalist organization, but more recently it has come to include gender, sexuality, and identity.

Some suggest that the development of critical management studies in the United Kingdom and later the United States, Scandinavia, and Australasia was the product of happenstance. The CMS tradition resulted from the unique amalgamation of management and the sociology of work. Following the Thatcherist purge of British sociology departments in the 1980s, a number of influential radical sociologists moved into management departments and business schools (Grey and Willmott, 2005). Thatcher's class offensive had the humorous and unintentional consequence of putting Karl Marx on the business education curriculum, usually under the innocuous guise of Organization Behaviour. From the early interest in Marx and the labour process, as well as the critical sociology of Weber, to the more recent turn to post-structuralism, the idea of criticism has obviously changed. CMS is today considered to be a critique of managerialism and the rituals that support it in organizations. According to a much-cited definition of CMS by Fournier and Grey (2000): 'CMS is unified by an anti-performative stance, and a commitment to (some form of de-naturalization) and reflectivity' (Fournier and Grey, 2000: 7). In other words, criticism creates knowledge about work organizations and contemporary managerialism that (*a*) is not designed to perpetuate it; (*b*) denaturalizes the status quo (since corporations often justify oppressive structures by acting as if the present has always been like this and therefore there is little alternative); and (*c*) promotes a reflectivity about one's own research protocols (something that distinguishes CMS from mainstream positivist social research).

Critical research as it has most recently been manifested in CMS has developed over a number of years. This development has by and large moved away from Marx (and synchronic concerns with exploitation, equality, unionism, and ownership patterns) to a more post-structuralist-inspired criticism focusing on the intersection of power and identity and/or discourse. More specifically, and following Gabriel's (2001) argument, critique in this format (which mirrors permutations in both cultural studies and sociological analysis) has become *aestheticized* in important ways. Let us trace these different currents in more detail to get a better picture of how scholarly criticism might relate to the nature of capitalism today.

From Structure to Identity

In presenting an overview of theoretical traditions and empirical analysis of organizations from a CMS standpoint one cannot help notice the almost inevitable divisions between Marx, Weber, and Foucault. Each involves different concerns and emphases regarding the nature of organized work. How is this so? As mentioned above, the use of Marxist analysis was a formative moment in CMS via labour process theory in the 1980s. Chapters on the labour process and the factory in *Capital* (Marx, 1867/ 1972) were of great importance to early CMS scholars. In order to understand work and its organization, one must not focus on managerial discourse or even societal structures, but on the concrete 'point of production' where value is created and expropriated. Alongside Edwards (1979) and Burawoy (1979), Harry Braverman's (1974) *Labour and Monopoly Capital* is one of the most influential applications of labour process theory, positing the idea that this 'point of production' utilizes deskilling and mechanization, be it in the factory or in the office. Notwithstanding the problems around the deskilling thesis (as well as questions about how we ought to understand management as a class), labour process theory inspired a number of important works that consolidated the CMS perspective (see Friedman, 1977; Salaman, 1981). Here, organizations are sites of managerial control, ideological mystification, exploitation, and class conflict.

It is more difficult to gauge the impact of Max Weber in the CMS community since there was never really a Weberian school of organization theory akin to the labour process movement. It was not until the tortuous collaboration of Gerth and Mills resulted in an alternative translation to Parson's tamed rendition that the full extent of Weber's criticality was recognized. This version of Weber's research was sometimes integrated into mainstream organization theory in order to highlight the importance of domination at work (Perrow, 1986). From this angle, the limitations, dysfunctions, and mythological status of bureaucratic rationality were also objects of critique (Blau, 1955; Meyer and Rowan, 1977). At the more radical end of the organization theory spectrum, Weber's insights were often blended with a Marxian concern with control, ideology, and exploitation (see Bendix, 1956; Mills, 1956; and Gouldner, 1955). Alvesson's (1987) analysis of technocratic consciousness, for example, was inspired by the Frankfurt School's preoccupation with the way in which rationalization operates as an ideological master trope governed by means-orientated efficiency. Clegg and Dunkerley's (1980) fascinating discussion of class and ideology in the modern corporation uses Weber's analysis of 'the work ethic' and rationalization to understand how employees are both physically and mentally harnessed to the rhythms of production.

Foucaultian thought has had a massive impact on studies of work in CMS over the past few years. Some have even suggested that the arrival of Foucault truly inaugurates CMS proper. This is also the case in organizational terms, given that there are now divided LPT and CMS conferences. In the 1990s the 'labour process debate' raged in which a number of critical scholars openly repudiated the Marxian framework in light of Foucault's problematization of economic determinism, ideology, and class. Knights and Willmott (1989) and Clegg (1990), for example, argued that LPT is no longer a credible framework for understanding the power relations of the modern firm, or the constitutive effects of discourse and the concomitant identity politics. Workers do not have 'true interests' outside the wider discourses that craft them as the subjects of labour. Nor do they suffer from a false consciousness if they fail to resist managerial control. From a Foucauldian perspective, then, work becomes a place where identities are regimented through disciplinary processes, micro-integration, and self-surveillance (Deetz, 1992). The role of discourse is constitutive since language constructs the realities that are enacted in the workplace. Power thus involves both a subtle disciplinary training of the body and mind via discontinuous techniques and a more raucous identity politics where discourses compete for expression, legitimacy, and institutionalization. It is not only the concrete 'point of production' that matters but also the plethora of discursive practices in and around organizations that constitute what work means (see Jacques, 1996). In this sense, the phenomenon of work cannot be disentangled from broader questions of identity, gender politics, and dominant discourses that frame the self and the individual's life project.

Aestheticizing Critique?

The popularity of post-structuralism and Foucault in the CMS field has seen emphasis move from structure to identity and subjectivity in important ways. As I suggested above, much of this re-emphasis results from CMS scholars abandoning a Marxist analytic given the insurmountable problems it was thought to harbour. For example, Marxian critique was said to adhere to an implausible distinction between reality and ideology; it involved economic reductionism and determinism; it saw struggle between capital and labour as the engine of all struggles; and so forth. With the arrival of Michel Foucault in particular, many of these assumptions were jettisoned in favour of a more pluralistic, discursive, and relativist understanding of corporate power. In many critical investigations of work organizations today, class, exploitation, ownership, and ideology are rejected as antediluvian concepts, and capitalism is hardly even mentioned. Attention is instead given to identity formation, flows of discourse, and the relationship between self and power. Much of this is indicative of the *aestheticization* of critique, an argument Gabriel (2001) succinctly makes in his discussion of recent trends in CMS research. He uses the views of Antonacopoulou (1999) as representative of this tendency in which critique is aimed primarily at the discursive practices that circulate in corporations, and is vigilantly reflective about the critic's own status as knowledge producer. In Gabriel's (2001: 26) words, this version of criticism is more about the 'ability to think differently, to see differently and to act differently... [it] seeks to vindicate critique not as the mechanizes of discovering a promised land of happiness and justice, but as a way of life, which leaves nothing unquestioned'.

In this approach to CMS and the critique of the firm we can note a number of important themes that demarcate it from earlier, perhaps more structuralist, readings. First of all, the object of criticism is a kind of universal everything since nothing is left to chance, and all aspects of society are ripe for deconstruction. Ironically, perhaps, such a criticism is reminiscent of an immature Marx when he propounded with romantic brio that his radicalism was interested in 'a critique of everything that exists'. The post-structuralist variant of this critique of everything is problematic, as the 'everything' here is more about what is immediately presented to bourgeois consciousness than the concerns of poor workers in Indonesia or the sex worker in Kings Cross – hence, the poverty of romanticism in critical social thought, as others too have pointed out. Echoing the anti-perfomativity axiom proposed by Fournier and Grey (2000), the key here in this aestheticized criticism is the eschewal of anything hinting at a programmatic formula for radical (even if modestly so) social change. The objective is to open up possibilities of difference rather than bluntly state what is wrong with an extant reality and how it might be changed. For if there is no 'Archimedean point' from which to speak and all discourses are ultimately of equal value, who then is the critic to say what is right and what is wrong? This brings us to the issue of motivation because if criticism is not informed by judgement, then why be critical at all? Warwick Organization Behaviour Staff's (WOBS, 2001) introduction to indicative articles in CMS pinpoints the motivation for criticism in the absence of any stable ground. Citing Nietzsche and Foucault as inspiration, they summarily dismiss the traditional foundations of critique, namely that it involves knowledge that is revelatory, emancipatory, or political. They go on to address the question that such a stance inevitably begs: '[W]hy bother developing a critical approach . . . contestation is life affirming . . . critique can even be fun' (WOBS, 2001: xxxv).

Gabriel (2001) rightly points out that this variation of critique reveals an aesthetic inclination in which self comes to the fore in both the object of analysis and the analyst. The emphasis is on the expression of identity in the corporation under analysis and the experience of self in the critical moment of scholarly production. The conventional features of criticism pertaining to patterns of exploitation, economic ownership, and multinational control are conspicuously absent. Gabriel's (2001) discussion goes on to pinpoint the effects of the CMS that Antonacopoulou (1999) is representative of. This type of criticism resembles or draws parallels with the movement of commodities since it is more about 'the look' rather than the structures operating behind the scenes. In a similar manner to Frank's (1998) argument that countercultural activism (the situationist critique of everyday life, for example) was frighteningly amenable to commodification, the same could be said for scholarly criticism itself:

It is this very aestheticization of critique that makes it instantly amenable to the logic of commodities and markets. Are you critical of traditional or modernist administration/literature/architecture/music/organization theory, etc? We can supply you with an 'alternative' . . . like rebellion, commodified critique disintegrates into dandyism, a highly narcissistic affirmation of one's difference and taste. (Gabriel, 2001: 27)[1]

This aesthetic shift in the object and tenor of criticism in the CMS field is no more evident than in the study of workplace resistance. After a long hiatus, the concept of resistance recently made a dramatic reappearance in CMS research. But compared to the Marxist concern with structural forces, a more Foucauldian analysis has tended to dominate the field. Many researchers withdrew from the classic Fordist image of worker resistance that privileges open, overt, and organized opposition (e.g. strikes and go slows) to focus instead on more quotidian variants like cynicism, foot-dragging, dis-identification, and alternative articulations of selfhood. Since selfhood and identity were deemed to be a major conduit and expression of power, it ought then to be studied as a site of opposition too. Hence the importance of alternative discursive enunciations, subversive expressions of personhood, and the subterranean infra-politics of everyday life. But is it not astounding that a scholarly tradition once concerned with mapping the often bloody clash between labour and corporate capitalism now sees aloof dandyism as a heinously subversive act?

The Industrialization of Critical Consciousness

While believing itself to be against the corporation, could CMS now be plying a logic that resonates with a new type of managerialism (that utilizes criticism of a particular kind)? Is not the aestheticization of critique in keeping with that aspect of contemporary managerial discourse promoting an expressive and empty radicalism under the auspices of authenticity (or 'just being yourself')? Such an observation has implications both at the level of analysis and that of pedagogy. In relation to major currents of CMS analysis, employee cynicism in the context of a culture management programme, for example, might challenge some features of power (e.g. the aim to create a biddable worker), but it will hardly dismantle the HR department of a firm or those local pillars of capitalism consolidating the managerial prerogative. Indeed, following the work of Žižek (1989), cynical dis-identification could provide the very breathing space that allows capitalism to function even better, quietly deflating more serious challenges to its hegemony (Fleming and Spicer, 2003). As we have noted in earlier chapters, this view is partially validated by the latest crop of managerial ideas inspired by Tom-Peters-like liberation management. Knowledge-intensive firms ought to hire zanies, radicals, and anti-authoritarian 'talent' in order to enhance innovation, creativity, and ingenuity. Much of the intransigent everyday resistance celebrated in organization studies is now encouraged by some firms and is an important support for the new spirit of capitalism. And at the level of pedagogy, is there not a danger that this poeticized criticism, which a CMS curriculum might impart to students (conceivably in the vein of an anti-establishment cool that is against everything), would be the very type of subject that fits the mould of the now much-celebrated creative Bobo?

As Harney and Oswick (2006) nicely put it, even management today has jumped on the anti-management bandwagon with all its talk about joyous anarchism, anti-authoritarianism, and the deconstruction of hierarchy (see also Messner et al., 2008). In this sense, contemporary corporate ideology resembles the intrepid commodity form that does not fear transgression so long as it is not its own founding principle that is being challenged. Others too have mentioned the uncanny symmetry between a broad CMS project that emphasizes a diffuse matrix of identity and discourse politics and the ideas from management gurus such as Peters and Semler. In a perceptive paper, Parker (2005) focuses on the anti-performative nature of CMS criticism as outlined by Fournier and Grey (2000), and the danger this presents for dismissing practical interventions from a critical standpoint. Health and safety, for instance, has rarely been picked up on the CMS radar, but it ought to be if we are interested in tackling political issues affecting the working lives of many. Parker also mentions Semler's *Maverick!* (1993) and the call for anti-hierarchical, democratic, and self-managing corporate structures. Are these ideas that CMS are in accordance with, and ought Semler, one of the top selling pop-management writers, be invited to the next CMS conference? Regarding the other features of Fournier and Grey's (2000) criteria for critical research, Parker adds: '[A]nd what about Tom Peters? He and a great deal of the business guru literature... announces itself as critical of the established order... it too is concerned to denaturalize and radicalize' (Parker, 2005: 357).

Parker suggests that these issues pose a problem for critical scholarship regarding its willingness to become a reformist movement. Does CMS attempt to humanize and improve workplaces (and thus court absorption by mainstream management) or does it ignore managerialism altogether and thus have little practical influence? I agree with Parker's analysis, but think the main problem is the nature of the critique involved and the underlying schematism of political economy it implicitly subscribes to. Semler and his Semco might make for a more human workplace, but it is hardly radical in the context of global capitalism (just as the welfare state wasn't either). Moreover, I suspect that if we were allowed to interview Semco workers we would probably find (as in the study of Sunray in Chapter 1) that much of it was perceived to be exaggerated hype (Semco is certainly not in the same league as Mondragon, for example). None of these reflections aim to dissuade the teaching of CMS in the university or business school setting. I will formulate my admittedly limited reflections regarding how we can avoid appropriation in the next section. The real question here is the kind of the criticism being articulated (the object and method of analysis) and the potential demeanour that is pedagogically engendered. It would be functionalist to state that CMS in the form that I have indicated above simply 'mirrors' the needs and conditions of the 'just be yourself' firm, but co-optation only needs points of sympathy and resemblance to operate. What are the dynamics of co-optation when critique is aestheticized in this way?

'Discipline and Punish' in the White House?

In an essay provocatively called 'Why Has Critique Run Out of Steam?' Bruno Latour (2004), initiates a plaintive dialogue with the most recent variants of French-inspired social critique. His main concern is that the conditions that gave the criticism by French postmodern theorists in the 1960s and 1970s a radical edge has changed dramatically. In its heyday, the main function of this kind of critique worked primarily against the ideology of science as it was shored up by the military–industrial complex. One of the significant analytical feats of Foucault, for example, was the way he incisively challenged the dogma of scientific discourse to reveal that reason has a political history – thus debunking the ideological myth of objectivism – and that power and knowledge are always intimate (we can also note this message echoed, although in a very different form, in the Frankfurt School, especially in the work of Adorno and Habermas). Such criticism was important, given how science has commanded such a privileged voice for sorting out what are historically arbitrary problems relating to crime, psychiatric concerns, medicine, racial and colonial policies, and so forth. Scientific discourse is considered a paradigm among many, and this pluralism was indeed radical in the context of scientific hegemony.

Latour argues that the cultural conditions that once made the critique of science a powerful, socially progressive tool have shifted. The discourse of uncertainty regarding the power of science has now been absorbed by some of the more dominant groups in society to further the needs of multinational capital, religious fanatical groups (at least in the West), and powerful nation states. Postmodern theory has entered the corridors of power where it is found to be very useful. Latour gives the example of global warming. In the United States, the environmental movement has been challenged by neo-conservatives exactly on the basis that science does not assure certainty and is in fact a vendor for influential interests (pro-environmental lobbies). What he terms obvious 'matters of fact' (such as global warming and climate change) is now undermined by distrust and uncertainty since all statements are indicative of an underlying power game for domination:

While we spend years trying to detect real prejudices hidden behind the appearance of objective statements, do we now have to reveal the objective and incontrovertible facts hidden behind the *illusion* of prejudices? And yet entire PhD programmes are still running to make sure good American kids are learning the hard way that facts are made up, that there is no such thing as natural, unmediated,

127

and unbiased access to the truth, that we are always prisoners of language, that we always speak from a particular standpoint, and so on, while dangerous extremists are using the very same arguments of social construction to destroy hard-won evidence that could save lives. (Latour, 2004: 227)

Latour is certainly not attempting to re-crown science as the only discourse. He is subtler than that. The argument shows that the cultural milieu in which a critique of science was useful has changed and it is using many of the pluralistic and relativist stances once held by social critics. Latour gives many other examples of officials dismissing social issues in the name of social construction. And can we not see a similar connection between the recent anti-management fad (e.g. Semler and Peters) and the neo-conservative debunking of a scientific point of view? Pluralism, denaturalization, and soft relativism are all the rage in the 'just be yourself' corporation (at least within the bounds of the pre-established relations of power that are, of course, beyond reproach).

When we teach business students CMS, what are the lessons from Latour's provocative piece regarding the conservative potential of denaturalization? Some important problems around the co-optation of critique by the corporation are certainly evident. Let us take the criticism of the corporation and the ethos inspired by the aesthetic moment in the classroom. In addition to the concern with paradigms and pluralistic frameworks designed to undermine mainstream management science, students are also taught, for example, that Marx's analysis of the firm is one perspective among many. A worldview is nurtured that is mistrustful of 'meta-narratives' or worldwide problems regarding global capitalism since we all have different views. Such a stance can undermine important criticisms. For capitalism is so established within the current political imagination that only grand scientific claims (especially with respect to the environment) can really do the job of challenging its hegemony. As Jameson points out, we are more comfortable imagining the end of the world caused by environmental disaster than a modest modification of the economic substructure. A reflective short circuit appears to be built into the critical moment in which subjects remind themselves that their perspective is only one among many. In relation to CMS pedagogy and the ethic it imparts, this might serve several functions important to capital accumulation today. When students enter the corporation with their critical notions of power and discourse, identity politics, etc., relativism around CMS fits nicely with the dynamic and multiple positions required by the consultant or banker. Moreover, in the classroom itself, some students challenge CMS analysis – say, of Foucault and power, or gender and politics – as one standpoint among a number of others. As we all know, this serves more to legitimate what it is not (in this case non-critical tolerance of corporate capitalism).

My justification to students for teaching critical and radical organization theory draws on the trope of necessity. Rather than stating that CMS is just one perspective among many, I argue that we cannot reasonably understand the world of work without being critical. Capitalism is a radical system and it requires a very strict critical view in order to make sense of it. Otherwise we are lost in the illusions and fantasies of outdated management ideologies. Latour (2004) also suggests getting closer to un-comfortable truths: '[M]y argument is that a certain form of critical spirit has sent us down the wrong path, encouraging us to fight the wrong enemies and worst of all, to be considered friends by the wrong sort of allies... the question was never to get away from facts, but closer to them' (Latour, 2004: 231). It is important to remember here that Weber was right regarding his admonitions about science as a vocation. Even if universities are highly political sites, classrooms are not soapboxes. But, following Latour, rather than turn away from matters of fact bolstered by science, truths ought to be selectively transformed into matters of concern. These are facts that one is close to, that mean something to people, and that are developed from the rigour of sustained investigation. Such a position thus deconstructs the simple boundary between science and interest in a man-ner that does not render the classroom as either a sterile business labora-tory or a platform for political agitation.

Artistic Critique and Capitalism

The anti-science spirit at the heart of a postmodern criticism of society that Latour identifies gains much of its drive from what Boltanski and Chiapello (2005) refer to as 'artistic critique'. Matters of fact have long been the staple justification of those in power, be it in the corporation or in the nation state. Moreover, the scientific worldview has often been associated with a petit bourgeois mentality, the direct opposite of the bohemian artist that exudes more of a subversive recklessness. It can be recalled from our analysis in preceding chapters that Boltanski and Chiapello demonstrate how mainstream managerialism appears to have absorbed or commandeered many of the catchphrases that were once part of the critique of a capitalist's everyday life. They make an ardent (if somewhat problematic) distinction between social critique – more syn-chronic considerations of exploitation, ownership patterns, and access to decision-making opportunities – and artistic critique. The latter derives from romantic and bohemian concerns with how capitalism damages selfhood and subjective experience. Criticism from this perspective focuses on questions of inauthenticity, alienation, and disenchantment. Of course, in the right context, artistic criticism was actually a fairly radical engagement with a very boring life and undermined the featureless landscape of an overly bureaucratized world. It was artistic critique as much as structural criticism that inspired millions of people to participate in protests during the 1960s. As one famous instance of street graffiti put it: '[S]tructures do not take to the streets!'.

According to Boltanski and Chiapello (2005), managerial discourse responded to such artistic criticism to ameliorate dissatisfied workers without challenging the system as a whole. While Boltanski and Chiapello's analysis is troubling in the way they equate capitalism merely with markets, their argument is useful for shedding light on today's corporate forms that require a subversive innovation and creativity without calling attention to the biggest problem of all (i.e. the existence of corporation itself). But as we mentioned in previous chapters, the mimetic function underlying the co-optation of artistic critique transforms this subversive consciousness into something else. It involves a kind of 'domination-by-gleaning', an act of recycling and repackaging. Such a transpositive reduction is inevitable if the radical spirit is to be made into a tool of production, as we have seen with the very privatized and individualized notion of personal authenticity. Latour points to the insights of the 'new spirit of capitalism' argument in relation to contemporary manifestations of critique:

[T]he new spirit of capitalism has put to good use the artistic critique that was supposed to destroy it. If the dense moralistic cigar-smoking reactionary bourgeois can transform him or her self into a free-floating agnostic bohemian, moving opinions, capital and networks from one end of the planet to the other without attachment, why would he or she not be able to absorb the most sophisticated tools of deconstruction, social construction, discourse analysis, post-modernisms, post-ology? (Latour, 2004: 231)

Artistic critique is potentially complementary to capitalism, especially in its most recent forms that we have discussed in this book regarding the 'just be yourself' business ideology. It imparts an ethos of criticism that encourages the personal detachment required in the contemporary firm we mentioned in Chapters 2 and 3. A cynical and sceptical consciousness is now required in order to survive in many occupations since it was discovered that identification with the corporation (especially in the context of high-commitment cultures) was frequently counterproductive to profit maximization. The cynical consciousness enables a semblance of distance that can buffer the individual from the shocks of corporate life. This is the 'workstyle' (Liu, 2004) of the detached bohemian that is 'cool' but works for the firm nevertheless. Criticism morphed into cynicism is now a resource in the 'just be yourself' context, a source of creativity, innovation, and motivation (since we can now express our most intimate and private authentic sides). Is there is not a danger that the aestheticized critique currently fashionable in CMS is unwittingly sympathizing with an emerging logic of the corporation?

On the Limits of Co-optation

There are two corollaries to this analysis regarding the industrialization of critical consciousness. The first concerns the obvious question about where the limits to co-optation might be found. The second concerns the model of the university that underlies the idea of co-optation. Before we briefly explore these corollaries, however, it must be pointed out that radical criticism – especially on the left in those many moments when it is the underdog or on a losing streak – has always been obsessed with the problem of co-optation and appropriation. The reasons for this are clear. Criticism gains impetus from a place outside the present, a point that makes for a troublesome *aporia* since this outside represents both a possibility and impossibility in its fullest sense (Piccone, 1976). One cannot step outside of history but obviously one needs to do so to envisage progressive alternatives (the failure to account for their *own* critical standpoint in this manner is the chief weakness of Boltanski and Chiapello, 2005). Moreover, given the penchant for dialectical thinking in critical social theory, is not the dialectic swinging most impressively when criticism itself joins the object of critique? The fact that we have knowledge of this inclusion, and this knowing too becomes part of the object of critique, is what Adorno's infamous 'negative dialectics' attempts to understand. Let us now briefly unpack the two corollaries to the investigation thus far.

On Limitations

It has hopefully been established that artistic or aesthetic critique is particularly susceptible to co-optation given its expressive and relativistic tendencies. Two issues are important when endeavouring to understand the limitations of co-optation, especially of artistic critique as we have rendered it above.

A limit can be studied as a border or boundary that separates certain spheres, spaces, or logics (as in a 'city limit'). The way to identify the limitation or border between criticism and capitalism is simply by asking a negative question rather than a positive one. We performed the same mode of analysis in relation to resistance and absorption in Chapter 4, where we did not get into the old debate about what is 'real' resistance but identified boundaries instead: What type of criticism could not be put to work in the corporation and would be considered inscrutable and dangerous? This would be a mode of critical awareness that is today continuously silenced in favour of the more streamlined version that is useful to the demands of the contemporary firm. And in terms of CMS in the business school classroom, a similar limit-defining question could be asked: What kind of critical pedagogy could not be put to service by the new spirit of capitalism as it is manifest in the corporate world today?

We need to add here that capitalism has all sorts of limits, forms of criticism that cannot be co-opted, some of which we would not want to support (think of the extreme neo-fascist, anti-corporate stance in the United States, for example). Thus the limit-defining questions must be guided by politics revealing more than just abstract possibilities but also progressive ideals. Such politics, I would venture, are more sympathetic with the structural or 'social' critique that tends to eschew poetics. It is guided by a kind of socialist imaginary addressing concerns with the environment, ownership, and exploitation, and would completely reconfigure the firm if enacted. In relation to critical research perhaps the concepts pertaining to this inscrutability would look quite old-fashioned, including radical unionization, health and safety, ownership of capital, and so forth, rather than merely 'the subject'.

In addition to the limit that defines the 'outside' or unco-optable identified above, a critical consciousness ought to be sensitized to a second limit. These are the borders that already exist inside capitalism. In other words, capitalism reveals its own margins in its very business-as-usual ideology, normalizing what other societies and times would have otherwise labelled 'demented'. Impending environmental catastrophe, increasing food riots, and energy wars are patent examples. A critical pedagogy demonstrating the profound impossibility of 'business as usual' (i.e. capitalism) is the limit that we are looking for here, a boundary that cannot easily be utilized by the corporation as yet another resource. This is because its effects are pragmatic and alien to the corporate gaze – exiting the system, making career choices that circumvent the corporation, and other modes of 'exodus'. One might call this an immanent limit to co-optation since it is defined by capital itself.

Socialization or Sites?

In discussing the co-optation of critique and its limits, it is often taken for granted that critique is born within the university. Thus we need to reflect on our assumptions about how the university and the business school operate in relation to the corporate world. In practical terms, it would be very difficult to discern the points of congruence between the business school CMS curriculum (of whatever form) and the attributes favoured by the current 'permissive corporation'. For sure, it would be very fascinating to conduct a study of the paths and careers of the CMS student, compared to a control group of mainstream business students. What differences would we detect and how would we measure such differences? Much critical management education justifies the difference CMS can make in terms of pedagogy. Progressive changes to capitalism might be achieved through an educational format in which students gain a critical consciousness and social awareness that changes their future corporate practices. The argument set out above relies on this causal vector too, but asserts a different meaning to it by suggesting that CMS may not have recognized the changes in corporate ideology pertaining to the 'new spirit of capitalism' and the utility for some kind of critical awareness in industry.

Much of the debate and discussion around co-optation may overly rely on the socialization model of the university and the business school. This is indicative of a broader problem in that the politics of CMS is compromised by making the business world outside the university its sole interest, treating the university as more of an ideological transit point for capitalism rather than being itself a site of politics. It is very doubtful that CMS pedagogy will change very much in the business world other than in its own conditions of labour and those of its students (which is not to say that the business world will not utilize aspects of critical consciousness for its own ends). Perhaps, then, we ought to refrain from thinking 'vertically' (with business at the end of the chain of socialization) and think more 'horizontally', with the university embedded within a constellation of capitalist relations, as a point of production in and of itself and as a political site par excellence. This *inter alia* is what Harney (2007) has recently argued. He develops his argument from an autonomist position in which 'social labour' and the 'social factory' stretch across the society, spreading the point of production outside the firm, as we discussed in Chapter 2. Here business schools are not considered to be institutions of socialization where CMS educators train potential managers. Indeed, this might very well be an outdated understanding of critical pedagogy given that we are not teaching managers anymore but 'producers' in a financialized social structure of accumulation. Therefore, the object of critique is not 'the manager' but business itself. In this sense, the business school ought to be reframed as a 'site of struggle between the society of producers and the "social undertakings" of finance capital' (Harney, 2007: 148–9).

This has three implications for critique and its industrialization or otherwise. First of all, criticism should not frame business in terms of the production of wealth and its unfair redistribution. Instead it can be viewed as a parasite feeding on the common wealth already present. From this perspective, then, business is 'the restraint on wealth-making capacities of a society of associated labour' (Harney, 2007: 141). This point resonates with the immanent limit mentioned above, especially when financial markets have recently been recipients of such a huge transfer of wealth from the working classes to avert its downfall. Second, there is no reason why criticism ought to take place only in the university. Indeed, it is easy to argue that universities are today amongst the most conservative institutions in society, and one would expect radical activism to flourish *outside* the confines of higher education institutions. It is a strange state of affairs in many UK universities when humanities departments look to business schools as being the most critically aware. This leads to the third point. Universities ought themselves to be considered sites of productive labour and exploitation. Most CMS scholars seem blind to the deprivation and degradation of their own position and that of their students, turning to critically investigate the corporation instead. Why not focus our critical praxis on the business school – not as a zone of socialization but as a site of politics involving a sub-commons of exploited labour?

Conclusion

The 'just be yourself' management approach to employee relations has implications for the very nature of critical scholarship in the business school. The concern with authenticity, expressive or 'designer resistance', and what I have referred to above as the industrialization of critique means that we need to think carefully about what criticism is attempting to achieve. The commons must feature prominently in this analysis because, as I have argued in earlier chapters, it is the raw source material that is being annexed to the corporate world as an instrument of self-maintenance. It is both the inspiration for authenticity – with its non-work focus and aura indicating something beyond the commodity form we explored in Chapter 6 – and that of grievance, criticism, and resistance. The limits of co-optation reside within the capitalist frame vis-à-vis the commons since the latter cannot be fully expressive in the firm without tremendously undermining the axioms of corporate domination.

Critics might also think in terms of the commons as it features both outside and inside the university system. The overtly aesthetic object and modality of critique as it has typically manifested in CMS represents, to some extent at least, a captured or enclosed commons. It is an outcome of domination and commodification. The sub-labour of the commons needs to be more fully expressed, free of the simulacratic form in which it now appears in the hallways of the corporation. The university also represents a commons that is being exploited both by the university system itself and by the corporate world that looks to it for a pliable critical spirit. And it is this concern with the commons that brings us back to the question of authenticity. If it is the wellspring for personal authenticity that the 'just be yourself' ideology seeks to tap, then what, if any, critical potential does the idea of authenticity still hold?

7

Authenticity, Solidarity, and Freedom

> The genuineness of need and belief, which is questionable anyway, has to turn itself into the criterion for what is desired and believed; and in this way it becomes no longer genuine. This is the reason why no one can say the word 'genuineness' without becoming ideological. . . . In the jargon [of authenticity] it stands out in the unending mumble of the liturgy of inwardness. Like a rag-picker, the jargon usurps the final protesting movements of a subject in which its downfall is thrown back on itself and hucksters those moments off. The edge is removed from the living subject's protest against being condemned to play roles.
>
> (Adorno, 1973: 57)

Can authenticity still be considered a viable site of political freedom at a time when it has been abridged into little more than a surface display of retrograde individualism? For sure, the preceding chapters have not been kind to the idea of personal authenticity. We have shown how it has been utilized in different ways, articulated to disparate political projects in the context of the corporation and beyond. In one sense, authenticity is a scaffold upon which the worker can situate a truth of themselves in a forest of illusions and cultural fabrications designed to enlist their most intimate emotions for the firm. In another sense, the latest wave of managerial discourse appears to have given up on the notion of a unified cult-like organizational value system and instead embraces difference, diversity, lifestyle, and real selves ('warts and all'). Much of this 'just be yourself' business ideology ironically draws upon a certain strain of anti-capitalist intimations, mimicking the rituals of aesthetic dissent and rendering it into a pro-business event. Anyone who enters the large corporations dominating the megalopolies of the West finds a weird amalgam of conservative pro-corporate ideology mixed with expressions of designer resistance and slacker cool. From yet another angle, we can identify a long-standing managerial dialogue with authenticity harking back to the paternalist company towns of the nineteenth century and subsequently the neo-human relations idea of self-actualization within the work task. In a number of ways the 'just be yourself' managerial approach echoes this concern to adjust the worker to the dissonance of work and discover ways to make them 'happy' and 'satisfied' in a space largely devoid of formal humanity.

What makes the most recent iteration of this technology of adjustment different is the way it parasitically draws upon the world of non-work, both outside the organization (in terms of leisure, lifestyle, and popular counterculture) and inside the formal organization (in terms of informal interactions, discretion, subcultures, and organizational 'slack'). In this sense, the 'just be yourself' management approach exudes a liberalist esteem for self-expression and individual freedom. The last three chapters have noted that the corporation is willing even to transgress its own pro-management ideology (if not the ideology of the privately owned for-profit corporation per se) and tolerate those who want to express their dissent against 'the system' through *pro bono* CSR initiatives and so forth. It is sometimes striking how anti-capitalist views can be turned inside out and put to work. Particularly prominent in the so-called permissive firm is an appeal to individual identity, difference, and diversity. While many non-work motifs are fabricated with the hope that work might appear not to be what it is, in fact it is an acute individualism that comes to the fore. To be authentic in this milieu is to express your individual self vis-à-vis those around you since conformity and homogeneity are a sign of corporate sluggishness and an inability to innovate.

Of course, just as the commons cannot properly exist in the corporation neither can any true form of individualism. It thus manifests in the space of production as a kind of expressive cipher. And this sign (if not substance) of individuality slots very well into the liberalist version of the organization, infused as it is with competitiveness, market rationality (in which one must sell oneself as a brand), and perfunctory appeals to diversity and difference around the unitary pursuit of surplus. While all of this must undoubtedly afford certain freedoms denied in past managerial regimes, this book has been fairly critical of this approach to personal authenticity since it trades in the silly Gatesian fantasy of a frictionless capitalism whereby control and class are finished. I argued in Chapter 1 that this liberty to 'just be yourself' does not free people from control at all. Given the expressive individualism in which corporatized authenticity is couched, we found it results more in freedom *around* control rather than *from* control. Moreover, workers felt that the celebration of personal identity and the conveyance of markers regarding sexuality, lifestyle, and leisure were more of a detraction from control. And finally, we recognized significant limits to the 'just be yourself' discourse: Be yourself, but only up to a point, only in a manner deemed useful and acceptable. All freedom is conditional, but the hyper-aestheticized version of personal authenticity analysed above has made identity somewhat ideological in the face of the continuing appropriation of surplus value.

We have developed a political economy to more broadly frame these permutations in the corporate world. Through the ideas of the Italian autonomist movement, Hardt and Negri (1999) demonstrate the parasitical proclivity of capital and its need to appropriate its 'other' in order to sustain itself. What is being arrogated in the sphere of non-work (fun, sexuality, lifestyle, domestic rituals, etc.) are signs of an 'elemental communism' whereby gestures of cooperation, non-market forms of life, and interaction (both inside and outside the firm) are reified into a productive resource. Co-optation relies upon a mimetic function that reveals some basic limits of capital since it cannot make itself into a work-free paradise with *duplicata* alone. It is this transposition process that has hastened the development of a universalizing immaterial labour and the social factory specifically peculiar to advanced capitalist societies. From this standpoint, we have not necessarily debated the ontological meaning of authenticity but explored its political effects and ramifications. Most importantly, who is being asked to be authentic? And what are the contours of the personal authenticity being asked for?

Having been filtered, twisted, and transmogrified into an appendage to the accumulation process, whither authenticity as both a critical concept and radical practice? The purpose of this final chapter is to think ahead and speculate about the future significance of authenticity. Is it still helpful for critical scholars and can it feature in progressive workplace politics in anyway? In the context of the above summary, I aim to outline the different ways in which authenticity and freedom can be linked in the context of the contemporary corporation. Having outlined three positions in which authenticity might result in certain emancipatory freedoms, we will be in a better position to decide whether it still has any radical and progressive political purchase. Before this, however, we need to pull together the argument thus far and map the model of self that underlies the very individualized notion of authenticity plied in organizations today. This will set the scene for the second section of the chapter, which aims to unsettle this pseudo-individualism and theorize how authenticity might be linked to other types of freedom in the workplace. More specifically, authenticity will be unpacked in relation to three kinds of freedom: freedom *through* work; freedom *around* work; and freedom *from* work. Each political trajectory yields an equivalent notion of personal authenticity and its relationship to labour.

The Individual, the Gaze, and the Act

As we have argued in the preceding pages, the conspicuous visibility of personal authenticity in corporate ideology sees it being cast in a very atomized manner. For example, in his analysis of some large corporations for which he has consulted, Bains (2007) proposes that generation-Y employees now want to express their difference and individuality in the corporate sphere. Managers must tolerate different lifestyle signifiers at work if they are to have a productive organizational environment. This line of thought pits the individual directly against the unthinking mass since the latter might ruin the corporation through its supposed lack of agility or creative quick thinking. For sure, the main 'reason why people have learned to be inauthentic in relating to others is the pressure to conform' (Bains, 2007: 249). Authenticity in the rhetoric of the 'just be yourself' business philosophy reflects the hallowed axioms of individual identity and difference.

There are some obvious reasons why authenticity is conceived like this. In modern liberal societies, the sanctity of the individual conveys a strong notion of a private interiority that is somehow sealed off from the perceived polluting influence of the crowd (Taylor, 1992). Intimate friends and family are often allowed to cross the rampart of selfhood, but even this permission may be rescinded at any moment if certain trusts are violated (Trilling, 1972). We traced the development of this 'cult of inwardness' in Chapter 1 and the way in which the isolated site of self becomes a theatre of authenticity and inauthenticity. Important here too is what Giddens (1991) calls reflective modernity, whereby subjects develop a sensitive self-awareness in a context where new-age self-fulfilment is considered paramount. The paradox of such an individualist algorithm of authenticity is well noted by Taylor (1992):

This can even result in a sort of absurdity, as new modes of conformity arise among people who are striving to be themselves, and beyond this, new forms of dependence,

139

as people's insecure identities turn all sorts of self-appointed experts and guides, shrouded with the prestige of science or some exotic spirituality. (Taylor, 1992: 15)

The avowed 'liberal corporation' reflects these assumptions about what an authentic (and inauthentic) self might mean, especially in terms of expressing a unique individuality that is presumed to exasperate the generic norms of the classic bureaucratized firm. Let us look at some important aspects of this individualized version of authenticity in both management ideology and broader social theory in order to gain a better grasp of its consequences.

Responsibility

It is no secret that the individualization of authenticity in the 'just be yourself' management philosophy serves very important production needs. Following Sennett's (1976) line of argument and his notion of the 'tyranny of intimacy', the celebration of the 'whole person' allows more of the subject to be monitored in terms of a 'responsible production'. This has two facets. First, the compulsion to display one's true self as it pertains to individual difference delivers a powerful current of subjectification to the formal sphere of work that might have been located elsewhere in the past (the family, the neighbourhood, the church, etc.). This power can be used in obvious ways, but the paradox is that at the same time as we see the evocation of non-work as a marker for authenticity, work itself comes to have principal sway over how a genuine subjectivity might be communicated.

Second, and as Adorno (1973) states in his characteristically vituperate tone, when authenticity is crafted as an expression of sincere truthfulness, it tends to psychologize the worker, whereby performance is linked to self and 'attitude' rather than to structure. Responsibility for one's *fortune* is removed from the ebb and flow of socio-political caprice and placed squarely on the shoulders of the individual. I observed this occurring in the call centre firm studied in earlier chapters. Once the employment relationship was read according to a script that prized personal attitudes, lifestyle displays, and other very individual attributes, it became an easy target for individualizing the injuries of work. This underscores the argument made in the first chapter that authenticity seems to become a problem mainly when it is absent. Focusing on the psychological 'health' of the worker is a convenient way to deal with the systemic failures of the corporation. Now to be fair to the neo-human relations movement, there we see a concern with the immediate in-house structural questions related to the task (via job-enrichment programmes). But it still necessarily removed the entrenched factors that had generated self-alienation in the first place (e.g. capitalism). Distinct from this semi-materialist feature of the neo-human relations movement, the current 'just be yourself' management approach operates almost purely at the level of identity and mimetic display. The individual is 'king' but with the added proviso that he or she rules only in a specified way, expressing difference only up to a point. Excess is still a sign of danger.

Adorno (1973) notes these depoliticizing consequences of the 'jargon of authenticity' in his criticism of the existentialist ideas of Heidegger and Buber (interestingly Adorno hardly mentions Sartre). The word 'jargon' implies a technical language specific to a particular body of knowledge and a certain thoughtlessness that results when it is dogmatically repeated. As for Heidegger, Adorno argues that the singularization of authenticity in his philosophy betrays an attempt to place a very conservative notion of truth at the heart of being (Marcuse [1955] conveyed this when he said that Heidegger pedalled a 'philosophy of death' in more ways than one). This places some very dubious political connotations regarding the subject outside of politics and naturalizes what Adorno calls the 'cult of inwardness'. Authenticity is approached by Heidegger as an ontic self-identity whereby being belongs to itself apart from the crowd, 'the they' or *Das Man*. Adorno levels considerable criticism at how this individualized authentic self must logically carry responsibility for societal forces. Anxiety, inwardness, and a private isolation (all the hallmarks of the modern individual) are ideologically cut off from the very social forces that produce it. The subject is reified and this serves the system in important ways:

Once such an ontology of what is most ontic has been achieved, philosophy no longer has to bother about the societal and natural–historical origin of this title deed, which declares that the individual owns himself. Such a philosophy no longer needs to be concerned with how far society and psychology will allow a man to be himself or become himself, or whether in the concept of such selfness the old devil is concentrated one more time. The social relation, which seals itself off in the identity of the subject, is de-socialized into an in-itself. (Adorno, 1973: 95)

The obvious trouble with this version of authenticity, according to Adorno, is that it ideologically converts a damaged empirical reality into a transcendental principle. That is to say, the neurotically disfigured individual that emerges from the tumult of class society is left high and dry to

141

account for him- or herself. This type of individualism often defies the very best of modernist individualism – self-reliance and independence – since it constantly looks to the group that produced it for leadership (this is why Adorno repeatedly argues that modern individualism is a travesty of the notion of the individual as such).

Display and Sight

The politics of selfhood mentioned above regarding the freedom of individual expression receives significant impetus from the liberalist fetishization of the visible individual. Sight and seeing has been noteworthy in both liberal political thinking and radical social analysis. Jay (1994) demonstrates this in his history of vision in French philosophical thought in particular, describing how the liberal assumption of 'being seen' has quietly entrenched itself in critical reason. Both the look of author and the audience of the spectacle draw upon a similar lineage of enlightenment thought that places the gaze and its object at the centre of political discourse, especially when public self-expression enters the scene with the invention of the state. In order to be heard and recognized, one must be seen. This is why some of the most poignant criticism of the liberalist state (like the one developed by Foucault) favour a kind of self-imposed *aphasia* to elude the constitutive force of self-confession.[1]

Sight and display are similarly essential in the 'just be yourself' business ideology. For how else does one convey their authenticity when it is articulated mainly through the medium of identity? For sure, the very term 'identity' is based upon a visual metaphor whereby an individual is recognized through visual characteristics. The politics of liberalism is preparatory here since the private subject emerges with the right and duty to speak. Combined with the aesthetic current of self-expression discussed above, then, we have a very display-orientated notion of authentic individualism. This, of course, holds it own tensions. The cult of inwardness must now be externalized and put on show. In an environment where one is constantly observed, self and identity are from the very start made to be seen. This reified notion of subjectivity makes the individual amenable to the 'just be yourself' business practice and its obsession with 'the look'. It might be recalled from the study of the call centre mentioned earlier that the celebration of gay sexuality, for example, involved the display of extremely stereotypical icons: 'colourful', 'flamboyant', and so forth. As Adorno (1963) nicely puts it, 'in the jargon [of authenticity] there remains from inwardness only the most external aspect' (Adorno, 1973: 61).

This 'politics of aesthetics' (Ranciere, 2004) functions by reducing the rich texture of visuality to a mere abbreviatory sign, disconnecting the working subject from the now invisible social formation that pushes him or her into work. The society of the spectacle is dominated by the sign, for sure, but never has the sign meant so little in practico-political terms. Let me use the example of designer resistance that I developed in Chapter 4 to explain my point. In the politically correct workplace (or what Ross [2004] dryly calls the 'transgressive firm', when referring to Razor Fish) the countercultural chic and decor is the result of an expressive truncation of resistance. When the company replicates anti-conformist lifestyle signifiers in the sphere of production it eviscerates resistance by making it more of a fashion statement. Subversion becomes fantasy (in the technical terms of wish fulfilment in the face of the reality principle), which especially revealed when the anti-conformist ethos rubs up against the realities of capitalism (e.g. when Razor Fish faced financial difficulties it reverted back to good old-fashioned domination). This is not to say that the aesthetic realm is inherently false, on the contrary the transposition of anti-corporate sentiment into a fashionable decor (often entailing a failed mimesis) makes the simulacra an instrument of corporate rationality. As Jay (1994) puts it in another context, this represents the denigration of vision.

Sight and display also play to a strong undercurrent of market rationality that frames the 'just be yourself' managerial ideology. For many commentators, a major dysfunction of the drive to build cultures of commitment during the 1980s and 1990s was the inadvertent complacency and lack of innovation it created among workers. The appeal to conformity in the culture paradigm was unsurprising given the Japanese origins of the corporate-clan ideal. Among US management gurus today there seems to be a strong aversion to homogenizing processes associated with culture, bureaucracies, and, perhaps, managerialism generally. They are considered synonymous with anonymous hoary collectives that reward dogma and social loafing (the supposed ills of communism). The rise of market rationality centres primarily on the individual and the 'freedom' of exchange inside the firm regarding one's labour and skills. Hired contractors, for example, are on their own bar their mobile marketability and personal 'brand'. And as we mentioned in Chapter 1, opposed to the uniform collective, the market is presumed to encourage and enhance difference and diversity. The importance of 'colourfulness' and 'brightness' in the parlance of corporatized authenticity resonates with the so-called transparency of the marketplace and its elegy to plurality. Of course, fitting with this reliance on sight, the parameters of the market remain invisible, like a sphere that curves back on itself.

The final aspect of sight and display important to individualized authenticity is the presumptive auto-translucency of the subject who is displaying his or her genuineness. As Bove (2008) has pointed out, the concept of authenticity (especially as it was developed in the post-Sartrean era of critical social thought) relies on an acute self-transparency. The Cartesian moment of reflection conveys a self-knowledge and truth of what one is (reflection, of course, makes this truth). If this self-knowledge was not assumed in the discourse of authenticity, then how would the subject know he or she was being authentic or not? Of course, such self-transparency (especially in the phenomenological tradition that alludes to a transcendental ego) has been problematized on a number of fronts. French post-structuralism suggested that the eye of self-awareness in the modern age might be more accidental than transcendental, indicative of the historical forces that operate behind the backs of individuals. But as was argued in Chapter 1, we can bypass these endless debates regarding the ontology of the subject by simply demonstrating how people do reflect on their own selves, how they do develop a heightened sense of self-awareness, and this has important political effects that require explanation.

The Authentic Act and Solidarity

We have established that if authenticity is somehow being 'true to one's self', then its individualization in current corporate trends relies upon collapsing the social into the individual. The fetishized result of this collapse then must be perversely displayed to contrast it from the crowd. From a more materialist perspective, this authenticity might be externalized onto the act. The authentic deed, of course, is a central feature of existentialist philosophy. The most recent analysis can be found in the Marxian psychoanalytic perspective of Žižek (2006a, 2006b, 2006c). According to Žižek, the authentic act is the only way to break through the ideological beliefs that others are performing in our place. I want to briefly outline and criticize his argument because ironically it reproduces many of the key problems with liberalist understandings of self-identity and the authentic individual (here liberalism and critical theory share a latent and uneasy family resemblance). The following analysis aims to set the scene to think about what a more collective understanding of authenticity might entail in critical thought and practice.

As opposed to traditional approaches to *ideologiekritik* that finds subjects believing in their own domination directly, Žižek maintains that in an era of permissive cynicism and personal distancing, ideological belief functions via displacement and transference. The first kind of transference is onto practice. The hyper-consumerist cynic is a classic example. These cynics do not believe in capitalism as they participate in its rituals and believe they are free from any mystification. As Žižek famously observes, however: '[C]ynical distance is just one way to blind ourselves to the structuring power of ideological fantasy: even if we do not take things seriously, even if we keep an ironical distance, *we are still doing them*' (Žižek, 1989: 32; emphasis in the original). Such a displacement is 'interpassive' in the sense that when I interact with objects, rituals, and others, 'the object itself takes from me, deprives me of, my own passive reaction of satisfaction (or mourning or laughter), so that it is the object that "enjoys the show" instead of me, relieving me of the superego duty to enjoy myself' (Žižek, 2006*a*: 5). In relation to practice, the key here is the opening gulf between the formal subject of belief and the objective practices that believe in our place. The objectivity of practice – the rituals, routines, and mind-numbingly ordinary vagaries of everyday life in the marketplace of commodities and employment – becomes the index of ideological devotion to the dominant economic order.

Our identification with domination is not only displaced onto objective practices but also onto other actors who believe for us in our place. The second displacement enrols other people who are within the imaginary network of social relations in any given political milieu (who may or may not actually exist). Žižek nicely demonstrates the fundamental exteriority of even our most intimate experiences. For instance, enjoyment and laughter might be experienced for us by canned laughter on television sitcoms. In some cultures mourners are hired to do the wailing for the bereaved at the funeral of a loved one. Žižek is particularly interested in those who feel they are radically transgressing the rules of society, and the mechanisms that displace their conservative beliefs onto others to perform in their place. The *inauthentic* act of transgression is one that relies upon an ultimate guarantor to believe in domination for us. Those who believe in our place do not have to actually exist – they can just be supposed to exist. This is because the displacement of belief onto others is a minimal *belief in the belief of the other*. To paraphrase Žižek, when I say 'I believe in the corporate culture', what I really mean is 'I believe there are some people who might believe in the corporate culture.' I need these imaginary believers to be a naughty subversive. This is the function of the guarantor, 'yet this guarantor is always deferred, displaced never present in persona...the point of course is that the subject who directly believes, needs not exist for the belief to be operative' (Žižek, 1997*b*: 44).

In *The Parallax View* (2006*b*), Žižek provides yet another instance of the 'Other' believing in our place that reveals the important ideological consequences of presupposing others who identify for us. The example is framed within a discussion of why it is difficult to be Kantian or at least 'enlightened' in the Kantian sense. For Kant, mature citizens do not fear their freedom – they do not rely on an external or natural master who sets the limits to their bad and unruly behaviour. Such a citizen realizes that there is no natural master to draw these limits since we are free to decide for ourselves what they might be. As a result, 'a truly enlightened mature human being is a subject who no longer needs a master, who can fully assume the heavy burden of defining his own limitations' (Žižek, 2006*b*: 90). According to Žižek, it is the inability to act maturely that fuels a particular type of ideological transference in today's promiscuous postmodern society. Underlying the chic transgressions of the avant-garde consumer culture, the ideological support of supposed *non-transgression* is never far away. In terms of Kantian immaturity, much pop-radicalism relies upon an external guarantor, another who represents pure conformity and lawfulness. As Žižek explains:

[A] promiscuous teenager may engage in extreme orgies with group sex and drugs, but what he cannot bear is the idea that his mother could be doing something similar – his orgies rely on the supposed purity of his mother which serves as the point of exception, the external guarantee: I can do what ever I like, since I know my mother keeps her place pure for me.... The most difficult thing is not to violate the prohibitions in a wild orgy of enjoyment, but to do this without relying on someone else who is presupposed not to enjoy so that I can enjoy...the same goes for belief: the difficult thing is not to reject belief in order to shock a believing other, but to be a nonbeliever without the need for another subject supposed to believe on my behalf. (Žižek, 2006*b*: 91)

The authentic act, therefore, must traverse the fantasy of the 'Other' we utilize within our ideological frame to believe for us: '[T]his allows us further to specify the Lacanian notion of an authentic act. Act is to be opposed to mere activity. Activity relies on some fantasmatic support, while the authentic act involves disturbing – "traversing" – the fantasy' (Žižek, 2006*c*). Žižek's singularization of the authentic act suspends the usual slippage of signifiers in the Lacanian subject as it comes to spontaneously posit itself *ex nihilo* during an event that renders experience acephalous (one is reminded here of Badiou's [2005] theory of the event).

The trouble with the heroic authentic act is that it works within such an anti-collectivist political horizon. Žižek's authentic act is too indebted to a childish existentialist notion that one can only find freedom in the singular act of obliterating the social as we focus the universe of existence into the pinpoint of self. Can we not imagine all sorts of situations in which the struggle is maintained through the belief that our comrades somewhere still believe in the cause, the revolution, the fight for indigenousness rights, attempts to radicalize popular sentiment regarding the natural environment, etc.? Individual transgression may certainly be propped up by a wily guarantor, rendering any subsequent subversion trite. But group solidarity in the context of certain types of struggle may yield cases in which the guarantor has progressive political outcomes. In times of weakness and fatigue, when the situation seems hopeless, sharing the burden of identifying with the cause might function as an exceptionally resistant moment. Why must the 'authentic' act be sited in such an atomized way and the truth of ourselves sought in the non-social abyss?

The digression above for the first time in this book broaches the connection between authenticity and solidarity. Can personal authenticity be found in a gesture of solidarity and a Jacobin conceptual politics? Here we must return to a prominent working definition of authenticity: *the truth of oneself*. The two operative terms here are 'truth' and 'oneself'. Various kinds of fascism certainly used a more communal approach to authenticity, as Adorno (1973) noted in relation to Heideggerian ethics. In this silly and regressive political ideology, the notion of a pre-historical radical purity is posited in order to 'sort' the insiders (the authentic ones) from the outsiders, with the folk and countryside definitive aspects of the authentic community in which the self disappears into a more totalizing social experience. As Adorno (1974) once remarked, even the social is sick in this regard. A more liberal democratic attempt to socialize authenticity can be found in the work of Taylor (1992). He argues that the term has become a synonym for self-obsession over difference. The paradox for him is that authenticity requires dialogue with the community in which one belongs. Just as the self is socialized to its very core, the moment of authenticity – the truth of oneself – may also be derived from a dialogical recognition that allows one to speak in a socio-political setting frequently defined by injustice. This theorization does not subsume the self into the social body, but nurtures one's truth of being in a community of mutual

awareness and respect. Belonging and democratic dignity are the foundations of authenticity whereby self is forged through society rather than
against it. As Taylor explains:

This is what is so self-defeating in modes of contemporary culture that concentrate on self-fulfilment, which shut out history and the bonds of solidarity. These
self-centred 'narcissistic' forms are indeed shallow and trivialized.... But this is
not because they belong to the culture of authenticity. Rather it is because they
fly in the face of its requirements. To shut out demands emanating beyond
the self is precisely to suppress the conditions of significance, and hence court
trivialization... it destroys the conditions in which the ideal can be realized.
(Taylor, 1992: 40)

Taylor's analysis is indebted to a communitarian position regarding
democratic inclusion and recognition, and thus suffers from many of the
problems that dog communitarian politics more generally. But it is useful
insofar as it places authenticity firmly within a social setting of intercon-
nectedness and solidarity, thus displacing the hyper-individualism that
has limited so many conceptions in both conservative and leftist camps.
In concrete terms, what exactly does personal authenticity look like when
coupled to the sentiment of solidarity – say, working-class unionism or
various forms of collective struggle against capital, gender oppression, and
so forth? And how does authenticity connect with the notion of freedom,
given the way in which prevalent appreciations are often pitted against
the social?

Authenticity and Freedom

While authenticity has largely been conceived within a matrix of hyper-
individualism, there is evidence of it having more communal connotations for workers (and we will unpack some of these connections to
solidarity shortly). One of the main reasons that corporate discourse
gives authenticity such individualistic overtones relates to the supposed
freedom from control it affords. It may be recalled from Chapter 1 that the
'just be yourself' business ideology was heralded as the demise of control
since workers could express their unique individuality rather than conform
to homogenizing processes (such as technical regimentation, bureaucratic
dehumanization, and cultural normalization). This definition of personal
authenticity is equated with freedom per se, and both are then pitted
against the standardizing order of collective controls.

We clearly established in Chapter 1 that there is little creditability in the equivalence drawn between freedom of self-expression and freedom from control. This is because self-expression is fixed in a very specific manner (identity displays mimicking non-work activities) and within fairly robust boundaries (be yourself, but only up to a point). Having said this, social theory has often given individual authenticity and freedom strong associations. From an existentialist standpoint that Sartre propounded, for example, realizing the 'truth of oneself' might be painful and involve a number of almost insurmountable dilemmas, but it frees the subject from the illusion of powerlessness cultivated by a reified social environment. The moment we create ourselves through our choices (if only within the sticky bounds of 'facticity') we are individually free, even in the most oppressive political nightmares. As Sartre would say, the French people were never so liberated than under Nazi occupation since the choices were stark and obvious. Another example demonstrating this relationship between freedom and authenticity is closer to the world of work. Corporate cynics might find themselves acting out the rituals of a team-building exercise, faking their way through whilst maintaining an inner preserve of self apparently free from managerial domination. While this 'freedom' may in itself be ideological (see Fleming and Spicer, 2003) in that management never really expects full-blooded identification anyway, the relationship between a personal authenticity and freedom is clear. Likewise, in terms of the aforementioned solidarity, moments of subjective and practical freedom can be forged from the connective associations of working-class unity. The ties and affiliations built from shared toil allow a more positive identity to be maintained, significantly liberating workers from the stigma of second-class status and degradation often attributed to them (Burawoy, 1979). This freedom through solidarity inscribes authenticity (who one feels one really is) with flows of communal experience.

I define freedom here simply as *having a life*, reclaiming it from work so that self-identity (or personal authenticity) might be achieved. Given its strong relationship with freedom, I now aim to map the concept of authenticity onto different kinds of freedom that can be observed in the contemporary organization. Three modalities of freedom are identified: freedom *through* work; freedom *around* work; and freedom *from* work; and each is framed in relation to a specific construction of personal authenticity involving both individualist and communal variants. The attempt to forge and/or find freedom in the corporation shapes the significance of work in very different ways. The first situates the capitalist labour process in reform, counter-identification, and engagement. The second moment-arily sets work aside and finds pockets of liberation outside the organiza-tion. The last negates any centring of work by choosing exit as the best strategy of emancipation. The aim of this differentiation is to spread out the components of authenticity in relation to the politics of freedom in the corporation. In doing so, we not only broaden the meaning of authen-ticity beyond the stereotypical individualism underscoring the 'just be yourself' managerial approach, but can also judge its viability as a useful vocabulary in emancipatory movements today.

Freedom Through Work

Critical research has frequently recognized how workers forge various forms of freedom within the confines of the organization. As a research agenda (if one could call it that), there is an interest in how pragmatic piecemeal improvements can be achieved. The labour process and the corporate form that embeds it within the political economy of capitalism can become a space of limited self-determination when the extant condi-tions are sufficiently radicalized. In other words, freedom of a particular kind can be achieved through work when individuals and/or groups at-tempt to garner from it something other than the detritus of exploitation. There are many cases in which the workplace is transformed into a set of bounded possibilities for micro-emancipation (as Alvesson and Willmott [1992] call it to distinguish it from revolutionary movements) – some large and others more modest. While unions have typically been instruments for distancing employees from the strategic command of work (Collinson, 1992), they can also tactically deploy the very dependencies of business to harvest certain liberties. The classic wildcat strike is an obvious example, in which the withdrawal of labour understands and exploits very well the weaknesses of capital (Gouldner, 1955). Another good example is workers showing a keen interest in the minutia of managerialism with the object-ive of partaking in partial control of the firm (Fleming and Spicer, 2007). This inscribes the corporation within a reformist politics and takes one step towards voicing the commons proper inside the logic of economic rationality.

Authenticity is articulated as 'freedom through work' in a number of forms, some of which are more amenable to co-optation than others. We can categorize these under the label *authenticity through work*. At the indi-vidual level, a well-known instance of this kind of authenticity was noted by Hochschild (2003). She demonstrates the tensions that develop around the allocation of time when demands are made on some women to fulfil the stereotypical role of the mother whilst earning an income. Many working mothers find what Hochschild once referred to as the 'second shift' (unpaid domestic labour) dull and alienating. A major reversal of the typical logic of alienation occurs whereby the home itself is more like a factory or prison setting in which archaic patriarchal domination denies women the power of self-determination. The seat of dignity and respect is found more in the standardized rituals of working. Mothers that Hochschild observed looked forward to leaving the home for the corporation since they could feel 'human' once again. In this sense, the workplace can engender an authentic identity as much as can the non-workplace. Hochschild's analysis is weakened by the class bias in the sample of mothers she studied (what about the immigrant toilet cleaner or the prostitute?) and by the implicit assumption that oppression at work is somehow better than oppression at home. Moreover, this search for freedom in work must certainly be open to the flows of co-optation in light of the technologies of authentization discussed thus far in this book.

A more solidaristic example of an attempt to galvanize personal authenticity and freedom through work can be seen in my own research of Sunray Customer Service. At Sunray, it can be recalled, much emphasis was placed on identities of difference, with extra-employment motifs especially prominently displayed. Some of the workers I interviewed, however, undermined the sentiment and celebration of diversity by emphasizing solidarity, uniformity, and collective subordination reflective of the standardized tasks and labour market position that defined their employment reality. As one worker put it, 'Well, to "succeed" at Sunray you are basically gay, have to be really "alternative" and Sunray likes people who have different colour hair and who are into [*in a sarcastic tone*] "being themselves". Now I'm not too sure which one we fit into, but basically we are all plebs. Just plebs' (insurance agent). This agent's colleague – an airline agent – also used the term 'pleb' as a more apt interpretation of call centre work given the mundane constraints of technological, bureaucratic, and cultural controls. Her discourse dismisses the idea that employees and management are equals:

> They [management] pretend we are equal to them. But when I see myself and my team, I know I'm just a pleb. I only wish they [management] would simply tell me the truth and not pretend it to be otherwise!

For these workers, the newly legislated freedom to 'just be themselves' did not sit well with the continued conformity to extant controls. This identity-addled detraction from control was experienced more as mystification, inspiring its own variants of resistance. They were critical of the aims and legitimacy of the 'just be yourself' discourse since it did not afford matter-of-fact freedoms *apropos* the concrete work tasks of the enterprise. This challenged the idea of individual difference as providing a road to freedom. The observations that 'we are all just plebs' partially undercuts the focus on monadic uniqueness by giving voice to shared experiences, commonality, and even solidarity (see also Vallas, 2003). The ultimate structural position of telephone agents at Sunray was one of uniform subordination and this became the truth of their being at work. But is there not a danger here in using subordination as the reference point for identity, perpetuating a kind of 'wound attachment' in which class injuries are celebrated?

Freedom Around Work

Freedom may be achieved outside of the corporation if its regimes of dependence and control are put aside and other pleasures and sources of authenticity are tapped in order to redefine self in supra-work terms. As we have mentioned in earlier chapters, the sphere of non-work (even inside the organization in the form of informal interactions) has typically been considered somehow more free than that of production. This is especially so in liberal political thought, in which choice, self-determination, and self-expression are the inalienable rights of the citizen. Outside the strictures of corporate control, people are presumed to have a greater say over their lives in the realms of leisure, consumption, sexuality, and so forth, and it is therefore a place where feelings of 'real' selfhood suggestive of personal authenticity might be experienced. This is an *authenticity around work*. This 'discovery', maintenance, and elaboration of 'the truth of oneself' can take a number of different forms, with varying political implications.

The most obvious form of freedom around work leaves itself very open to the regulatory power of the 'just be yourself' managerial ideology. One expresses identifications and lifestyle signifiers that reveal to a corporate audience the apparent truth of ourselves. I have spent a good deal of time in this book articulating the development and structure of this management ideology. We have done this from an ethico-political point of view, linking it to a broader framework of immaterial labour and the commons. But even inside these regimes of control, the freedom to express one's 'gay' identity or 'class' background, for example, is still noteworthy. In the context of conventional workplace controls (unenlightened by the 'just be yourself' business model), such expressions of self may indeed develop into a politically recalcitrant axis of personal authenticity (see Creed,

Scully, and Austin, 2002). Many workplaces certainly continue to frown upon the evocation of non-work themes. Under these conditions, in which the cogs of power and domination operate on a different register to that discussed in this book, there may be opportunities for significant freedoms. However, as may be expected, the likelihood of co-optation in the 'just be yourself' corporation must remain a danger.

Another way in which freedom around work might be enjoyed builds on decidedly communal notions of authenticity. Working class and ethnic neighbourhoods, for example, can frequently afford a strong sense of belonging alongside dull and alienating work. These extra-work identifications can even overwhelm the significance of employment as a marker for selfhood ('its just a job and has nothing to do with me'). In the case of ethnicity, the vector of group affiliation signifies a truth that might not be accepted at work (other than through its mere visible presence). In the case of class identity the workplace is an important counter-point to flows of solidarity around family, tradition, cooperation, and shared experience. A classic analysis of this authenticity around work can be found in Goldthorpe et al.'s (1969) classic analysis of 'patterns of sociability' in the United Kingdom:

> The tightly knit network of kinship and the close ties of familiarity between neighbours are the products of successful generations of families living out their lives alongside each other; the strong sense of communal solidarity and various forms of mutual help and collective action reflect the absence of any wide economic, cultural or status differences. (Goldthorpe et al., 1969: 86)

While the above account was written in the context of declining class identity in the Luton area, the solidarity described gave people a sense of genuineness around the degradation and humiliation of work or employment, and generally in the case of unemployment.

Freedom From Work

The logical extension of the sequence we have outlined above is those refusals that widen and deepen the time and space for non-work. This is especially so in the context of any corporate form representing a greedy institution whereby almost anything is ripe for co-optation. We can call this position 'freedom from work'. Personal authenticity is formed by way of a non-reliance (even vicariously) on the expectation that one must return to an alienating social relationship once one has finished 'being oneself'. If work is the source of continuing economic and subjective injury (a lack of a life), then a radical politics ought to forge alternatives by extending the realm of non-work, freeing subjects from the very notion of modern corporate employment in significant ways. Emancipation here blends the idea of work as both discursive and economic reality, usurping its ideological predominance and crafting substitutes to the current rule of 'a normal job'. This sentiment is echoed in the 'down-shift' and 'slow down' movements in which the high-stress and fast-paced lifestyles of, say, the management consultant, is unsustainable. These movements are often brought about following compulsory retrenchment and redundancy. Indeed, in light of the oncoming 'social factory' in which non-work and work are forcibly placed on the plane of production, the best course of action might be simply to opt out all together.

A version of this position can be seen in the advocates of the work-less movement prevalent in France during the 1980s (Gorz, 1988). Gorz focuses on the efforts to reduce the amount of time spent at work and builds upon a Marxist analytic regarding labour time and value. He is especially worried about the ways in which the leisure industry is speciously defined as a place of freedom in popular consciousness. Leisure is symbiotically linked to alienated labour in a number of ways since it provides an outlet and support for an unpleasant world of work. As well as being sceptical about freedom around work (e.g. working class culture and communal forms of life around the factory, call centre, or corporation), Gorz is similarly troubled about the hope that work might eventually provide self-actualization (freedom through work). The ideology of work draws upon semi-religious ideas regarding the 'joy of labour' and the work ethic. Gorz suggests this is more about enticing employees, managers, and other members of the firm to enjoy their alienation:

I cannot emphasize this too strongly: *A job whose effect and aim are to save work cannot, at the same time, glorify work as the essential source of personal identity and fulfilment.* The meaning of the current technological revolution cannot be to rehabilitate the work ethic and identification with one's work. It only has meaning if it broadens the field of non-work activities in which we can all, the new type of worker included, develop that dimension of our humanity which finds no outlet in technicized work. (Gorz, 1988: 88; emphasis in original)

The problem with Gorz's formulation is obvious. In the 'just be yourself' enterprise these extended narratives of non-work are fertile for absorption and corporate transposition. In other words, the numerical reduction of work time could potentially slip into a 'freedom around work' stance with all its attendant problems. In this sense the Leftist slogan of 'Working Less

So Everyone Can Work' remains attached to a capitalist frame and might actually embed the for-profit rationality more acutely in the social body (e.g. the idea of paid domestic labour). In the social factory where immaterial labour aspires for universality the autonomists argue that the non-work tactic ought to be taken to its radical conclusion. This is not a rejection of labour per se, but a very narrow definition of labour called 'work' (since they evoke non-capitalist rather than non-economic coordinates; Wright, 1995). For sure, the ideology of contemporary employment functions through our neurotic attachment to work. If we are not working, then surely a kind of spiritual wasteland must emerge and barbarism will descend. Hardt and Negri (1999) rightly point out that for the multitude or the global commons this wasteland is already here. For them exit is a more desirable path. The Refusal of Work movement extends the 'freedom from work' strategy by emphasizing the networks of labour or the commons that the social factory parasitically feeds upon. Like the petit bourgeois celebration of productive work, they too draw upon religious imagery of 'the exodus' to emphasize the importance of politically activating the under-commons already existing in and outside of the corporation. This too might serve to bolster a feeling of personal authenticity – a self-fulfilled life not outside of work but *without* work as it is defined today. Not a life that is partial (authenticity around work) or vicariously wedded to capitalism (authenticity through work) but completely autonomous to the commodity form and productive labour. At last life escapes the need to be defined in terms of its negative absence (like authenticity itself) and becomes a positive force in and of itself.

Conclusion

It is perhaps this version of authenticity that overcomes or simply bypasses the problems that afflict both the freedoms through and around work. Freedom through work runs the risk of glorifying the source of alienation rather than overcoming it, and is also closely linked to the work ethic in which a kind of psychic self-flagellation is transformed into a principal of pride. Freedom around work also runs into a number of problems, since authenticity is sourced in a manner that can reinforce the work–leisure dichotomy sustaining the labour process. Moreover, the freedom around work that relies upon a display of difference and/or diversity at the mere visual level can lend itself to co-optation by the 'just be yourself' managerial discourse.

Freedom from work presents authenticity in a different light and could be lived in either a communal or individualistic manner. To qualify this point we must remember that authenticity becomes a managerial concern when it is a problem, when it is absent or wanting. It is symptomatic of a fundamental 'lack' (what we called in the Introduction to the book a *lack of life*). When the sphere of non-work (which is very different to non-labour, since work is a very specific rationalization of labour) spreads out across the commons and is subsumed under the rubric of pleasure and struggle, the dialectic of work and non-work ceases to function as a centripetal conservative force. A plane of immanence emerges in which authenticity is everything and nothing – a life of full positivity. Here we move from contradiction to a smooth surface that overcomes the divisions of work and life, the public and private, labour and non-labour. Exodus is a point of departure but also a modality of life in itself. Viewed from this perspective, it is very possible that the idea of personal authenticity might cease to function as a pragmatic cognitive map when engaging with the contemporary cultural politics of work. Authenticity fails as a radical gesture in the context of a 'workers' society' the very moment the antagonism that makes it a problem is overcome.

Conclusion: Authenticity and the Joy of Non-work

> The factory has invaded the territory of everyday life. Illicit pleasures are banned until they become profitable. Our apparent freedom to do whatever we like shows how whatever we choose serves the economy.
>
> (From Vaneigem's *Book of Pleasures*, 1983)

There is no doubt that authenticity is now big business consisting of a large market for a particular kind of 'real' and its attendant aura of organic truthfulness. Management books, consultants, and human resource managers of different stripes fervently espouse the jargon of authenticity in order to make for a more productive workplace. The suite of investments around the ideal of self-expression and personal genuineness is formidable. Marketing and branding experts argue that consumers want a unique realism in their products. In the age of organic food, reality TV, vegan hairbrushes, and exotic 'true to life' holidays, an authentic experience and 'being' are big sellers. Fakeness or falsity are 'uncool' since the consumer gaze expects products and services that are bona fide so that they too can display their realness to significant others. The music industry abounds with allusions to 'keeping it real', especially music branded with edgy or rootsy origins (gangster rap, reggae, etc.).

In the realm of corporate ideology and employee relations many organizations attempt to ooze an authentic air in which CSR programmes give the impression that stakeholders really matter. Moreover, as we noted in Chapter 5, employees can derive a sense of personal integrity working for these firms, making money whilst remaining faithful to their values as tempered radicals or progressive leftists. The countercultural rally against the poverty of everyday life is prominent in recruitment advertising, corporate training manuals, and recruitment agencies. The supposedly radical cyber-Marxist statement regarding the potential freedoms of technology found in the *Hacker Manifesto* fits almost perfectly with a reinstated capitalist imperative whereby profit is pursued in the name of an anti-profit nimbus. IT firms, advertising companies, and even call centres are located in the urban areas of cities known for their artistic, loft-living, bohemian atmosphere. The fake, plastic, and glitzy decor of the corporate 1980s has been replaced with warehouse style visuals, providing workers with an authentic underground feel as they toil for the firm's owners and customers.

The cities are particular redolent with this turn to the real. Perhaps this is unsurprising since the idea of personal authenticity was born as neo-romantic philosophers attempted to retain the 'truth of oneself' amidst the dirty, sprawling metropolis. But the reverse logic of authenticity appears to be on the march in the city. Capital and rent-seekers are moving into the once poor neighbourhoods of London and New York, for example, because the underground scene is considered to yield more authentic cultural networks. The rise of the so-called creative class has ushered in a gentrification process that trades in the chic alternative cool of real neighbourhoods (Florida, 2005). Corporations have located offices in the soviet-style buildings of former East Berlin in order to tap the creative and artistic flows considered more genuine compared to typical corporate districts (Pasquinelli, 2008). And the 'creative cool' of Barcelona that was developed over many years of struggle, autonomy, and self-determination has been targeted by rent-seekers to exploit the demand for housing in neighbourhoods considered more authentic (Harvey, 2002). The fakeness that Rousseau might have found in the sprawling neighbourhoods of the metropolis is now ironically the source of authenticity. Even more incongruous is the fact that for many the gentrification of these cityscapes no doubt renders them increasingly superficial.

It has been argued in this book that with the rising prominence of authenticity in Western consumer and corporate culture its meaning has been scripted in important ways. First, only authenticity of a particular type is considered a moral and social good. The boundary patrolling mechanisms of the corporate social order are certainly activated when unacceptable kinds of self-expression are detected. Commodifiable versions of being authentic are circumscribed within broader political flows of domination and are overlaid with 'fun', 'designer cool', 'exoticism', and other expressions of abstract difference. Second, if authenticity is meant to stand for an original – an assumption in the managerial discourse that the source of authenticity is outside the corporation – then it is ironic that such a substantial machinery of mimesis is required to create authentic products, cultural icons, and experiences. If the affluent society of late capitalism is governed by simulacra, as Baudrillard (1995) proposed, where the original is no longer meaningful, then the veritable explosion of discourses around authenticity is doubly perplexing. The transferability of the 'original' non-work experience of freedom into the workplace renders it instantly infelicitous for many. The development of this abstraction is dynamic since the original is manufactured as much as discovered. Non-work and other associatives of the commons is a screen upon which certain managerialist projections unfold (in a similar way, the mafia in the United States began to imitate film portrayals of their lifestyle). Perhaps the original does not even exist. But its supposition is important here for the *duplicata* of non-work to manifest in the corporation. Did we not see this in the case of corporatized 'fun' where staged 'play' failed to be very fun in the end and was even experienced by some as inauthentic, phoney, and fake? Ross's (2004) superb depiction of the warehouse decor in Razor Fish also revealed this fragile mimetic function at work.

The book has also endeavoured to point out that the recent turn to authenticity in the 'just be yourself' ideology is linked both to broader changes in society and a continuation of earlier managerial rhetoric. This is why we ought to think of the language of authenticity as a *symptom* of more profound questions troubling Western social structures of accumulation. As I have stated several times, personal authenticity becomes a concern when it is perceived to be absent or even unattainable. What are the contours of the generative structure of absence or 'lack' that gives rise to the notion of fakeness and the quest for personal authenticity? And what do such contours mean for the very idea of authenticity in relation to the corporate world and the political counter-tactics of those employed there?

This book has tackled these questions in a manner that does not assume that the 'just be yourself' business ideology is something concerning all corporations. A global division of labour ought to disabuse us of the temptation to generalize. The 'humanizing' veneer that we might see in a London call centre might have little weight in, say, the factories of South-East Asia. Moreover, even within the structures of Western employment, many jobs lie outside this new-age concern with personal authenticity (that involves fun, sexuality, etc.). For example, the 'play ethic' would seem out of place in the official mission of the hospital or prison. Its superficialities make it particularly suitable to the corporate sphere of production. In the occupations and corporate cultures in which the 'just be yourself' management approach does have purchase, a number of more symptomatic factors currently underlie its

159

popularity. We have discussed many of these in the preceding chapters. The challenge of enticing and motivating a new generation of workers who think work 'sucks' and have been reared on the countercultural (or even anti-capitalist) values of popular culture is relevant. This generation-Y ethic is contradictory since it is sceptical about capitalism but still seeks to gain from it. Take the classic example of the business school student immersed in critical theory, eagerly waiting to join the ranks of a management consulting firm. When evaluating this apparent contradiction it would be too crude to put it down to hypocrisy. The different layers and social spheres that bind us to the production process are overdetermined, consisting of a complex generative matrix of rationales. On the side of the corporation, not only is there a sub-commons of intellectual creativity flowing from this radical chic, it is also concerned with its internal legitimation among savvy employees.

This attention to internal legitimation may take two forms, involving a 'weak' and 'strong' appeal to authenticity. In its 'weak' form, the corporation and managerial function simply avoids raising expectations regarding the reciprocal chains of commitment and loyalty in the firm, treating it more as a marketplace defined by the cold cash nexus. There is little hype and this suits the part-time contractor, for instance, who does not want to be bombarded with 'Californian bathtub crap'. Here the employee is pushed back onto him- or herself as a brand and bundle of skills that extracts the most he or she can from the corporation with little long-term desire to stay. As we mentioned in Chapter 1, this sits in contrast to the distinct drive around building cultures of commitment in the 1980s that touted regimented values. The firm that promotes a 'weak' authenticity strips back the HRM hype and plastic commitment exercises to reveal the organization in a particular light. As Kunda and Ailon-Souday (2005) put it, this changes the capital–labour relationship from something like a long-term marriage (i.e. cultures of commitment) to a one-night stand. Workers in these firms view any attempt to facilitate 'strong cultures' with cynicism, and managers also think it is either a waste of resources or counterproductive, given the dysfunctions associated with normative control in relation to creativity, innovation, and 'flexibility'.

Next is the 'strong' version of authenticity, which has been the main focus of this book. This is where we see the social factory coming into its own since the non-work realm is particularly prominent in the quest to render work a propitious space for self-actualization. While the social factory and prevalence of labour outside the walls of the corporation still underpins the 'weak' version of authenticity, it is with the 'just be yourself' ideology that the legitimation-by-appropriation mechanism becomes important. Capital depends upon what we have called, after Hardt and Negri (1994), 'the commons', both as a source of energy and value, and as a dumping ground for the externalized traumas of production. Its symbolic duplication inside the organization provides a prop for capital since the corporation can never reproduce itself. The appearance of the commons in such an abbreviated form also intends to legitimate the firm to the generation-Y employee who thinks the corporation 'sucks'. This pervasive mistrust is articulated to other signifiers so that anti-business sentiment ('cool') can coincide with the goals of the corporation. This book has detailed the specific kinds of appropriative techniques that make this possible pertaining to radical chic, CSR initiatives, and managed pleasure.

Legitimating capitalism in the eyes of the swarming teams of disbelieving generation-Y employees is not the only driver for the recent salience of the 'just be yourself' managerial discourse. The emphasis on self, difference, and lifestyle is symptomatic of a shift in the cultural politics of the firm whereby the traditional coordinates of worker activism have been supplanted by a more identity-orientated ethic. In earlier chapters we traced the concern with 'identity' in both theory and practice. The turn to identity does not automatically make for conservative politics. Anti-racist and pro-gay social movements have all challenged the corporate hegemonic norm in significant ways. With the turn to aestheticism in critical theory and practice, struggles around discourse have often replaced practical engagements with structures upholding oppressive arrangements. In relation to this permutation in US radicalism, Sanbonmatsu (2004) laconically puts it thus: '[S]ubversion of language and speech, rather than transformation of consciousness or material institutions, came to be seen as the proper method and proving ground of praxis' (Sanbonmatsu, 2004: 51). When identity politics is subsumed by liberalist ideology and is reduced to a mere gesture of lifestyle difference, it is ripe to be exploited by the so-called new spirit of capitalism. In this sense, the importance of personal authenticity in the context of the corporate form represents a displacement of struggle from structure to social poetics, a displacement that weaves in and out of the continuing grass-roots concern among workers about the damage done to their everyday experience.

The hyper-reflexivity marking this era of modernization must also be implicated in these transformations around corporate management as employees seriously ponder 'what it all means'. In popular culture, McGee (2005) has traced the rise of the self-help industry in which authenticity is the holy grail of the disenchanted (post)modern denizen. In this excellent historical study she argues that the personal 'truth of oneself', in the United States at least, has always underpinned the self-help industry. But the most recent manifestation – from Tony Robbins 'Personal Power' to new-age Buddhist-oriented spiritualism – is more a symptom of translating the responsibility of a precarious employment into psychological categories that impute personal responsibility. In this sense, work and the corporate production of exploitation or 'wasted lives' (to use Bauman's compelling phrase) is intimately linked to the quest to 'find oneself' and to find happiness. This overblown reflexivity, involving a heightened sense of self-awareness bordering on narcissism, is part and parcel of the modern consciousness, as Giddens' (1991) too has well documented.

The firm is also entangled in this reflexive turn as it captures and sublimates the energies of self-exploration within the corporate setting. Rather than prohibit the spiritual self-fulfilment of workers in the labouring moment, the enterprise can become a therapeutic and playful zone of self-discovery. But a double moment of reflective buffering is operating here. In addition to the initial inward turn to 'find oneself', the somewhat artificial vehicles for achieving this are also authenticated with a varnish of ironic self-awareness by the authorities. In this way the otherwise ludicrous 'fun' exercises designed to draw out authentic expressions of self are inoculated from serious criticism. They are wheeled out in staff meetings and Away Days with an ironic smile among the 'fun-sultants' who do not seem to take them seriously either. The knowing smile makes these exercises even more insidious and difficult to escape. Moreover, the translation process that maps structure onto self sits well with the individualization tendencies of the firm such as the growing importance of the 'portfolio career' we discussed in Chapter 7.

A central thesis discussed in this book is that authenticity in the 'just be yourself' vein is mostly a symptom of an antagonism between capital and labour in the broadest sense. Personal authenticity becomes an issue most notably when it is absent. This is what connects this managerial discourse most closely to older industrial schematics like the neo-human relations movement. There are certainly other parallels and antecedents, especially with the culture management tradition and the attempt to manage meaning in the sphere of production. What I mean by the proposition that antagonism is the driver of the most recent pursuit of authentic selves can be unpacked on a number of levels. That authenticity is on the radar at all is indicative that something is inherently missing in the contemporary workplace. We argued in the Introduction that what is missing most is 'a life', which explains why non-work and an instrumentalized commons features so much in the 'just be yourself' discourse. Perhaps work has never been more unpopular than today (notwithstanding the contradictory sign that we are all obsessed with having it). The recent attempt to *act as if* work is a sphere of non-work and thus a zone of life is driven by this antagonism, especially when it intersects with the recruitment problems raised above and a wider 'new spirit of capitalism' where artistic grievances are partially incorporated. The liberal or humane organization tries to smooth over the trauma of contemporary labour – the chronic lack of life at work – by colonizing the wider life-giving energies of the commons.

This tells us that work is still a problem that needs solutions. The many managerial solutions posited today focus on 'self' and 'integrity' within the unchanging structures of corporate non-life. Crisis and solution are dialectically entwined in a call-and-response dialogue between capital and the commons as the autonomist tradition of critique points out. I have utilized this variant of Marxist thought because it best allows us to place the emergence of the 'just be yourself' business ideology within a broader political economy. The notion of the social factory captures Vaneigem's suspicion (opening this conclusion) that the factory mentality has invaded almost every facet of life. In Chapter 2, I referred to this as the 'haemorrhaging organization' because the traditional boundary between work and non-work has been unsettled in an unprecedented fashion. This has involved a dual process of refracting the pleasure of non-work through the act of productive labour and casting the logic of accumulation into everyday life. Autonomist thought allows us to understand the rationale behind these movements (although there is no need to posit an intentional string-pulling agent). The commons is the site of creative energies, co-operation, and mutual aid that occurs in between the structures of capitalist competition. We have argued that the immaterial worker or 'social worker' (in the autonomist sense) represents the contradictory confluence of a capitalist 'partial' moment generated out of its antagonistic contrary. The 'just be yourself' managerial approach represents a complex intersection involving the non-work life-affirming commons being inscribed into the firm. Transposition reduces the commons to an individualistic aestheticism that is both practical ('slack in the system') and symbolic, alluding to something not present and that can never be in the space of production (at least, not without seriously undermining it).

Given the partial capitalist moment of the immaterial worker and the political uncertainty that ensues when the commons is invited into the office, authenticity might yet be the watchword of radical labour. That is to say, we must not assume the desire to be 'true to oneself' only serves the corporation. In the last chapter we linked authenticity (both in the corporatized sense and in alternative reconfigurations) to different forms of freedom. The freedom analysed there was not the pure freedom of the totally emancipated subject – the authentic act that Žižek celebrates in relation to transgressing the fantasy of the guarantor – but freedoms inspired by a certain relation to the organization. We noted that freedom in work and around work (with the equivalent denotations of personal authenticity) were problematic in their own ways in light of the social factory. Indeed, as Vaneigem puts it, the freedoms that each authentic moment involves only reinforce the fact that whatever we choose serves the economy. It is the third approach to freedom and authenticity that provides the only viable avenue of political strategy in the context of the universalizing social factory and the cunning new spirit of capitalism: *freedom from work*.

We briefly mentioned the refusal of work movement in Chapter 7 and as this book comes to a conclusion, I want to argue that this is perhaps the most sensible response to the current intersection of corporate power and personal authenticity. It is the logical corollary to the 'social factory' framework that has been developed in this book to fathom the mechanisms underlying the 'just be yourself' managerial vision of the corporation. Authenticity cannot be achieved in or around the corporation without its conceptualization and enactment being implicated in reproducing the production process. Moreover, if we accept that the pursuit of authenticity is more a symptom of the everyday crisis that the regime of employment exacts on millions of workers, then maybe we need to think beyond authenticity – or at least rethink it in a way that turns it into a line of flight outside of itself, to a time and place where the search for personal authenticity is no longer necessary. Given that the usual spaces for gathering the materials of an authentic self (to be expressed at work) are frequently the myriad moments ostensibly outside of work (what the autonomists call the commons), then it is this underbelly of living labour that needs to be universalized.

The Refusal of Work movement has been growing in popularity over the last few years, with the Krisis Group and Work Less party prominent examples. Tronti (1966/1979) first theorized this argument in his essay 'The Strategy of Refusal' in terms of capital's dependency on labour as the engine of accumulation and the social factory, with the refusal to work being the most useful way to bypass the accommodating logic underlying the tokenistic democratization of the factory. The notion of exodus is both a description and prescription regarding the best way to deal with the traumas of the social factory when almost everything is fungible. It entails not an escape but a more forceful realization of the extant commons, a set of social, communicative, and symbolic valuing activities that capital parasitically co-opts for its own purpose. The sovereignty of empire (the nation state and capital) can be resisted and usurped by the swarming multitude of cooperative workers that shape the quality of the corporate form. As Hardt and Negri (2004) put it: '[T]his act of refusing the sovereign is a kind of exodus, fleeing the forces of oppression, servitude and perse-cution in the search of freedom. It is an elemental act of liberation and a threat that every sovereign constantly has to manage, contain or displace' (Hardt and Negri, 2004: 334). This is not a rejection of labour, per se, in favour of hedonistic abandon. It is a reconstitution of labour in the Marxist sense of it being 'living, life-forming fire'. Hardt (1993) points out elsewhere that 'the refusal of work (lavoro) was never the refusal of labour (lavoro) as such; it was never directed against productivity, creativ-ity or inventiveness. Rather it was the refusal of a specific relation between capital and labour' (Hardt, 1993: 114, quoted in Wright, 1995: 28).

And where does this leave authenticity? The 'just be yourself' mode of self-expression is so intimately entwined in the political economy of accu-mulation that there is little left of much use outside of the conservative parameters in which we find it being pursued today. The ruse of leisure and free-time cradling the traditional point of capital accumulation (relations that have become a network of production beyond the office walls) ultim-ately functions to support the very source of alienation that the culture industry attempts to ameliorate. Moreover, the personal authenticity being formulated in the large corporations of the West is far too atomized given how selfhood is raised out of the tissue of social relations and transformed into a narcissistic obsession. Self becomes a slave to itself. The universal-ization of the commons – that appears to inspire the notion of personal authenticity – would invariably entail de-subjectification politics whereby the social networks of the co-operative community render obsolete the symptomatic fetishization of self. Indeed, the inspirational source of what passes for 'authentic' might ultimately bring an end to the very demand for authenticity if realized in its full positivity. For the pursuit of authenticity in the sphere of work is indicative of a desire for self-identity that can only be properly realized when the commons moves out from the shadow of the corporation. Until that happens, authenticity still matters, but not for the reasons for which we think it does.

Notes

Introduction

1. Hardt and Negri (2004) explicitly state they prefer the word 'common' rather than 'commons' since it avoids any possible nostalgia regarding the enclosure movement under primitive capitalism. I use the plural 'commons' for purely stylistic purposes.

Chapter 1

1. This extremely individualistic and privatized reading of authenticity fits with other changes in employment patterns, namely the rise of market rationalism. A number of commentators have noted a shift or surge towards an era of 'market rationality' in which normative alignment is downplayed or even redundant (Foster and Kaplan, 2001; Barley and Kunda, 2004; Kunda and Ailon-Souday, 2005). Of particular importance is the proposition that 'market rationalists seem to have little patience for culture, no matter how strong' (Kunda and Ailon-Souday, 2005: 203). As opposed to the normative rhetoric of strong unitary values and extreme loyalty, we instead find pseudo-individualism, entrepreneurial risk-taking, and self-reliance to be key signifiers.
2. See Parker (1992) for a useful analysis of cynicism about management and corporation in popular culture.

Chapter 2

1. A number of very useful overviews of Italian autonomism are available. Wright (2002) and Mandarini (2005) are excellent for this purpose.

Chapter 3

1. For an extended empirical investigation of managed fun in the corporation, see Fleming (2005).
2. The notion of mimesis and repetition has a long tradition in psychoanalytic (Freud, 1920/1961), philosophical (Deleuze, 1968), and anthropological (Taussig,

1993) thought, which I don't have the scope to unpack here. I approach it as simulation and adhere to the basic principle regarding its relation to power: 'mimesis is repeating and not a *re-presenting*' (Bhabha, 2004: 88; emphasis in the original). All repetitions fail in some form or another, which is important for its politics in the 'just be yourself' firm.

Chapter 5

1. For an extended analysis of this 'ideology of cynicism', see Fleming and Spicer (2003, 2007).

Chapter 6

1. The mention of the dandy here (as the key embodiment of an artistic critique) represents for McGee an intersection of antisocial individualism and the poeticization of everyday life: 'The nineteenth century witnessed the emergence of an aestheticization of everyday life in figures such as the dandy, for whom superior taste and an uncompromising style were tools that set him apart from the masses, who were held in contempt' (McGee, 2005: 45).

Chapter 7

1. Foucault discusses the importance of silence (in the context of the petit bourgeois compulsion to speak) in a number of texts. For me, the most interesting text is Foucault (1982/1997).

Bibliography

Abrahamson, E. (1991). 'Management Fads and Fashions: The Diffusion and Rejection of Innovations.' *Academy of Management Review*, 16: 586–612.

Adorno, T. W. (1973). *The Jargon of Authenticity*. Trans. K. Tarnowski and F. Will. London: Routledge.

—— (1974). *Minima Moralia: Reflections on a Damaged Life*. London: Verso.

Alvesson, M. (1987). *Organization Theory and Technocratic Consciousness: Rationality, Ideology and Quality of Work*. New York: de Gruyter.

—— and Willmott, H. (1992). 'On the Idea of Emancipation in Management and Organization Studies.' *Academy of Management Review*, 17(3): 432–65.

———— (2002). 'Identity Regulation as Organizational Control: Producing the Appropriate Individual.' *Journal of Management Studies*, 39(5): 619–43.

Anteby, M. (2008). 'Identity Incentives as an Engaging Form of Control: Revisiting Leniencies in an Aeronautic Plant.' *Organization Science*, 19(2): 202–22.

Antonacopoulou, E. P. (1999). 'The Power of Critique: Revisiting Critical Theory at the End of the Century.' First International Critical Management Studies Conference, Manchester.

Arendt, H. (1958). *The Human Condition*. Chicago, IL: University of Chicago Press.

Avolio, B. J., Howell, J. M., and Sosik, J. J. (1999). 'A Funny Thing Happened on the Way to the Bottom Line: Humor as a Moderator of Leadership Style Effect.' *Academy of Management Journal*, 42(2): 219–27.

Badham, R., Garrety, K., Morrigan, V., and Zanko, M. (2003). 'Designer Deviance: Enterprise and Deviance in Culture Change Programmes.' *Organization*, 10(4): 707–30.

Badiou, A. (2005). *Being and Event*. Trans. Oliver Feltham. New York: Continuum Press.

Bains, G. (2007). *Meaning Inc: The Blue Print for Business Success in the 21st Century*. London: Profile Books.

Banerjee, B. (2007). *Corporate Social Responsibility: The Good, the Bad and The Ugly*. Cheltenham: Edward Elgar.

Barker, J. R. (1999). *The Discipline of Teamwork: Participation and Concertive Control*. London: Sage.

Barley, S. R. and Kunda, G. (1992). 'Design and Devotion: Surges of Rational and Normative Ideologies of Control in Managerial Discourse.' *Administrative Science Quarterly*, 37: 363–99.

———— (2004). *Gurus, Hired Guns and Warm Bodies*. Princeton, NJ: Princeton University Press.

Barsoux, J. (1993). *Funny Business: Humor Management and Business Culture*. London: Cassell.

—— (1996). 'Why Organizations Need Humor.' *European Management Journal*, 14(5): 500–8.

Baudrillard, J. (1995). *Simulacra and Simulation*, trans. S. Glaser. Ann Arbor, MI: University of Michigan Press.

Baughman, W. E. (2001). 'Making Work Fun: Doing Business with a Sense of Humor.' *Hospital Materials Management Quarterly*, 22(3): 79–83.

Bendix, R. (1956). *Work and Authority in Industry: Ideologies of Management in the Course of Industrialization*. Berkeley, CA: University of California Press.

Berman, M. (1970). *The Politics of Authenticity: Radical Individualism and the Emergence of Modern Society*. New York: Atheneum.

Beynon, H. (1980). *Working for Ford*. Harmondsworth: Penguin.

Bhabha, H. (2004). *Locations of Culture*. London: Routledge.

Bhattacharya, C., Sen, S., and Korschun, D. (2008). 'Using Corporate Social Responsibility to Win the War of Talent.' *MIT Sloan Management Review*, 49(2): 37–44.

Blau, P. (1955). *The Dynamics of Bureaucracy*. Chicago, IL: University of Chicago Press.

Blowfield, M. and Murray, A. (2008). *Corporate Social Responsibility: A Critical Introduction*. Oxford: Oxford University Press.

Boczany, W. J. (1985). 'Productivity Improvement: Making Work Fun.' *Journal of Systems Management*, 36(4): 20–3.

Bolman, L. G. and Deal, T. E. (2000). *Escape from Cluelessness*. New York: Amacom.

Boltanski, L. and Chiapello, E. (2005). *The New Spirit of Capitalism*. Trans. G. Elliott. London: Verso.

Bove, A. (2008). 'Affect and the Language of Authenticity.' Paper presented at Cambridge Workshop on Authenticity. Cambridge University, 16 May.

Boyle, D. (2004). *Authenticity: Brands, Fakes, Spin and the Lust for Real Life*. London: Harper Perennial.

Braudel, F. (1961). *Chapters in Western Civilization*. New York: Columbia University Press.

Braverman, H. (1974). *Labor and Monopoly Capital*. New York: Monthly Review Press.

Brooks, A. (2004). *Bobos in Paradise: The Upper Class and How They Got There*. New York: Simon and Schuster.

Burawoy, M. (1979). *Manufacturing Consent: Changes in the Labour Process Under Monopoly Capitalism*. Chicago, IL: University of Chicago Press.

Callinicos, A. (2006). *Resources of Critique*. Cambridge: Polity Press.

Casey, C. (1995). *Work, Self and Society: After Industrialism*. London: Routledge.

Bibliography

Casey, C. (2002). *Critical Analysis of Organizations: Theory, Practice, Revitalization.* London: Sage.

Caudron, S. (1992). 'Humor is Healthy in the Workplace.' *Personnel Journal*, 71(6): 63–72.

Chadderdon, L. (1997). 'Director of Fun.' *Fastcompany.com* <http://www.fastcompany. com/magazine/12/jobcabler.html> Accessed 20 October 2008.

Champy, J. (1995). *Reengineering Management: The Mandate for New Leadership.* New York: Harper Press.

Chow, R. (2002). *The Protestant Ethic & the Spirit of Capitalism.* New York: Columbia University Press.

Clegg, S. (1990). *Frameworks of Power.* London: Sage.

—— and Dunkerley, D. (1980). *Organization, Class and Control.* London: Routledge and Kegan Paul.

Clouse, R. W. and Spurgeon, K. L. (1995). 'Corporate Analysis of Humor.' *Psychology*, 32(3–4): 1–24.

Cogman, D. and Oppenheim, J. (2002). 'Controversy Incorporated.' *McKinsey Quarterly*, 4: 1–4.

Collinson, D. (1988). 'Engineering Humour: Masculinity, Joking and Conflict in Shopfloor Relations.' *Organization Studies*, 9(2): 181–99.

—— (1992). *Managing the Shopfloor: Subjectivity, Masculinity and Workplace Culture.* Berlin: de Gruyter.

—— (2002). 'Managing Humour.' *Journal of Management Studies*, 39(3): 269–88.

Coser, L. A. (1974). *Greedy Institutions: Patterns of Undivided Commitment.* New York: Free Press.

Costas, J. and Fleming, P. (2009). 'Beyond Dis-identification: A Discursive Analysis of Self-Alienation in Organizations.' *Human Relations*, 62: 353–78.

Courpasson, D. (2006). *Soft Constraint: Liberal Organizations and Domination.* Copenhagen: Copenhagen Business School Press/Liber.

Crane, A. and Matten, D. (2007). *Business Ethics.* Second edn. Oxford: Oxford University Press.

Creed, W., Scully, M., and Austin, J. (2002). 'Clothes Make the Person: The Tailoring of Legitimating Accounts and the Social Construction of Identity.' *Organization Science*, 13: 475–96.

Crofts, N. (2005). *Authentic Business: How to Make a Living by Being Yourself.* London: Capstone Publishers.

De Angelis, M. (2007). *The Beginning of History: Value Struggles and Global Capital.* 2007. London: Pluto Press.

De Man, H. (1927). *The Psychology of Socialism.* New York: Henry Holt and Company.

Deal, T. and Kennedy, A. (1982). *Corporate Cultures: The Rites and Rituals of Corporate Life.* Addison Wesley.

—— —— (1999). *The New Corporate Cultures.* London: Orion Business.

—— and Key, M. (1998). *Celebration at Work: Play, Purpose and Profit at Work.* New York: Berrett-Koehler.

Deetz, S. (1992). *Democracy in the Age of Corporate Colonization: Developments in the Communication and the Politics of everyday Life*. Albany, NY: State University of New York Press.

Delbridge, R. (1998). *Life on the Line in Contemporary Manufacturing: The Workplace Experience of Lean Production and the 'Japanese' Model*. Oxford: Oxford University Press.

Deleuze, G. (1968). *Difference and Repetition*. Trans. P. Patton. New York: Columbia University Press.

——(1992). 'Postscript on the Societies of Control.' *October*, 59(Winter): 3–7.

Dockery, R. (2008). 'Are Companies' Corporate Social Responsibility Initiatives Authentic?' *Epoch Times* <www.epochtimes.com> Accessed 30 October 2008.

Donzelot, J. (1991). 'Pleasure in Work.' In G. Burchell, C. Gordon, and P. Miller (eds.), *The Foucault Effect: Studies in Governmentality*. Chicago, IL: University of Chicago Press.

Duncan, W. J. (1982). 'Humor in Management: Prospects for Administrative Practice and Research.' *Academy of Management Review*, 7(1): 136–42.

——Smeltzer, L. R., and Leap, T. L. (1990). 'Humor and Work: Applications of Joking Behavior to Management.' *Journal of Management*, 16(2): 255–64.

Dwyer, T. (1991). 'Humour, Power and Change in Organizations.' *Human Relations*, 44(1): 1–19.

Edwards, R. (1979). *Contested Terrain: The Transformation of the Workplace in the Twentieth Century*. New York: Basic Books.

Ehrenberg, A. (1998). *La faitgue d'être soi*. Paris: Editions Odile Jacob (excerpt trans. Arianna Bove 2008).

Ferrara, A. (1998). *Reflective Authenticity: Rethinking the Project of Modernity*. London: Routledge.

Fierman, J. (1995). 'Winning Ideas from Maverick Managers.' *Fortune*, 6 February: 40–6.

Firth, D. (1998). *The Corporate Fool*. London: Capstone.

Fleming, P. (2005) 'Workers' Playtime? Boundaries and Cynicism in a "Culture of Fun" Program.' *Journal of Applied Behavioral Science*, 41(3): 285–303.

——(2007). 'Sexuality, Power and Resistance in the Workplace.' *Organization Studies*, 28: 239–56.

——and Spicer, A. (2007). *Contesting the Corporation: Power, Resistance and Struggle in Organizations*. Cambridge: Cambridge University Press.

————(2003). 'Working at a Cynical Distance: Implications for Subjectivity, Power and Resistance.' *Organization*, 10: 157–79.

——and Sturdy, A. (2008) '"Just Be Yourself" – Towards Neo-normative Control in Organizations?' Working Paper, Queen Mary College, University of London, London.

Florida, R. (2002). *The Rise of the Creative Class*. North Melbourne: Pluto Press.

——(2005). *Cities and the Creative Class*. London: Routledge.

Foster, R. and Kaplan, S. (2001). *Creative Destruction: Why Companies That Are Built to Last Underperform the Market And How to Successfully Transform Them*. New York: Currency.

Foucault, M. (1963/1998). 'A Preface to Transgression.' Trans. D. Bouchard and S. Simon. In Donald Bouchard (ed.), *Language, Counter-Memory, Practice*. Ithaca, NY: Cornell University Press.

—— (1982/1997). 'Michel Foucault: An Interview By Stephen Riggins.' *Ethics: Subjectivity and Truth*. Ed. P. Rabinow. London: Allen Lane.

—— (1983). 'Preface.' In G. Deleuze and F. Guattari (eds.), *Anti-Oedipus: Capitalism and Schizophrenia*. Minneapolis, MN: University of Minnesota Press.

Fournier, V. and Grey. C. (2000). 'At the Critical Moment: Conditions and Prospects for Critical Management Studies.' *Human Relations*, 53(1): 7–32.

Frank, T. (1998). *The Conquest of Cool: Business Culture, Counterculture and the Rise of Hip Consumerism*. Chicago, IL: University of Chicago Press.

Freire, P. (1970). *Pedagogy of the Oppressed*. New York: Continuum Publishing Company.

Frenkel, S., Korczynski, M., Shire, K., and Tam, M. (1999). *On the Front Line*. New York: Cornell University Press.

Friedman, A. (1977). *Industry and Labour: Class Struggle at Work and Monopoly Capitalism*. London: Macmillan.

Friedman, M. (1970). 'The Social Responsibility of Business is to Increase Profits.' *The New York Times Magazine*, 13 September.

Freud, S. (1920/1961). *Beyond the Pleasure Principle*. Trans. J. Strachey. London: Hogarth Press.

Gabriel, Y. (1999). 'Beyond Happy Families: A Critical Re-evaluation of the Control–Resistance–Identity Triangle.' *Human Relations*, 52(2): 179–203.

—— (2001). 'The State of Critique in Organizational Theory.' *Human Relations*, 54: 23–30.

—— Fineman, S., and Sims, D. (2000). *Organizing and Organizations*. London: Sage.

Giddens, A. (1991). *Modernity and Self-Identity: Self and Society in the Late Modern Age*. Cambridge, MA: Polity Press.

Gilmore, J. and Pine, B. (2007). *Authenticity: What Consumers Really Want*. Harvard, MA: Harvard Business School Press.

Goffman, E. (1959). *Presentation of Self in Everyday Life*. Harmondsworth: Penguin.

Goldthorpe, J. H., Lockwood, D., Bechhofer, A., and Platt, J. (1969). *The Affluent Worker in the Class Structure*. Cambridge: Cambridge University Press.

Gorz, A. (1988). *Critique of Economic Reason*. London: Verso.

Gouldner, A. (1955). *Patterns of Industrial Bureaucracy*. London: Routledge and Kegan Paul.

Greenwich, C. (2001). *Fun and Gains: Motivate and Energize Staff with Workplace Games, Contests and Activities*. Sydney: McGraw-Hill.

Grey, C. and Willmott, H. (2005). 'Introduction.' In C. Grey and H. Willmott (eds.), *Critical Management Studies Reader*. Oxford: Oxford University Press.

Guignon, C. (2004) *On Being Authentic*. Abingdon, Oxon: Routledge.

Hamper, B. (1992). *Rivethead: Tales from the Assembly Line*. New York: Warner Books.

Hanlon, G. (2007). 'Rethinking Corporate Social Responsibility and the Role of the Firm – On the Denial of Politics.' In M. Crane, A. McWilliams, D. Matten, J. Moon, and D. Siegel (eds.), *Oxford Handbook of Corporate Social Responsibility*. Oxford: Oxford University Press.

—— (2008) 'HRM Is Redundant? Professions, Immaterial Labour and the Future of Work.' In S. C. Bolton and M. Houlihan (eds.), *Searching for the Human in Human Resource Management*. Basingstoke: Palgrave Macmillan, pp. 263–80.

Hardt, M. (1993). 'Il volo attraverso le alpi.' *Riff Raff*, April.

—— and Negri, A. (1994). *The Labor of Dionysus: A Critique of the State Form*. Minneapolis, MN: University of Minnesota Press, 1994.

—— —— (1999). *Empire*. Cambridge, MA: Harvard University Press.

—— —— (2004). *The Multitude: War and Democracy in the Age of Empire*. New York: Penguin.

Harney, S. (2007). 'Socialization and the Business School.' *Management Learning*, 38(2): 139–53.

—— and Oswick, C. (2006). 'Regulation and Freedom in Global Business Education.' *International Journal of Sociology and Social Policy*, 26(3/4): 97–109.

Harvey, D. (2002). *Spaces of Capital: Towards a Critical Geography*. New York: Routledge.

Heath, J. and Potter, A. (2005). *The Rebel Sell: How Counterculture Became Consumer Culture*. West Sussex: Capstone Publishing.

Heilbroner, R. (1986). *The Nature and Logic of Capitalism*. New York: W.W. Norton.

Hemingway, C. and Maclagen, P. (2004). ' "Manager's" Personal Values as Drivers of Corporate Social Responsibility.' *Journal of Business Ethics*, 50: 33–44.

Hemsath, D. and Sivasubramania, J. (2001). *301 More Ways to Have Fun at Work*. San Francisco, CA: Berrett-Koehler.

Heuberger, F. and Nash, L. (eds.). (1994). *A Fatal Embrace? Assessing Holistic Trends in Human Resources Programs*. New Brunswick, NJ: Transaction.

Hochschild, A. (1983). *The Managed Heart: Commercialisation of Human Feeling*. London: University of California Press.

Hollway, W. (1991). *Work Psychology and Organizational Behaviour: Managing the Individual at Work*. London: Sage.

Holmes, J. and Mara, M. (2002). 'Having a Laugh at Work: How Humour Contributes to Workplace Culture.' *Journal of Pragmatics*, 34(12): 1683–710.

Hudson, K. M. (2002). 'Transforming a Conservative Company: One Laugh at a Time.' *Harvard Business Review on Culture and Change*. Cambridge, MA: Harvard Business School Press.

Jacques, R. (1996). *Manufacturing the Employee: Management Knowledge from the 19th to 12th Centuries*. London: Sage.

Jameson, F. (1991). *Postmodernism, or the Cultural Logic of Late Capitalism*. London: Verso.

Janssens, M. and Zanoni, P. (2005). 'Many Diversities for Many Services: Theorizing Diversity (Management) in Service Companies.' *Human Relations*, 58(3): 311–40.

Jay, M. (1994). *Downcast Eyes: The Denigration of Vision in Twentieth-Century French Thought*. Berkeley, CA: University of California Press.

Johnson, P. and Gill, J. (1993). *Management Control and Organizational Behaviour*. London: Paul Chapman.

Kahn, W. A. (1989). 'Towards a Sense of Organizational Humor: Implications for Organizational Diagnosis and Change.' *Journal of Applied Behavioural Science*. 25(1): 45–63.

Kane, P. (2004). *The Play Ethic: A Manifesto for a Different Way of Living*. London: Macmillan.

Kanter, R. (1989). *When Giants Learn to Dance*. New York: Simon and Schuster.

Kinnie, N., Hutchinson, S., and Purcell, J. (2000). 'Fun and Surveillance: The Paradox of High Commitment Management in Call Centres.' *International Journal of Human Resource Management*, 11(5): 967–85.

Kline, E. and Izzo, J. B. (1999). *Awaken Corporate Soul: Four Paths to Unleash the Power of People at Work*. London: Fair Winds Press.

Knights, D. and Willmott, H. (1989). 'Power and Subjectivity at Work: From Degradation to Subjugation in Social Relations.' *Sociology*, 23: 534–58.

Kunda, G. (1992). *Engineering Culture: Control and Commitment in a High Technology Corporation*. Philadelphia, PA: Temple University Press.

—— and Ailon-Souday, G. (2005). 'Managers, Markets and Ideologies – Design and Devotion Revisited.' In S. Ackroyd et al. (eds.), *Oxford Handbook of Work and Organization*. Oxford: Oxford University Press.

Laclau, E. (1996). *Emancipations*. London: Verso.

—— and Mouffe, C. (1985). *Hegemony and Socialist Strategy*. London: Verso.

Lasch, C. (1979). *The Culture of Narcissism, American Life in an Age of Diminishing Expectations*. New York: W.W. Norton.

Latour, B. (2004) 'Why Has Critique Run Out of Steam? From Matters of Fact to Matters of Concern.' *Critical Inquiry*, 30(Winter): 225–48.

Lazzarato, M. (1996). 'Immaterial Labor.' In P. Virno and M. Hardt (eds.), *Radical Thought in Italy*. Minneapolis, MN: University of Minnesota Press.

Leavitt, T. (1958) 'The Dangers of Social Responsibility.' *Harvard Business Review*, 36: 41–50.

Liu, A. (2004). *The Laws of Cool: Knowledge Work and the Culture of Information*. Chicago, IL: University of Chicago Press.

Lundin, S. C., Paul, H., and Christensen, J. (2000). *Fish: A Remarkable Way to Boost Morale and Improve Results*. London: Hodder and Stoughton.

Malone, P. B. (1980). 'Humor: A Double-Edged Tool For Today's Managers?' *Academy of Management Review*, 5(3): 357–60.

Mandarini, M. (2005). 'Antagonism vs. Contradiction: Conflict and the Dynamics of Organisation in the Thought of Antonio Negri.' *Sociological Review*, 53(S1): 192–214.

Marcuse, H. (1955). *Eros and Civilization*. Abacus: London.

Mariotti, J. (1999). 'A Company that Plays Together, Stays Together.' *Industry Week*, 248(6): 63–5.

Mars, G. (1984). *Cheats at Work: An Anthropology of Workplace Crime*. London: Allen and Unwin.

Marx, K. (1867/1976). *Capital: Volume One*. London: Pelican.

Maslow, A. (1954) *Motivation and Personality*. New York: Harper & Row.

Mayo, E. (1945). *The Social Problems of an Industrial Civilization*. London: Routledge.

McGee, M. (2005). *Self-Help, Inc: Makeover Culture in American Life*. Oxford: Oxford University Press.

Messner, M., Clegg, S., and Kornberger, M. (2008). 'Critical Practices in Organizations.' *Journal of Management Inquiry*, 17(2): 68–82.

Meyer, J. W. and Rowan, B. (1977). 'Institutionalized Organizations: Formal Structure as Myth and Ceremony.' *American Journal of Sociology*, 83(2): 340–63.

Meyerson, D. (2003). *Tempered Radicals: How Everyday Leaders Inspire Change at Work*. Cambridge, MA: Harvard University Press.

Michelli, J. (2007). *The Starbucks Experience: 5 Principles for Turning Ordinary into Extraordinary*. New York: McGraw-Hill.

Miller, J. (1996). 'Humour: Empowerment Tool for the 1990s.' *Management Development Review*, 9(6): 36–40.

Mills, C. W. (1956). *The Power Elite*. New York: Free Press.

Mirvis, P. H. (1994). 'Human Development or Depersonalization? The Company as Total Community.' In F. W. Heuberger and L. L. Nash (eds.), *A Fatal Embrace? Assessing Holistic Trends in Human Resources Programs*. New Brunswick, NJ: Transaction.

Negri, A. (2003). *Time for Revolution*. Trans. M. Mandarini. New York: Continuum.

New York Times (2006). 'Can Google Come Out to Play?' 31 December.

Nippert-Eng, C. (1996). *Home and Work: Negotiating Boundaries Through Everyday Life*. Chicago, IL: Chicago University Press.

O'Reilly, C. and J. Chatman (1996). 'Culture as Social Control: Corporations, Cults, and Commitment.' In B. Staw and L. Cummings (eds.), *Research in Organizational Behavior*. Greenwich, CT: JAI Press, pp. 157–200.

Parker, M. (2002). *Against Management: Organization in the Age of Managerialism*. Oxford: Polity Press.

——(2005). 'Writing Critical Management Studies.' In C. Grey and H. Willmott (eds.), *Critical Management Studies Reader*. Oxford: Oxford University Press.

Pascale, R. and Athos, A. (1982). *The Art of Japanese Management: Applications for American Executives*. Harmondsworth: Penguin.

Pasquinelli, M. (2008). *Animal Spirits: A Bestiary of the Commons*. Rotterdam: NAI Publishers/Institute of Network Cultures.

Perlow, L. (1998). 'Boundary Control: The Social Ordering of Work and Family Time in a High-Tech Corporation.' *Administrative Science Quarterly*, 43(2): 328–57.

Perrow, C. (1986). *Complex Organizations: A Critical Essay*. Third edn. New York: McGraw-Hill.

Peters, T. (1989). *Thriving on Chaos*. London: Pan.

——(1992). *Liberation Management: Necessary Disorganization for the Nanosecond Nineties*. London: Pan.

——(1994). *The Tom Peters Seminar: Crazy Times Call for Crazy Organizations*. London: Macmillan.

——(2003). *Re-Imagine! Business Excellence in a Disruptive Age*. London: Dorling Kindersley.

——and Austrin, N. (1986). *A Passion for Excellence: The Leadership Difference*. London: Fontana.

——and Waterman, R. H. (1982). *In Search of Excellence*. New York: Harper & Row.

Piccone, P. (1976). 'Beyond Identity Theory.' In J. O'Neil (ed.), *On Critical Theory*. New York: Seabury.

Pickard, J. (1997). 'You Cannot Be Serious!' *People Management*, 3(25): 34–5.

Pollard, S. (1965). *The Genesis of Modern Management*. London: Edward Arnold.

Raeburn, N. C. (2004). *Changing Corporate America from Inside Out: Lesbian and Gay Workplace Rights*. Minneapolis, MN: University of Minnesota Press.

Ramsay, H. (1977). 'Cycles of Control.' *Sociology*, 11(3): 481–506.

Ranciere, J. (2004). *The Politics of Aesthetics*. Trans. Gabriel Rockhill. New York: Continuum Press.

Ray, C. A. (1986). 'Corporate Culture: The Last Frontier of Control?' *Journal of Management Studies*, 23(3): 287–97.

Reeves, R. (2001). *Happy Mondays: Putting Pleasure Back into Work*. London: Pearson Education.

Roethlisberger, F. and Dickson, W. (1939). *Management and the Worker*. Cambridge, MA: Harvard University Press.

Rosica, C. (2007). *The Authentic Brand: How Today's Top Entrepreneurs Connect with Customers*. London: Noble Press.

Ross, A. (2004). *No-Collar: The Humane Workplace and its Hidden Costs*. Philadelphia, PA: Temple University Press.

Roy, D. (1952). 'Quota Restriction and Goldbricking in a Machine Shop.' *American Journal of Sociology*, 57(5): 427–42.

——(1958). 'Banana Time: Job Satisfaction and Informal Interaction.' *Human Organization*, 18: 158–68.

Rushe, D. (2007). 'Forget Work, Just Have Some Fun: Office Jollity is Replacing Drudgery for Today's Staff.' *Sunday Times*, 16 September. <http://business.timesonline.co.uk/tol/business/industry_sectors/technology/article2459581.ece> Accessed 25 August 2008.

Salaman, G. (1981). *Class and the Corporation*. Glasgow: Fontana.

Sanbonmatsu, J. (2004). *The Postmodern Prince: Critical Theory, Left Strategy and the Making of a New Political Subject*. New York: Monthly Review Press.

Sartre, J. P. (1943/1969). *Being and Nothingness*. Trans. H. E. Bares. London: Routledge.

——(1948). *Existentialism and Humanism*. London. Methuen.

Scase, R. and Goffee, R. (1989). *Reluctant Managers: Their Work and Lifestyles*. London: Unwin Hyman.

Semler, R. (1993). *Maverick! The Success Behind the World's Most Unusual Workplace*. London: Arrow.

——(2004). *The Seven-Day Weekend*. New York: Penguin.

Sennett, R. (1976). *The Fall of Public Man*. New York: Penguin.

——(2008). *The Craftsman*. New York: Allen Lane.

——(1998). *The Corrosion of Character: The Personal Consequences of Work in the New Capitalism*. London: W.W. Norton.

Serres, M. (1982). *The Parasite*. Trans. L. R. Schehr. Baltimore, MD: Johns Hopkins University Press.

Sloterdijk, P. (1987). *Critique of Cynical Reason*. Minneapolis, MN: University of Minnesota Press.

Sunday Times (2005, 2006). '100 Best Companies to Work For.' *Sunday Times*.

Sutton, R. (2001). *Weird Ideas that Work: 11 1/2 ways to Promote, Manage and Sustain Innovation*. New York: Penguin.

Tannebaum, A. (1967). *Control in Organizations*. New York. McGraw-Hill.

Taussig, M. (1993). *Mimesis and Alterity*. New York: Routledge.

Taylor, C. (1992). *The Ethics of Authenticity*. Cambridge, MA: Harvard University Press.

Thompson, E. P. (1967). 'Time, Work Discipline and Industrial Capitalism.' *Past and Present*, 38: 56–103.

——(1968). *The Making of the English Working Class*. Harmondswood: Penguin.

Trilling, L. (1972). *Sincerity and Authenticity*. Cambridge, MA: Harvard University Press.

Tronti, M. (1966/1979). 'The Strategy of the Refusal.' *Working Class Autonomy and the Crisis: Italian Marxist Texts of the Theory and Practice of Class Movement: 1964–1979*. London: Red Notes and CSE Books.

——(1971). 'Il piano del capitale.' *Operai e Capitale*. Torino: Einaudi Editore.

Trosclair, A. (2008). 'Authentic Marketing Strategies' <http://www.advertising.suite101.com/article.cfm/authentic_marketing_strategy> Accessed 30 October 2008.

Vallas, S. (2003). 'The Adventures of Managerial Hegemony: Team Work, Ideology and Worker Resistance.' *Social Problems*, 50(2): 204–25.

Van Maanen, J. (1991). 'The Smile Factory: Work at Disney Land.' In P. Frost, L. Moore, M. Lewis, C. Lumberg, and J. Martin (eds.), *Reframing Organizational Culture*. Newbury Park, CA: Sage.

Vaneigem, R. (1983). *The Book of Pleasures*. Trans. J. Fullerton. New York: Pending Press.

Virno, P. (2004). *A Grammar of the Multitude*. New York: Semiotext(e).

Vise, D. (2005). *The Google Story*. New York: Pan.

Warwick Organizational Behaviour Staff (eds.) (2001). *Organizational Studies: Critical Perspectives on Business and Management*. London: Routledge.

Watson, T. J. (1994). *In Search of Management: Culture, Chaos and Control in Managerial Work*. London: Routledge.

Weber, M. (1930). *The Protestant Ethic and the Spirit of Capitalism*. London: George Allen and Unwin.

—— (1947). *The Theory of Social and Economic Organization: Being Part I of Wirstschaft and Gesellschaft*. Trans. A. Henderson and T. Parsons. London: Hodge.

—— (1948). *From Max Weber: Essays in Sociology*. Ed. and trans. H. Gerth and C. W. Mills. New York: Oxford University Press.

Whyte, W. H. (1956). *The Organizational Man*. New York: Doubleday.

Willmott, H. (1993). 'Strength Is Ignorance; Slavery Is Freedom: Managing Cultures in Modern Organizations.' *Journal of Management Studies*, 30(4): 515–52.

Wright, S. (1995). 'Confronting the Crisis Around Fordism: Italian Debates Around Social Transition.' *Reconstruction*, 6(Summer): 25–34.

—— (2002). *Storming Heaven: Class Composition and Struggle in Italian Autonomist Marxism*. London: Pluto Press.

Žižek, S. (1989). *Sublime Object of Ideology*. London: Verso.

—— (1997*a*). *Plague of Fantasies*. London: Verso.

—— (1997*b*). 'The Supposed Subjects of Ideology.' *Critical Quarterly*, 39(2): 39–59.

—— (2006*a*). 'The Interpassive Subject' <http://www.lacan.com/interpass.htm> Accessed 22 September 2006.

—— (2006*b*). *The Parallax View*. London: Verso.

—— (2006*c*). 'From Passionate Attachments to Dis-identification' <http://www.Gsa.buffalo.edu/lacan/zizekidentity.htm> Accessed 05/11/2006.

—— (2008). *On Violence*. London: Profile Books.

Index

DATE DUE